MW00992837

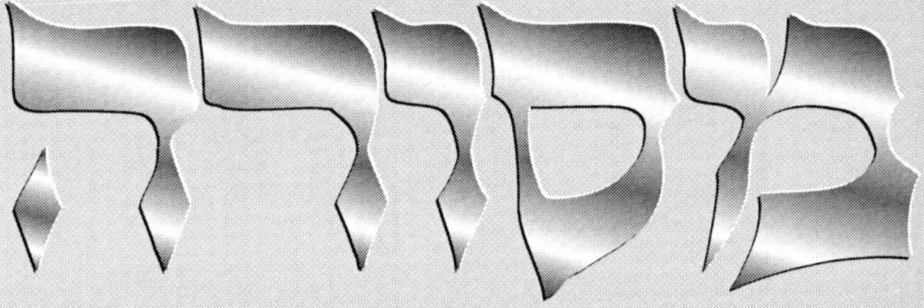

ArtScroll Series®

Rabbi Nosson Scherman / Rabbi Meir Zlotowitz

General Editors

Stories That Awaken

Published by
Mesorah Publications, ltd

the Heart

RABBI BINYOMIN PRUZANSKY

FIRST EDITION
First Impression ... August 2011

Published and Distributed by
MESORAH PUBLICATIONS, LTD.
4401 Second Avenue / Brooklyn, N.Y 11232

Distributed in Europe by
LEHMANNS
Unit E, Viking Business Park
Rolling Mill Road
Jarow, Tyne & Wear, NE32 3DP
England

Distributed in Israel by
SIFRIATI / A. GITLER — BOOKS
6 Hayarkon Street
Bnei Brak 51127

Distributed in Australia and New Zealand
by **GOLDS WORLDS OF JUDAICA**
3-13 William Street
Balaclava, Melbourne 3183
Victoria, Australia

Distributed in South Africa by
KOLLEL BOOKSHOP
Ivy Common
105 William Road
Norwood 2192, Johannesburg, South Africa

ARTSCROLL SERIES®
STORIES THAT AWAKEN THE HEART

To contact the author with inspiring stories or comments, he can be reached via e-mail at bpruz@yeshivanet.com

ISBN 10: 1-42261-108-6 / ISBN 13: 978-1-42261-108-1

Typography by CompuScribe at ArtScroll Studios, Ltd.

Printed in Canada
Bound by Sefercraft, Quality Bookbinders, Ltd., Brooklyn N.Y. 11232

הרב דוד קוויאט
ר"מ בישיבת מיר
ורב דאגודת ישראל סניף חפץ חיים

בס"ד   בין המצרים תשס"ז

לכבוד תלמידי ידידי יקירי הרב ר' בנימין יהודה פרוזאנסקי שליט"א. שכתב ספר ושמו הוא "Stories For The Jewish Heart".

והוא נכתב לעורר הלב היהודי לעבודת ה' יתברך. וזהו כשמו כן הוא, שמלהיב הלבבות לאביהם שבשמים, שמעשה של קידוש השם ומעשה חסדים של עבדי ה' הם מעוררים את האדם שגם כן הוא בעצמו יכול לעשות כזה מכח הכוחות הטובים מה שיש בהאדם עצמו בכל יהודי ויהודי בפנימיותו מכח אבותיו הקדושים. ואל יאמר האדם שאין זה עבורי, רק שיש בכוח שלו שיעשה נמי דוגמתו.

ואכן ספרו הראשון כבר פעל בו גדולות, ואברכהו שיצליח בספרו השנית להגדיל תורה ולהאדירה, כחפצו הטהורה ויפוצו מעינותיו חוצה לברכה ולהצלחה.

ממני ידידו, ומכירו שהשקפותיו הם בדרך התורה והיראה, ומברכו באהבת נפשי בכל לב.

דוד קויאט

דוד קויאט

Michtav Berachah from Rabbi Dovid Kviat זצ"ל for *Stories for the Jewish Heart*

Table of Contents

Chapter 3: Judgment Day

Chapter 4: Hear My Voice

Chapter 5: Forever Inspired

Author's Preface

Awakening the Slumbering Giant

How does one awaken his heart? How does one even know his heart is asleep?

These are the questions I pondered in the course of writing this book, and I have discovered that, though we may not usually be aware of it, our hearts and our passion for growth may indeed be in a deep slumber, eagerly awaiting the day they are awakened.

In this book, you will read about individuals who were inspired to renew their belief in Hashem and to redefine their lives on the force of this inspiration. As Elul is upon us, it is fitting to dwell on this concept of rousing our hearts and souls to make ready for the King to arrive. This time of year is a powerful opportunity to awaken our spirits, and thus it is my pleasure to present a book full of stories that illustrate this very idea. It is my hope that these stories will enter your heart as they did mine.

Yet, before we move on together to experience the stories in this book, let us take a moment to examine the workings of the heart. The beating heart is the center of our physical well-being and the source of our vitality, but it is far more than that. We are taught that the *lev* is the source of spiritual vitality, as well, that a healthy heart, full of enthusiasm for Hashem's Torah, is vital to our success in this world and the next.

The sounding of the shofar in the month of Elul is a rousing reveille to our hearts. Rav Sholom Schwadron, the famed Maggid of Jerusalem, expounds on the verse in *Shir HaShirim* (5:2): *Ani yesheinah v'libi er, kol Dodi dofek, pischu li.* ("I am asleep but my heart is awake; the voice of my Beloved calls to me to allow Him in.")

Hashem comes to each of us and knocks on the door of our heart, pleading to be allowed in. This is likened to a father who has not seen his son in many years. Finally, the opportunity arises for the father to visit, and he excitedly sends his son a telegram detailing the date of his intended arrival.

You can imagine the excitement of the father when his ship arrives; surely his son will be waiting for him on the dock, his arms wide open! But to his surprise, the son is nowhere to be seen. Undeterred, the father imagines that perhaps his son is just leaving his house to come greet him, and so, his heart filled with hope, the father walks to his son's home.

There, too, the dismayed father sees that his son is not waiting to greet him. He takes one last gamble and carries his heavy bags to his son's doorstep, certain that his son has at least left the door open for his beloved father. Imagine his sorrow when he discovers that the door is bolted tightly shut! Finally, in desperation, the father begins knocking on the unyielding door pleading for his son to open it and allow him in.

"During the Yamim Noraim," Rav Schwadron explained, "Hashem is closer than ever. He has traveled to us, and we cannot imagine His disappointment at finding the doors to our hearts bolted shut. How much more disappointed would the father have been if he had heard the son through the door, yelling, 'I'm too tired to get up now, I've already gone to bed for the night'?

"Our Father is knocking on the door. We can't afford to remain asleep."

A Call to Action

Rav Shabsi Yudelovitch, in his *sefer Derashos HaMaggid,* explains the same verse as follows:

"Though it may appear that the Jewish people are asleep and our mitzvah observance is like one sleepwalking, our hearts are truly wide awake. Deep within us, we are all looking for opportunities to become closer to our Father in Heaven. However, having our hearts awake is not enough. We cannot be children to Hashem only at heart; we must show Him our actions, as well! We need to show Him our willingness to act in order for our hearts to be truly set aflame.

"That is why Hashem tells us, 'Open your heart as the eye of a needle, and I will open it wide as a banquet hall.' "

To illustrate his point, Rav Yudelovitch shares an interesting story:

I was once on a flight to America, seated next to a Jewish—though irreligious—doctor who turned out to be a renowned heart specialist from Hadassah Hospital in Israel. We made some small talk before the flight took off, and he explained to me a little about what he does. Primarily, he specialized in treating those who had suffered heart attacks; he provided regular examinations, procedures, medication, and diet regulation. He stressed to me how crucial it was that his patients eat the right foods in order to avoid future heart issues.

In the middle of our conversation, a stewardess began distributing supper to the passengers. I received my glatt kosher meal, and my neighbor happily accepted his nonkosher meal, which he dug into with a gusto that made something inside me cringe terribly. I schooled myself into silence, but soon my strong reaction to his indulgence gnawed at my conscience too deeply to allow me to keep quiet.

"You're a Jewish person," I burst in astonishment. "How can you eat this food?"

The doctor turned to look at me, disdain plain on his face. "Rabbi, don't worry," he said thickly, through a mouthful of food. "I promise you that this won't give me a heart attack."

I couldn't accept his dismissive response. "Look, I'm sorry," I continued, "but if you don't think that eating nonkosher food stands in contrast to being a Jew, then what do you do differently to express your Judaism?"

He swallowed his mouthful, and he had a ready response for this question. "Eating nonkosher food is no big deal, Rabbi. It doesn't hurt me and it doesn't hurt anyone else; the main thing is that I have a Jewish heart! I give charity to many important causes in the State of Israel."

I sighed and leaned back. What could I say to a person who felt that a "Jewish heart" was enough? There was no other recourse but silence.

A few hours passed, and some of my fellow travelers were forming a *minyan* for Minchah in the back of the plane. I and many other religious Jews on the plane were rising to join, and so I asked my neighbor, the doctor, if he wanted to join us. He flatly declined.

Following Minchah, I returned to my seat. "My friend," I asked, "why didn't you join us for Minchah?"

He snorted. "Rabbi, I already explained to you that I am a Jew at heart, but I don't see any real reason to do the mitzvos."

I decided to try a different tack. "Look, doctor, my understanding is that you are a heart specialist. So tell me: what exactly is the cause of heart attacks? What brings them on?"

The professor smiled. This was a far more comfortable area for discussion. He delved into a detailed explanation of the way fatty foods cause buildup in the arteries that ultimately cause a dangerous rise in blood pressure as the heart works in overdrive to distribute blood throughout the body. The heart, he explained, can become overburdened with this work, at which point it will fail.

"Wow," I said, after he had finished. "Now I really understand what causes the heart to give out. I do have another question, though, if that's okay?"

The other man nodded.

"Well," I began, "you've told me a couple of times now that you have a good Jewish heart. In other words, all the mitzvos and obligations Hashem asks of us are, in your opinion, encompassed by the goodness of that heart, though not the rest of your body.

"Now I, on the other hand, acknowledge that G-d wants us to incorporate *all* of the body into performing His mitzvos, so that the responsibility is spread equally upon every limb and feature. My question is: is it not unhealthy to throw the entire weight of G-d's Torah onto your heart? Do you not worry about overburdening it to the point of causing a heart attack?"

The doctor chuckled lightly at this, and I realized that he had not accepted what I had to say. He was resolved to remain a "Jew at heart."

"It's unfortunate," Rav Yudelovitch concludes, "that this man did not understand that Hashem requires a lot more of us than a heart that is awake. He needs to see that we are Jews in every facet of life, performing his mitzvos with our hearts, our souls, and all of our bodies. That is why he calls to us: *Kol Dodi dofek, pischu li.* He asks us to reveal that small opening in our hearts so that He can widen it as much as necessary.

A Jewish Heartbeat

In truth, those Jews who are distant from Torah observance really do have a strong Jewish heart. Though years of neglect may have muffled their souls to the point that they can barely be detected, there will always be a faint, Jewish heartbeat that can be heard if one only listens closely. Sometimes, Hashem will present them with a challenge in order to breathe new life into their hearts. If absorbed correctly, these tests can serve as a powerful wake-up call to a higher truth, as the following story illustrates.

Seated in the busy waiting room of the Bikur Cholim hospital in Jerusalem, Ari poured his heart and soul into the *Tehillim* open before him, entreating Hashem to make the operation his mother was undergoing successful, so that she could finally return to her family who sorely missed her.

So absorbed was he in the immortal words of King David that he would have completely missed the elderly, secular *kibbutznik* in shorts and sandals who walked in just then, had it not been for the man's very obvious snort of disgust. Ari looked up.

The old man was watching him, his face twisted into an expression of pained disbelief. "Young man, what is it you think you're doing?"

"I'm waiting for my mother," Ari replied. "You see, she's going for an operation that..."

"That's not what I meant," interjected the other man. "I was asking what you're reciting."

"Oh, I'm saying *Tehillim*." Ari explained. "I'm asking Hashem to watch over my mother and see to it that everything goes well."

The old *kibbutznik's* face darkened. "Ha!" he barked. "You think that stuff works? What century are you from? Believe me: it's all a bunch of superstitious nonsense. Things happen the way they happen, and life isn't worth the effort of praying."

The younger man stared at the older one, wondering how someone could be so removed from Hashem right in the middle of the Holy Land. He had always thought that prayer was the one thing everyone believed in, in some way or another. Though this man was probably a long way from a Jewish lifestyle, didn't he believe in G-d?

"Well, why are you here?" Ari asked after a moment.

The old man didn't meet his eyes this time, and he responded in a hoarse voice. "I'm here to collect the body of my son."

Ari felt his heart lurch. Perhaps this was the reason for the man's bitterness. "I'm sorry that your son has died," he finally said.

"No," the old man clarified, "he hasn't died yet, but the doctors told me I should be prepared to take his body home, since there's nothing they can do for him, anymore. They're going to try some experimental surgery today, but really, nothing short of a miracle would save him now, and I don't expect anything like that."

With that, the man went to take a seat not too far away, looking spent. After a while, Ari moved quietly to the other end of the room so that he could continue praying for his mother without being disturbed. Let his neighbor believe as he pleased, but Ari was certain that his prayers were being heard.

It was about an hour later when Ari lifted his face from his *Tehillim* again, this time because a doctor had come rushing into the waiting room.

"Is there a Mr. Rafi Cohen in here?" the doctor asked, breathlessly.

The old man rose from his seat, his expression tight. "I'm here..."

"Mr. Cohen," the doctor exclaimed, "it's a miracle! It was the smallest of chances, but your son made it! He's going to have a complete recovery!"

"My son is...alive?" Mr. Cohen whispered, incredulously. Slowly, a fire seemed to light itself behind his eyes and an amazed smile appeared on his face. "Thank You, Hashem, thank You! *Shema Yisrael, Hashem Elokeinu, Hashem Echad!"*

Ari watched all this in awe, his mind reeling. One moment ago, this man did not believe in G-d, and the next moment he was praising that same G-d as loudly as possible, tears streaming down his cheeks. What had happened?

The following morning, upon returning to yeshivah, Ari presented this question to his rebbi, asking what the explanation for Mr. Cohen's behavior could be.

The rebbi smiled. "Ari, I'm going to explain this as I understand it.

"Every Jew intrinsically loves Hashem and believes in Him. He may deny it vigorously, and he may act like he doesn't, but there's a small part of him that never forgets the truth. This old man at the hospital reacted the way he did when he saw you davening because he wanted to daven, too! He was torn, because he had spent most of his life suppressing this desire to pray and telling himself that it doesn't mean anything, but suddenly his *neshamah* began to make itself heard, clamoring to daven. He ridiculed you for that reason.

"Yet, when the doctor came in to give news of the miracle, this man's *neshamah* could no longer be contained, and it burst forth to proclaim his *emunah* and his buried knowledge that Hashem truly runs the world. What else could express that better than the words of *Shema*?

"This is something to remember always, Ari. Every Jew really loves Hashem, even though it's sometimes hard to see that under all the hardened layers of materialism. We must always seek ways to pry the Jewish heart free so that it can see the light of day."

The Real Me

In the pure core of every Jew, there is a holy spirit that has no desire to sin. The problem is that the *yetzer hara* is a devious, overpowering force that often sways the body and mind to act inappropriately against the word of Hashem.

An essential part of the *teshuvah* process is the realization of who we really are and a return to that pure essence. We must tell ourselves the truth: that the "real me" loves Torah and mitzvos. The real me prays with passion and a desire to cling to G-d; the real me wants nothing more than to do His bidding here in this world. Sinning is not really who we are; it is merely the result of the *yetzer hara* seizing hold of us momentarily.

Rav Yankel Galinsky explains this concept in a particularly beautiful manner, using an incident he witnessed many years ago.

During the war, I was imprisoned in a Siberian labor camp. Imprisoned along with me were many Lithuanian military leaders and government officials who had been deemed a danger to the Soviets.

One night, as I struggled to sleep in the crippling cold, I noticed a tall fellow rise from his pallet and look around swiftly to make sure the rest of us were asleep. When he was satisfied that he remained unobserved, he withdrew a package from under his bedding and pulled a military general's uniform out of it.

Looking around once more, he hastily removed his prisoner's clothes and donned his uniform; I understood it to be the uniform he must have worn before being incarcerated. Well, what was most amazing about this all was the sudden transformation. His back straightened, his arms stiffened at his sides, and he marched about smartly for a little while, his carriage utterly different from the bowed, defeated slump of most inmates. When this ritual was complete, he changed back into his usual clothing, stuffed the package back into its hiding place, and peacefully went to sleep.

The next morning, as we were marched to work, I fell into step with this former general. "What was it you were doing last night?" I asked him point-blank, my voice a surreptitious murmur.

"You saw?" he hissed in return, missing a step.

"I won't tell anyone," I reassured him. "I was just curious."

He leaned in a little closer to make sure we weren't caught conversing, barely moving his lips. "They think we are their slaves," he whispered, fury in his voice, "but I will not forget that I am a general. I commanded troops! I decided that at least one moment of every day, I must remind myself of the real me. The real me is not a Soviet prisoner; the real me is the man you saw for only a moment."

Rav Galinsky says: "We must learn to apply these words to ourselves. A Jew must realize that he is only the 'real me' when he performs a mitzvah, or when he rises in the morning to serve Hashem. If he sins, it isn't because that's who he is; it's because he is a prisoner to evil forces for a little while. But the 'real me' never forgets who he is underneath it all."

Teshuvah Transforms

The Rambam, in Hilchos Teshuvah (7:6), states: Teshuvah is great because it brings a person, who was far from Hashem, close. Yesterday, he may have been hated (because of his sins) and seen as disgusting, cast-off, abominable, but then today he is beloved, desired, and close to Hashem.

Rav Yitzchok Zilberstein relates a story about how a person can be completely transformed through the power of *teshuvah*.

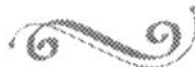

Amnon was a secular Israeli who would only occasionally appear in shul to daven. Although members of his community worked tirelessly to convince him to keep Shabbos, kashrus, and other mitzvos, their efforts never bore fruit. For a time, Amnon would halfheartedly attempt to keep one mitzvah or another, but he would always slip gradually back into the comfortable, obligation-free lifestyle he simply could not let go of.

And then, one day everything changed. Amnon showed up in shul, determination on his face, and declared to the Rav that he was ready to do sincere *teshuvah*. Surprised, the Rav asked Amnon what had caused this new resolution. Amnon's response was a fascinating story.

"Earlier today I was driving on the highway, and I passed an area that I remembered had once been a garbage dump. In fact, the entire area used to smell so horrible that closing the windows never helped; you had to find some way to plug your nose, too! Today, however, I noticed that the legendary stench was completely gone. Instead, a beautiful park was there, full of grass, trees, and strolling families.

"For a bit, I wondered if I had made a mistake and taken the wrong route. I couldn't imagine how a place that had been so awful, so memorably rancid, could have undergone such a total transformation. It was impossible! Or was it?

"Curiosity made me pull my car to the shoulder and go investigate. I hopped the barrier, headed to the park gate, and asked one of the officials standing there if this was indeed the same place that used to be a garbage dump.

" 'Yes, it was,' he told me, 'but a few years ago, they decided to turn it into a park. See those tractors over there? They're still finishing the last part of the job, but it's already the most beautiful park in Israel. You should walk around a bit and take a look.'

"And so I did. I breathed in the air, fragrant with flowers, and marveled at the greenery, the shady trees, and the sheer number of people clearly basking in what was once a giant mound of garbage. How could such a place have become such a gorgeous park? Suddenly, the answer struck me.

"Hashem wanted me to see this park today and learn a lesson from it. If a place that had once been the most loathsome, disgusting location in the country can be transformed into something so beautiful, certainly I can hope to remove from upon myself the filth of sins that creates such a horrible spiritual stench! Perhaps I can turn myself into one of the most beautiful of Hashem's children. One day, I might even merit having children and *talmidim* who can bask in the sweet, beautiful fragrance of my *neshamah*."

May it be the will of Hashem that we all succeed in our quest to awaken our hearts and souls to the beauty of genuine *teshuvah*. May this book serve as an inspiration throughout Elul and the year to come as we open the door to our dear Father and allow Him into our hearts. Let us never forget that our Father wants us to be close to Him for our *own* good, so that we may merit to be showered with all the love and blessing that He has to give.

Elul is upon us. May we heed the call.

Ani l'Dodi v'Dodi li.

Dedication

As I completed this book I turned my attention to formulating a dedication. To whom should this book be dedicated? Who was someone close to my heart, who has inspired me to grow? Then it dawned on me; I had the perfect choice. I remembered an incident that occurred earlier this year.

As an author, I always like to keep my eyes open for a good story. There are those fortunate occasions when such a story develops right before my eyes; this past Simchas Torah was one of those times.

The shul was filled to capacity with people from my community, all of us buzzing with the excitement of this special Yom Tov. Parents and their children stood at the ready for their chance to dance with the Torah, beaming smiles on their faces. My gaze swept the room, taking in with pleasure the ranks of yeshivah *bachurim* and neighborhood men who were eagerly awaiting the start of the *Hakafos*.

Abruptly, my gaze settled on a lone teenager sporting a long mane of hair, jeans, and the sort of shirt that stood out sharply amid the pool of black hats and dark suits. The next thing I noticed was the way he was praying *Shemoneh Esrei*: swaying gently, his eyes squeezed closed in concentration as he recited the words of davening long after everyone else had finished. There was something mesmerizing about the fact that his mode of dress and the passion of his *tefillah* could convey such starkly opposing messages about his connection with his heritage.

Curious to learn more, I approached the young man after his davening was completed and introduced myself. We stood at his table and chatted for quite a while; Yoni,* as he called himself, had a pleasant way of speaking that—again—seemed to belie the coarseness of his appearance.

"I grew up in New York," he told me after a while, "and I went to a regular yeshivah. The problem was, I struggled endlessly with my learning to the point that I just became disenchanted with the whole thing. No one seemed willing to help me, so I took up with a whole new group of friends and began to hit the streets. Eventually, I just dropped out completely. At least now, I'm somewhere where people accept me. The last two years have been tough on me—I've seen a lot that I wish I could forget—but now I'm good."

"What about your family?" I wanted to know.

He shrugged indifferently, but cast his eyes down. "Well...we don't really get along since I stopped footing their path. There used to be a whole lot of arguing, but now I've grown up and I can take care of myself."

"Would you consider going to a yeshivah in Israel to learn?" I suggested. "It might be nice to get a new start in a new place."

His lips twisted. "Nah, Rabbi, I'm done with that sort of stuff. Look, it was really nice to meet you...maybe we'll speak later."

I walked away from my new friend in a bit of a shock. Here was a boy who had come from a Torah-true background and now, at the tender age of 16, had simply decided he was "done with that stuff." I couldn't fathom being so cynical as to drop a centuries-old heritage at such a young age! Even so, something about Yoni struck me. His davening had been conducted with such intense concentration and love; it seemed that there was still a strong spark of Yiddishkeit within him that simply didn't spread outward anymore.

The *Hakafos* began, and the room shook with the force of people dancing, singing, and lifting their eyes and hearts to Heaven. Throughout the dancing, my gaze shifted to Yoni. I even managed to take his hand and dance with him a little, and I was pleasantly surprised to notice the broad smile on his face as he threw himself into the festive spirit. He might have felt out of place, but his dancing was just as joyous and as soaring as anyone else's.

The following day, I met my new friend again, and we spoke briefly about life and about Simchas Torah. It was a short chat, but I felt that we had made a deeper connection; I concluded that Yoni was inescapably pulled toward the yearning of his soul, but he simply didn't know where to go. He was wandering in the wilderness and searching for water, but he couldn't find enough of it to quench the thirst of his *neshamah.*

But then it happened: *Hakafos* began, and Yoni was given a Torah to hold. And hold it he did! I watched in amazement as he clutched the Torah to his chest, and began dancing vigorously with the circle. He seemed to grow more energetic as the dancing went on, and suddenly he leaped into the middle of the circle, holding up the Torah ecstatically as he whirled around. The joy in his voice was pronounced as he sang: *shivti b'veis Hashem, kol yemei chayai...*

Unable to contain myself, I leaped into the middle with him, held onto his shoulders and danced right along. I felt emotion rushing through me as I realized the importance of what Yoni represented. So many youth among us seem hardened and unreachable, but within them are powerful sparks that are waiting to be fanned into roaring flames. All we need to do is hand them the Torah, no questions asked. In Yoni's blissful face as he clutched the Torah, I saw his message as though he were screaming it:

I am alive, and I have a beautiful neshamah, just like you! Don't write me off because I look and dress a little differently than you; I, too, love Hashem and I, too, want to celebrate with His Torah! I, too, can shine.

As I danced with Yoni, I thought about how this message was shared by so many other lost *neshamos* across the world. Perhaps genuine *simchas haTorah* might ignite their hearts as well.

At the end of the exhilarating day, I parted with Yoni, securing his promise that we would keep in touch. I was deeply moved and inspired in a way I have never been before. Suddenly, it had all become real to me: the idea that a lost *neshamah* can be found and the spark within it can be made to blaze brightly once again.

The story of Yoni and his Torah reminded me of a very different story from many years ago. Ultimately, though, the messages are the same.

Warsaw Ghetto, 1942

The war on the Jews had been underway for a long while. Thousands of well-known faces and families were loaded onto cattle-cars every day, to be shipped off to places they were never meant to leave. Once-bustling yeshivos stood abandoned, shuls lay in ashes, and the skeleton Jewish community that remained in the city tried desperately to cling to hope.

Morale was as low as it could be; Warsaw had once boasted a community of over half a million Jews, but that was like a dream that had evaporated. The current population of Jews counted barely several thousand, and now it was Simchas Torah.

At a time that was once so full of happiness, the holiday dawned with an almost palpable bleakness in the air. Fifteen people were gathered at the home of the famous *tzaddik*, Rav Menachem Ziemba, on 37 Navelki Street. They were there for the *Hakafos*.

The *Sifrei Torah* were dutifully removed from the *aron kodesh* and the men began to circle the tables slowly as they sang the songs they knew from years past. It was dull singing: the kind that ached with the sound of broken hearts and crushed spirits. This year, there were no happy young children dancing with their fathers. There were no children left in the ghetto at all; they had been taken away weeks ago to be shipped off to their deaths in Treblinka.

Among the gathered men was Rav Yehuda Leib Orlean, a towering figure of the prewar Bais Yaakov movement. He had directed the seminary in Krakow. If Sarah Schneirer could be called the mother of the Bais Yaakov movement, Rav Orlean was the father. He had spent years instructing girls in the ways of the Torah and teaching them of their responsibility for the propagation of its study. Rav Orlean had once had great plans for Bais Yaakov, before the war turned all of Jewish life into a surreal nightmare.

As the men shuffled around the tables with the *Sifrei Torah*, Rav Orlean heard the door of the house creak open. A young boy, no older than 12, sidled into the room and shyly joined the circle, wonder stamped on his dirty face. Somehow, impossible though it was, this child had hidden and survived!

Rav Orlean was deeply shaken by the sight, and he ran over to the child, his heart pounding with joy. He swept the boy into a hug along with the Torah he already clutched in his arms. Holding them both to his heart, he cried out in a broken voice:

"*A yunger Yid mit der heilige Torah!*" ("A young Jew with the holy Torah!")

He broke into a joyful Chassidishe dance and began singing as loud as he could. Spontaneously, their faces filled with wonder, the other men formed a circle around the small group—boy, renowned *mechanech,* and *Sefer Torah*—and began dancing with renewed vigor and strength. As Rav Orlean's voice sang, *A yunger Yid mit der heilige Torah,* the assembled men realized what the Rav had seen right away: this young boy represented their future.

Rav Orlean was lost in another world, his singing capturing all of his love for the Torah and the Jewish children to whom he had dedicated his life. To him, this child stood for the hope that there would be another generation of young Jews who would survive the war and continue to grow in Torah and *yiras Shamayim*. This one young child meant that Hitler had failed, that Jewish children would continue to learn, and that the spark of our people would never be extinguished.

One young boy gave a roomful of broken men a powerful reminder that the spark of the Jewish people can never be extinguished by a physical force. In our own times, Yoni reminded me of that same resilient, everlasting spark. The eternal torch of the Torah will keep our souls alight forever. We need only remember to keep fanning the flames.

I dedicate this book to all the Yonis out there: to all the young men and women who have drifted off the path of their heritage. Although they appear physically to have left their Yiddishkeit behind, there is a powerful spark within them that is waiting to be reignited. Their *neshamos* are shouting:

I am alive, and I have a beautiful neshamah, just like you! Don't write me off because I look and dress a little differently than you. I, too, love Hashem and I, too, want to celebrate with His Torah! I, too, can shine.

Show them unconditional love, warmth, and acceptance. Give them a chance to hold a Torah close to their hearts, by showing them the depth and beauty of a Torah lifestyle. Show them how to dance with a Torah, by infusing your own service of Hashem with enthusiasm. Perhaps your actions will awaken the fire that is burning within their hearts. And hopefully, one day soon they too will sing, "*shivti b'veis Hashem, kol yemei chayai...*"

Together, dancing hand in hand, may we be *zocheh* to greet *Mashiach tzidkeinu bimheirah v'yameinu. Amen.*

Acknowledgments

Several months ago I sat down at my desk to begin work on a new book. Having already written four books in this series of inspiring stories for the heart, I wanted to do something a little different. While still aiming to present stories that are inspiring or entertaining, my priority was to find stories that challenge the reader to grow. I sought out stories that would strike the depths of the heart and awaken deep feelings and emotions: food for thought for the days of Elul, leading up to and through the Yamim Noraim.

I did not really know, however, where I would find the stories to fit my goal. Nevertheless, I got started, and as I began to write, with a great deal of *siyata d'Shmaya,* the stories began to roll my way: incredible stories the likes of which I had never heard before.

Today, I am proud to present a collection of **Stories That Awaken the Heart.** These are stories of ordinary people whose hearts were touched, warmed, and awakened by incidents and situations that led them to see Hashem's wondrous guiding "hand" in their lives, and to realize the greatness stored within themselves. I thank Hashem for leading me on this amazing and enriching adventure, and for giving me the opportunity to make a *kiddush Hashem.*

Writing a book of this nature is not the sort of project one can accomplish alone. There were many people who were involved in making this book a reality.

I am thankful to the following people, who were gracious enough to share their stories and experiences with me.

Rabbi Lazer Brody (Israel), Rabbi Shlomo Price (Israel), Rabbi Shmuel Grama (Lakewood), Rabbi Moshe Tuvia Lieff (Brooklyn), Rabbi Yerachmiel Milstein (Brooklyn), Rabbi Ahron Naftoli Heisler (Lakewood), Rabbi Kalman Krohn (Lakewood), Rabbi Moshe Grossman (Brooklyn), Rabbi Baruch Lederman (San Diego, CA), Rabbi Avi Fishoff (Brooklyn), Rabbi Heshy Pincus (Brooklyn), Rabbi Leibish Langer (Brooklyn), Rabbi Benzion Klatzko (Monsey), Rabbi Yonason Schwartz (Brooklyn).

Special thank goes to **Rabbi Duvi Bensoussan (Lakewood) and Rabbi Zecharia Wallerstein (Brooklyn)**, for sharing with me a number of their incredible stories and thoughts.

Thank you, **Rabbi Zalman Leib Meisels** and **Rabbi Moshe Yosef Unger**, for allowing me to reprint the stories about the Veitzener Rav, Rabbi Tzvi Hirsch Meisels *zt"l*, from the *sefer*, "*Mekadshei Hashem.*"

Although my rebbi, **Rav Dovid Kviat**, has passed on, his memory lives on in my heart, and continues to inspire me to reach new heights each and every day.

My Rav, **Rabbi Gavriel Finkel**, has encouraged me in this series from its inception. Thank you; your support really means a lot to me.

I would like to thank my dynamic editing team. The chief editor for this book was **Ari Nestlebaum**. Ari has polished and crystallized my stories, infusing them with heart and soul. His contribution will be appreciated by my readers as he has helped me to bring the stories in this book to life. Ari was joined by his talented mother, **Mrs. Chana Nestlebaum**, who has been the editor for the "Stories for the Heart" series since its inception. Her insightful editing and approach to the written word has helped make this book a real pleasure to read. May you both continue to enhance the Torah world with your writing talents for many years to come.

Thank you, **Rabbi Meir Zlotowitz** and **Rabbi Nosson Scherman**, for welcoming me into the ArtScroll family. It is an honor to be part of a movement that has awakened the hearts of thousands of Jews across the globe. May you both continue to spread the light of Hashem with good health, *berachah*, and *kol tuv* for many years to come.

The **ArtScroll team** has done a superb job once again. I am always amazed by the professionalism of their talented and dedicated staff. Thank you, **Rabbi Avrohom Biderman**, for always being there for me, and getting the job done. Thank you, **Reb Mendy Herzberg**, for coordinating, and seeing this project through from start to finish. Thank you, **Mrs. Mindy Stern**, for your insightful editing and comments. Thank you, **Mrs. Faygie Weinbaum**, for your meticulous proofreading. Thank you, **Reb Eli Kroen**, for producing another striking cover.

My good friend **Rabbi Zalman Feuer** has been instrumental in helping me with source material in this book and others. He has been a wellspring of knowledge from which I often draw. Thank you.

Thank you, **Rabbi Shea Rosenfeld**, rosh yeshivah of Yeshivah of Central Park, where I have the great *zechus* of serving as the *mashgiach ruchni*. I also thank my *talmidim* in yeshivah with whom I have had the opportunity to share my stories on many occasions.

My parents, **Reb Yosef and Marsha Pruzansky**, have always been my role models in *chesed* and life. My father, through his catering business and beyond, has always warmed people's hearts through his middos and *lev tov*. My mother's *ayin tov* and cheer are traits I will forever admire.

My in-laws, **Rabbi Shmuel Gedaliah and Raizel Pollak**, are everything a son-in-law can ask for. My father-in-law has always been a great role model for me and my family. His dedication to Torah and *tefillah* is something to which I continue to aspire.

Thank you to my siblings, **Avi and Rivky Pruzansky, Michoel and Raizy Pruzansky, Shea and Baila Caller**, and **Shmully and Shulamis Sussman**, for your continuous support.

Finally I would like to thank my wife **Rochie** for her constant support in all of my endeavors. This book and my other projects take up a lot of my time, and I deeply appreciate her patience and dedication in helping make my dreams come true. She is truly a partner in all of my work. May we continue to see *nachas* and *berachah* from our dear children, **Avrohom Yaakov, Shaindy, Simcha, Chayala, Miriam, and Batsheva**.

It is my hope that this book will inspire and uplift those who read it.

Binyomin Pruzansky
Lakewood NJ
Av 5771 / August 2011

Chapter 1: Answering the Call

The Slonimer Rebbe, in his work Nesivos Shalom, offers us a powerful assertion about the often mysterious ways in which Hashem runs His world and our lives: there are times when He calls to us in a hidden manner. The call may arrive via an incident in our lives, a difficult challenge, or an accidental, unusual occurrence that begs our attention. These are ways in which Hashem calls us to action, begging us to realize that He is calling our name and waiting for our response. In this series of stories, we will meet people who heeded this call, and perhaps we will be inspired by their experiences.

Lazer's Mission

Rabbi Lazer Brody has touched thousands of lives through the books he has written and translated on emunah and Jewish ethics. In particular, the book, "Garden of Emunah," a translation of the teachings of Rabbi Shalom Arush, has become quite popular and is often cited by countless individuals as a life-changing force. Rabbi Brody has dedicated his life to spreading the light of Hashem to those who founder in the darkness. But what of Rabbi Brody's own journey to teshuvah? In this story, Rabbi Brody describes a miraculous event that happened to him when he was a young, secular soldier in the midst of a war.

The year was 1982, and northern Israel found itself under heavy rocket fire from neighboring Lebanon. Katyusha rockets were terrorizing Israeli civilians and rendering them nearly senseless with fear; at any moment, sirens could send parents and their children scrambling to find shelter before projectiles slammed into their midst. Israel was effectively under siege, and the Lebanon war had begun.

At the time, Menachem Begin was prime minister, Ariel Sharon was the defense minister, and Rafael Eitan was the chief of staff of the IDF. Together, they conceived of a plan to end the rocket fire once and for all; they summoned an elite team of commandos of which I was a part. We were told that we would answer only to the commander in chief himself, and then we were informed of the dangerous mission we had been chosen to undertake. It was a moment I would never forget.

I hadn't started out in life imagining that I would be where I was in '82. I had led a mostly traditional, irreligious Jewish life when I was growing up in Maryland, and it was only after graduating college in 1970 that I acted on my strong attachment to my ancestral homeland and made *aliyah*. There I built myself the Israeli dream, settling on sprawling moshav farmland in the mountaintops of Shomron and living the good life.

I joined the IDF almost as soon as I was settled, and I rose rapidly in rank and acclaim, leading many daring counterterrorism missions during and after the Yom Kippur War. Many of these missions took place in locations throughout Lebanon. When I was summoned from the reserves to take part in a commando strike on the source of the rocket fire, I knew they had chosen me because I knew Lebanon almost as well as my own backyard.

As a reconnaissance sergeant, intelligence and maps were my specialty. For this mission, my job was to clear the way for the army by mapping their path into enemy territory based on the information that had been gathered. I was to lead them to their main target and avoid ambushes along the way. It was a highly dangerous operation, and I was honored to be asked to do it.

We discovered that the heavy missile fire was originating from the Russian Embassy in Beirut. Well aware that the Israelis wouldn't risk provoking war with the Russians by air-striking the embassy, terrorists had planted four batteries of Katyusha rockets right in the courtyard. These batteries were capable of launching 38 rockets per minute, and they needed to be neutralized.

On Saturday morning, General Eitan flew us to base via helicopter, where he met our group of 12 men to inform us of our mission and outfit us with heavy-duty equipment. Our unit was to infiltrate West Beirut and take out the missile batteries at close range. It was essentially a suicide mission, as we were being asked to directly face the den of terrorists who would be waiting for us in that courtyard. Though I had my doubts about successfully proceeding four kilometers into Beirut in broad daylight, I had received my orders and there was no turning back.

At exactly noon, our mission commenced. We split into four groups of three — my group consisted of myself, a radioman, and a tank hunter with a shoulder-mounted missile launcher — and began our sprint through the streets of Beirut.

All seemed to be going well for the first two kilometers, but then it became suddenly and frighteningly clear that the Lebanese had simply been holding their breath. All at once, the world seemed to cave in on us. Snipers rained fire upon us from rooftops south of our position. Other snipers were mounted in the north, stationed near the University of Beirut. From behind us, rockets streaked at us from the Syrian mountains while Katyushas targeted us from the Russian Embassy.

We did our best to avoid the hail of sniper bullets as the Katyushas began pounding into the earth closer and closer to our position. One fell 300 meters away, but then the next ones hit 200 and then only 100 meters from our location. At that proximity, it's all a person can do to keep his insides from leaping out of his mouth from panic and the sheer vibration of the impact. The roar of sound itself numbed my senses; my heart seemed to be pounding much faster than I thought possible, and the smoke choked us in the already sweltering 95-degree weather. A 10-story building right next to us suddenly collapsed before our eyes.

Then a Katyusha thudded right into our midst, and we experienced our first casualty as the commander of our unit was killed in the ensuing blast of glass and concrete. Before I could even draw another breath, my radioman, Rafi, went down in agony, with shrapnel embedded in his torso. The bleeding was profuse, and I immediately knelt by him to tie a tourniquet and prevent him from bleeding to death.

"Don't leave me to die!" Rafi screamed in naked fright. "Lazer, please don't leave me!"

Looking around desperately, I hauled Rafi under the relative safety of a vegetable cart that had flipped over in the pandemonium. I didn't get there in time to prevent a piece of shrapnel from slamming into my eye. I screamed in agony as I felt blood begin to pour from my wound; I was certain that I had lost the eye, but I didn't have much time to dwell on the pain in the face of my more important goal: survival.

The situation did not look promising in that respect. Bullets and Katyushas zipped toward us from all sides, my commander was dead, my radioman was bleeding slowly, and my own face was so smeared with blood that I could barely see anything at all. Smoke was filling my lungs and throat, and metal, glass, and concrete shards were flying everywhere that I could see. Katyushas were landing closer yet; one landed only 60 meters away, and I could hear the hiss of shrapnel in the air above my head. Glancing at my watch with my good eye, I estimated that I probably had about 30 to 40 more seconds to live.

Unbidden, my life began passing before me in the feverish racing of my mind. I could imagine my parents: the years I had spent with them, and how stricken they would be when they learned I was dead. To think that my mother was a Holocaust survivor who had already lost her daughter — my sister — to cancer! Now she would lose her oldest son as well.

And what have you to show for yourself, Lazer?

I began considering my own life, and in that regard I felt even more sorrow. Here I was, living in a *chiloni* (secular) paradise. I had my college degrees, a beautiful farm, made a good living, and enjoyed the local culture. In addition, I had a high-profile career in the special forces to brag about, and I was fighting for my country, a lofty cause indeed. I really had it all, didn't I? But suddenly, it wasn't enough. What about my soul? What would I take with me on my personal Day of Judgment, when I faced my Creator to give an accounting of my life? Why, I barely had any connection to Him whatsoever! At this realization, I was suddenly awash with the kind of despair that defies description. My life had no real meaning. I was about to die, and the world would not suffer in the slightest from my removal.

Oxygen was almost completely cut off now, and I dully noted the thud of yet another Katyusha touching down almost on top of me. I was beginning to black out, and I estimated another 20 seconds of precious life were left to me. I was prepared for the end, and I was only sorry that I hadn't really had a chance to truly live.

Suddenly, as though jolted by an invisible electric prod, I felt a surge as my body and soul joined to call out one last time to the only One Who might save me.

Hashem, Hashem! Save me, please! Please!

It may have been a silent scream, but the whole of my body shook with the force of it. Reeling with emotion, I promised G-d that I would dedicate my life to Him should I be given another chance to live it. Right then, with only 15 seconds left of my calculated lifespan, something unbelievable happened.

A voice thundered within me, resonating throughout my entire body.

Eliezer Rafael!

It was my full Hebrew name, such as I hadn't heard since my bar mitzvah.

Don't worry, My son, I will help you get out of here! You must change your life, for this is not your war. You must fight a different war.

With only seconds remaining, I nodded sluggishly. I understood. I was to fight a war within myself, against my Evil Inclination. I was willing to do it, of course, but it didn't seem to matter anymore. After all, I was about to die…

BOOM!

A thunderous noise above my head grabbed hold of my rapidly

waning consciousness. Was it a bomb? Looking up dimly, I noticed an airplane screaming over the scene. There was a Star of David on it. Two Israeli fighter jets trailed it, firing rapidly at the snipers to the south, killing them where they stood. On the second loop, the fighters destroyed the building that the northern snipers were shooting from. Then, with a vengeance, they streaked toward the rocket fire emanating from the Syrian mountains.

The air was suddenly clear, as the rocket fire from the embassy had inexplicably halted as well. I took a deep, shuddering, cleansing breath, and my senses and consciousness began to return. I became aware of the wail of a siren as Israeli Army ambulances came our way. Tears of pain and relief began to flow from my eyes, and I experienced my next shock: my wounded eye was fine! My tears had cleared away the blood and grime from my face, and I realized that I had not lost any vision at all. The miracle I had prayed for was coming together right before me.

As the medic saw to Rafi and other soldiers dealt with the commander who had been killed, I felt my energy returning in a flood. My unit regrouped under my lead, and together we sprinted the remaining two kilometers to the embassy and reached it at last. There were hardly any pockets of resistance left there, as many terrorists had fled in the face of the air strikes. Those who remained were easily disposed of, and it seemed mere minutes before we were mounting our shoulder missiles and, at close range, destroying every last scrap of the Katyusha batteries in that courtyard. Our mission was complete, and the way was cleared for the IDF to completely take over West Beirut.

After the war, I lived up to my promise to the One Who saved me that day. He became my new Commander in Chief, and I was honored to be His soldier in a very different sort of war. I found my way to Aish Hatorah and began to study my own rich heritage: an entire world I hadn't even known was there. Torah and halachah lent my life the depth and meaning I had been lacking, and I remained immersed in it until I eventually received *semichah* from the yeshivah and discovered my newest mission as a commando in G-d's army.

I was to spread the knowledge that I had learned to my fellow Jews across the world. I was to help them find the voice within themselves that is calling their names, to hear it as clearly as I heard it that day in Lebanon. Through increasing simple *emunah*, a Jew has the power to tune himself into this voice and listen to its instructions about attaining true happiness.

I believe that is why Hashem called to me that day and, as a good soldier, I will do my utmost to fulfill my mission: to fight a war.

My Brother's Keeper

People often fail to recognize the power of their words, and their responsibility to use this power with care and compassion for others. The Torah teaches us that Hashem holds us responsible for the pain we cause. In the very first dispute between two human beings, Adam's son Cain kills his brother Hevel. When Hashem, in an effort to pique Cain's conscience, asks Cain, "Where is your brother," Cain responds, "I do not know. Am I my brother's keeper?" Hashem answers with the words, "What have you done? The voice of your brother's blood cries out to Me from the ground."

In this rebuke, Hashem is telling Cain, "Yes, you are your brother's keeper. And had you treated your brother as a true brother, then you would never have spilled his blood. His blood is screaming out, 'Why didn't you treat me as a brother, Cain?'"

Although harsh words might not physically spill our brother's blood, they may emotionally and spiritually destroy him. Hashem *expects more from us — He expects us to be our brother's keeper, as Yossi Steinfeld* learned in this amazing story.*

Once upon a time, I was one of those rare, fortunate people who could look at my life and say, "I have everything I could possibly ask for." My real-estate business was thriving, built on my reputation for hard work and honesty. My family was thriving as well. My wife Sarah was a true *eishes chayil* devoted to raising our lively, adorable son, who had just had his *upsherin*, and my sweet 14-month-old daughter, who was beginning to toddle around the house on her unsteady legs. I was living a dream, until one day, I received a rude and terrifying awakening.

I was in the middle of an important business meeting, and I had instructed my secretary to hold all telephone calls until the meeting was concluded. Nevertheless, just as the meeting began, my phone began to ring. My secretary apologized for the interruption, but she knew I would want to take the call. It was my wife, and there was an emergency at home.

"Yossi, Yossi!" Sara called to me in a low, mournful tone. My stomach suddenly fluttered with a sense of foreboding.

"It's about Dovi," she continued. "You know how he hasn't been feeling well for the past week, and the doctor couldn't figure out what was going on, so he took some tests. Well, the results just came back and the doctor wants to see us. He says it's very serious, Yossi. Oy, my poor little boy!"

I canceled my meeting and drove home muttering silent prayers to Hashem. "Let it be a false alarm," I pleaded. "Let my Dovi just go back to normal, please, Hashem. He's just a little boy!"

When I arrived home, Dovi suddenly looked so much frailer to me than he had just that morning. We thought perhaps he had a flu or a virus — something that would run its course. Now, as I lifted him into my arms, he seemed weightless. I gently placed him into the car, feeling as if he could break like a fragile piece of crystal. As we drove to the doctor's office, there was silence in the car, my wife and I each lost in our thoughts and prayers, and the usually energetic Dovi sitting spent and listless in his car seat.

We were ushered directly into Doctor Rubin's office. One look at his face confirmed our worst fears.

"I'm sorry to tell you this, but the results of Dovi's blood tests show that Dovi has a very serious and rare disease. He needs immediate medical attention. Time is of the essence and if we don't act fast we are in danger of losing him."

My wife's face collapsed and tears coursed down her cheeks. Tears filled my eyes too, as this sudden, harsh new reality set in. But this wasn't time to mourn; it was time to act.

"Okay, then, what do we have to do? We'll take him to the best doctor there is, anywhere in Manhattan. Anywhere in the world!" I proclaimed.

Dr. Rubin had already done our homework for us. He had contacted doctors in the speciality that pertained to Dovi's condition, and had singled out the most renowned expert in this field. Dr. Green,* located in Boston, was the man who could save our son. Dr. Rubin had already contacted him; he was a religious Jew himself, eager to help a Jewish family. An appointment had been made for us for the coming Tuesday at 4 p.m.

"I suggest you book a room in a hotel there for a few days, and pray for the best," Dr. Rubin concluded.

"Thank you for taking care of everything," my wife told the doctor gratefully. "At least we know which way to turn. Thank you."

Early Tuesday morning we drove up to Boston and settled into our hotel. As my wife was drained both physically and emotionally, she stayed in the room to rest while I took Dovi for the appointment, arriving at Dr. Green's office a few minutes early, with enough time to fill out the paperwork required for our visit. I provided all of my, my wife's, and Dovi's personal information, and described the ailment that caused our visit. I handed the paper to the receptionist, who gave it a quick glance, smiled reassuringly at me, and said, "Don't worry. You are in great hands. Dr. Green is the best. He has a lot of experience in this field, and has had a lot of success."

With those words of hope to hold onto, I sat down and cradled Dovi in my lap. I opened my *Tehillim* and began to recite its soothing words, until I heard my name being called. My heart pumping fiercely with both hope and trepidation, I followed the nurse into the doctor's office, with my little son draped limply over my shoulder.

I had expected to encounter a sympathetic, or at least interested, attitude from Dr. Green, and therefore, I was puzzled by the cold, detached look on his face as he introduced himself.

"Mr. Steinfeld, I have reviewed your case," he said deliberately, looking me hard in the eye. "And after having given it much thought, I have decided that there is no way that I can treat your son. I'm sorry."

"What? Why not? You have to help us! You're our only hope!" I cried in shock.

"I'm sorry, but you will have to leave now. I will not be the one to help you," the doctor said with quiet, rock-hard firmness. "Goodbye, Mr. Steinfeld."

"But I don't understand," I kept arguing. I felt I could not leave this doctor's presence until I had secured the help for which we had come. "I was told that you were the only man in the country who would know how to treat my son, and now you are telling me that you can't help him?"

"I didn't say I can't help your son, Mr. Steinfeld. I said that I won't!"

The scene was unfolding like a nonsensical, yet horrifying nightmare. "What are you talking about? Why not? What's going on here?"

The doctor tilted his head slightly upward, giving me a full view of his face. "Yossi Steinfeld, look at me. Do you remember me from anywhere?"

Now I was puzzled. He had called me "Yossi," and obviously knew who I was. Yet his face stirred no memory in my mind.

"Think back, Yossi. Maybe you don't remember me, but I'm sure you remember my son, Reuven Green."

The mention of Reuven's name aroused a vaguely uncomfortable feeling inside me. "Reuven Green…yeah, I think I do remember him. He was a blond-haired boy who was in my seventh-grade class. Now that you mention it, I do remember him. Why do you ask?"

The coldness in Dr. Green's eyes dissolved in the film of tears that formed there as he related the heretofore unknown tale of Reuven Green.

"We moved to New York from out of town about 15 years ago; the school year had already begun when my son entered the seventh grade of your yeshivah. He was a bright boy who had loads of potential, and we thought he would settle in fast and make lots of friends.

"But he wasn't given a chance. You were one of the leaders of the class and you picked on my son. He was an out-of-towner, a little different in his ways, and you ridiculed him and called him names. You excluded him from the gang, and he was so very hurt. I spoke to your parents and your rebbi, but to no avail. I even spoke to you one day after school, hoping that you would feel some remorse, but you never let up. You destroyed my son.

"After eighth grade, my son had totally lost interest in yeshivah. He hated it, he hated his classmates and he hated Judaism. He refused to go to any high school in New York, so we decided that it would be best to move back to a smaller community. That's when we moved to Boston.

"But my son never recovered from his yeshivah experience and he slowly went off the *derech*. He stopped going to shul, stopped keeping mitzvos, and didn't even keep Shabbos unless we begged him. Eventually, he took off his yarmulke, changed his name to Robert, and moved away. I haven't seen Reuven in five years. I don't even know where he is. You destroyed my son and now you want me to save your son. I won't."

My tears and my pleading were of no avail. Finally, in defeat, I carried my son out of the doctor's office and placed him gently into his seat in the car. I sat down in my seat and burst into tears.

Images from the past played out in my mind. There was blond-haired, confident Reuven, the new kid in seventh grade, a contender for my position as king of the class. I had to protect my popularity, so I turned on him and of course, my friends followed suit. We didn't let him play our games or tag along with us at recess.

I knew Reuven was bothered, but I didn't care. I was protecting my turf, and quite successfully, too. My rebbi spoke to me, his father spoke to me, but no one succeeded in making me feel any remorse for Reuven's pain. All was fair in classroom politics, as far as I was concerned. Truthfully, I couldn't imagine that it really mattered that much to Reuven. I was playing my part and he was playing his, which unfortunately for him was not so choice a role. I remembered hearing that Reuven and his family had moved to Boston, but it never occurred to me for a moment that I had anything to do with that decision. I was just a kid!

Now, that whole long-ago era had come back to haunt me. Dejected, I headed back to the hotel to tell my wife the terrible news. Sarah was heartbroken by this unexpected turn of events, and although I tried to assure her that there must be another doctor that could help us, we both knew that Dr. Green was our son's best chance for recovery.

Nevertheless, we immediately began to make calls to doctors and specialist to see if there was another option in Boston or elsewhere. In every case, however, the trail led back to Dr. Green.

After davening Maariv and eating some supper, I sat down on

the couch, opened my *Tehillim,* and began to pour my heart out to Hashem, begging for some indication of which way to turn. After a while, the sheer emotional exhaustion of the day overcame me and I fell asleep.

Incredibly, that night I had a vivid dream. My grandmother, who had passed away earlier that year, came to me and said, "Yossi, go to Maine. That is where you will find a *yeshuah.*"

I woke up with a start. The dream was so real, but what did it mean? What was there for us in Maine? I did some research to find out if perhaps there was a specialist there whose name had so far eluded us, but there seemed to be none.

"I don't know what it's all about," I told my wife, "but I feel certain that this was not merely a dream. It was a message that we can't ignore. Tomorrow, I'm driving to Maine!"

"But where in Maine?" she asked. "It's a big state. What will you do when you get there?"

"I don't know," I admitted. "But this is all we have to go on right now, and Dovi's life is at stake. I'm willing to try."

Early the next morning, I set out on my journey, finally arriving after a 5-hour drive. With no specific destination in mind, I decided that the best place to stop would be the nearest shul. Of course, I had no idea where that might be either. So I pulled into a gas station to ask directions.

There was a mechanic bent over the open hood of a car. I walked over to him and asked for directions to the nearest synagogue.

"Sorry, sir, but there's no synagogue around here. Probably isn't one for another 50 miles," he said, barely looking up from the engine.

"Are you sure?" I persisted. I hadn't traveled five hours just to turn around and go back to Boston, but if I couldn't get to a shul, I had no idea where I would go.

Now the man looked up, a trace of annoyance showing on his face. "Let me ask one of my workers if he knows where there's a synagogue. Hey, Robert!" he shouted at a man who stood inside the garage, working on a car boosted high on a lift. "Come on out for a minute. A guy here needs some directions."

"I'll be out in a second, boss," the man responded, wiping his greasy hands on his work pants.

When I heard the boss call the name "Robert," my heart began to race. Didn't Doctor Green say that his son changed his name from Reuven to Robert? Could this be where the dream was leading me?

I could barely breathe as I awaited Robert's appearance. He emerged from the garage, and the moment he saw me, his face turned red. It was hard to discern the old Reuven from under the long disheveled hair and rough appearance, not to mention the many changes wrought by 15 years. Clearly, though, my appearance hadn't changed much and he recognized me.

"Can't help you, sir," he stated flatly. "Goodbye."

"Reuven, is that you?" I responded.

With an expression fierce as a warrior's, he stepped close to me and thrust a pointed finger at my face.

"Get out of here, Yossi," he said. "I don't know how you found me here, but I'm telling you that if you don't get out right now, I'll kill you with my bare hands!"

"Please listen to me, Reuven," I pleaded, trying to break through to the human heart beneath the anger. "My son is dying, and only you can help me."

"Leave now or I will call the cops," he retorted, as uncaring about my pain as I had once been toward his.

"Let me explain…" I began. But he cut me off with a blast of long-smoldering anger. "Now you want to explain? What about when we were in yeshivah and you ruined my life and I begged you to stop? Then you didn't want to talk it over with me. Get lost!"

Before I allowed him to cut me off completely, I managed to inject that the only hope for my son's survival was his father's medical treatment, but his father had refused to help me. With that message delivered, I went back to my car. On one hand, I was dejected over Reuven's refusal to help me. On the other hand, however, I could not help but feel Hashem's strong hand guiding me, bringing me to exactly the place where Reuven was to be found. The answer to my problem had been revealed to me, but accessing the help remained a frustrating puzzle.

Arriving back at the hotel, I related my incredible journey to my wife. "It's so frustrating," I told her. "There he was. In the whole state of Maine I just happened upon the exact person I needed to find. But he won't do a thing to help us!"

"Let's go back there together tomorrow, Yossi," she suggested. "We'll take Dovi with us, and when he sees this poor, sick little boy, I believe he will change his mind."

The next morning, we set out once again on the road to Maine. Again, I pulled up to the garage where Reuven worked, and we emerged from the car together, as a family, with the limp little Dovi borne like an infant in my wife's arms. I saw Reuven's expression as we approached. It hadn't softened in the least.

"Didn't I tell you to get out of my life?" he shouted as we got closer.

"Well, I figured I would give it one more chance," I replied softly. "It's my son…and well, I have to try."

We stood there like three beggars hoping for a few stray coins. I saw Reuven glancing at my wife with Dovi in her arms. His eyes lost some of their fierceness, for how could anyone be unmoved by the innocent suffering of a mother and child.

"All right, talk," he said begrudgingly. "I can spare a few minutes."

I explained to him what had happened to my son, and that the only person who could save him was his father. It was difficult to read the expression on his face as he heard the story. Did he truly lack any sympathy whatsoever, or was he just trying not to betray his emotions?

"Well, I'm sorry for your son. But what do you want from me?" he asked.

"Listen, your father blames me for causing you to leave Judaism and move out of the house. I believe that the only way he will take my son as a patient is if you come back with me to see your father again."

"Go back to my father? I can't do that anymore," he stated irritably. "Please…just leave me alone. It's too late to change things. You ruined my life and you can't turn the clock back. I can't forgive you for the way you tormented me and ruined my name, and I'm certainly not putting myself through a reunion with my father just to help you."

If it were just me needing the help, perhaps I would have quit right then and there, believing that I was probably getting just what I deserved. But it wasn't just me. It was an innocent baby and a heartbroken mother who had to bear the brunt of the damage I had caused. I had to make Reuven see that his revenge, though aimed at me, was literally killing a child.

"Please, Reuven, I beg of you. Look at my baby. He's dying in front of your eyes and you are his only hope," I said in a choked voice. My heart felt as though it would crack under the pressure of my fears for my child and my regret for the angry, bitter man that I, with my ignorant bullying, had helped to create.

"I know I messed you up, Reuven," I told him. "But it's not too late. It's true that we can't turn back the clock, but we can move ahead. I promise I will make it up to you somehow, I promise you. Please, please forgive me."

By this time, I was no longer attempting to hold back my tears. I was sobbing, begging for my son's life, begging for forgiveness, and sick with shame for all the troubles my cocky 13-year-old self had set loose in the world. Then, at last, my tears and pleas reached Reuven's heart.

"All right, I'll try to help — just for your son's sake. But what can I do?"

The next day, an odd foursome comprised of me, my wife, Dovi, and Reuven traveled back to Boston. Reuven made a stop at a barbershop for a very short haircut, and clapped one of my extra yarmulkes on top of his newly groomed head before we headed into Dr. Green's office. Reuven led the way into the reception area and marched straight up to the secretary. She stared at him a moment, and then exclaimed in a flash of joyful recognition, "Reuven, is that really you? Dr. Green, Dr. Green, come quick!"

Dr. Green emerged from a door behind the reception desk, no doubt expecting to see a medical emergency playing out in the waiting room. Instead, he looked up at the young man standing at the desk and he seemed ready to vault through the Plexiglas divider to embrace his son on the other side.

In seconds, he had dashed through the door and into the waiting room, calling, "Reuvy? Reuvy?" He reached his son and enveloped him in a tight embrace. "Oh, *baruch Hashem*! You're back!" the father cried into his son's shoulder.

The father and son continued hugging, crying, and repeating each other's names as if to reassure themselves that the reunion was real.

At last, Reuven pulled away from his father's shoulder and said, "Oh, Daddy, I'm so sorry for everything I put you through. But listen, please help Yossi's son. Everything is forgiven and things will be different now."

With that one statement, Dr. Green's heart was released from the pain that had prevented him from doing what he knew had to be done: to give his utmost effort to save a precious child. He took Dovi on as his patient, and true to his reputation, the surgeries and treatments he provided saved little Dovi's life.

Dr. Green got his son back as well. Reuven traveled to Israel to study in a *baal teshuvah* yeshivah where he found the inspiration he needed to return fully to Hashem and His Torah. Two years after he embarked on his return journey, his rebbi introduced him to a young woman who was studying with his wife. They married, and today they are the parents of a beautiful Jewish family, far from the gas station in Maine, and very close to a shul.

I share this story to serve as a lesson to all. Words can destroy lives. Even when we are young and carefree, we have to understand that our words can hurt more than anything in the world. Had I realized all the damage my words would cause, I am sure I would never have spoken them. Through all that happened to me, Hashem taught me this lesson, and He showed me as well the power of apology and forgiveness. If you do slip up and hurt someone, it's always worthwhile to try to make amends, for you never know what you might accomplish.

The Winning Numbers

I was present at a parlor meeting on behalf of Moreshes Yehoshua, a yeshivah in Lakewood, NJ, led by veteran mechanech, Rabbi Dovid Trenk. At a point where other yeshivos might give up on their troubled talmidim, Rabbi Trenk sees only their potential and he opens his doors and his heart to them, offering them the confidence and warmth that brings out their best. The guest speaker at this parlor meeting was Rabbi Moshe Tuvia Lieff, the Rav of Flatbush's Agudah Beis Binyomin. Rabbi Lieff addressed the theme Rabbi Trenk represents — believing in every bachur — with a few magnificent stories.

There was a very important visitor to Rabbi Heshy Pincus' *sofer stam* store in Flatbush: Rabbi Avi Fishoff, accompanied by two of his young students. Rabbi Fishoff is the founder and director of "Home Sweet Home," a place he established in Flatbush for teenagers who find themselves facing difficult life situations. "Home Sweet Home" is a judgment-free safe house where teenagers can always find a warm welcome and steady encouragement to develop into the fine adults they have the potential to become.

The two young men who accompanied Rabbi Fishoff today had finally reached the monumental decision to don their tefillin once again. It had been years since either of them had done so, and Rabbi Fishoff did not treat their change of mind lightly. In his opinion, this called for a special trip to a *sofer stam* store, where his boys would see the detailed beauty and pinpoint accuracy required to produce the tefillin that their fellow Jews donned every morning.

Rabbi Pincus was often called upon to display his wares to upcoming bar mitzvah boys, but he had found that people of all ages gained by touring his establishment. Something about seeing the countless rolls of parchment with their painstaking lettering helped ignite a unique kind of love and appreciation of Yiddishkeit.

Rabbi Pincus treated his visitors that day with a special respect; the roughness of their speech and dress was enough to indicate to him that these boys had come a long way. After Rabbi Fishoff and his students had observed the marvel and beauty of tefillin, *mezuzos*, and Torah scrolls in the making, Rabbi Pincus asked if there was anything in particular he could do for them.

"Actually," replied Rabbi Fishoff, "these boys would like you to examine their bar mitzvah tefillin to see if they are still kosher."

The Rabbi smiled and accepted a pair of tefillin from the first of his young visitors. "I'd be glad to check these for you," he said, with feeling.

Rabbi Pincus disappeared into the back of the store for a little while, only to emerge a little while later with a stunned expression on his face.

"Where did you get these tefillin?" he asked the student who had given them over.

He looked puzzled. "My father gave them to me."

"Do you have any idea what these are worth?" Rabbi Pincus asked, breathlessly. "These are rosh yeshivah tefillin — they're the top of the line! Your father must love you very much!"

The young man smirked uncertainly. "Oh, c'mon, rabbi. They're just tefillin."

"See for yourself!" The store owner excitedly motioned the boy over to his table in the back of the store, where even untrained eyes could see that the *parshiyos* in these tefillin were markedly different — far better formed — than other parchments nearby.

Incredulity was stamped on the young man's face. "I don't believe it, rabbi. These *are* beautiful."

"What does your father do?" inquired Rabbi Pincus softly.

"He's a rebbi in Boro Park," replied the student absently, his eyes still trained on the parchment of his tefillin.

It was the rabbi's turn to look unbelieving. "Young man, do you realize how much this man must love you? Do you realize how long he must have saved his money to even have a *chance* to buy tefillin like these? If I were you, I would never forget how much your father loves you."

The boy finally raised his eyes to Rabbi Pincus, and they shone with a film of tears. He nodded silently.

"Would you be able to find out which *sofer* made these?" pressed Rabbi Pincus.

The young man hesitated. "Sure, rabbi."

Taking his cell phone out, he strode past Rabbi Fishoff and his friend and went outside for a couple of minutes. When he returned, Rabbi Pincus met him at the front of the store.

"I texted my father, and he called me back and said the tefillin were written by a Rabbi Holtsberg," the student announced.

"I know Rabbi Holtsberg," murmured Rabbi Pincus in amazement. "His work really *is* the top of the line..."

But a few feet away, Rabbi Fishoff jumped as though he had just touched a hot stove. "Yitz!" he called, the shock blatant in his voice, "you *talked to your father?* You haven't communicated with your father in five years!"

The young man named Yitz gave a small smile, his eyes shining. "Rebbi, I just had to thank him for buying me tefillin as beautiful as these..."

"Five years!" thundered Rabbi Lieff at the parlor meeting. "This boy had not spoken to his father in five years, and yet he returned to him that day because he realized the strength of the unconditional love his father had for him! In chinuch, we must remember that there's no such thing as too late to reach a bachur.

"You should know that Yitz has never missed an opportunity to wear his beautiful tefillin since that day. He has begun to keep Shabbos again, and has rebuilt his relationship with his father. It may have taken years, but ultimately unconditional love is the best way to show a young man that he can always come home."

An 81-year-old Jewish man was seeking an attorney to help him with a very special situation: his winning $8 million in the state lottery!

Now richer than he could have ever dreamed of being, the old man wanted to apportion his newfound wealth to each of his seven children, all of them G-d-fearing Jews with beautiful families, one of whom even worked as a *kiruv* rabbi.

It was only when an acceptable Jewish lawyer had been located that the old man revealed the second part of his request: that a check for $10 was to be sent to the government of Germany, along with this fascinating note:

To Whom It May Concern:

My name is Yosef Klein, * *and I am a Holocaust survivor.*

When I was a child, the Nazis invaded my town in Poland and stuffed me and my family into one of the Auschwitz-bound cattle-cars. There was no food or water for the two days of the trip, and barely any room to breathe.

When we arrived, weak and sickly from the days of deprivation, my parents were immediately sent to their deaths. My siblings followed soon after. Only I, who was young and strong, was permitted to live. Then, they branded my arm as though I were an unknowing animal, changing my identity from Yosef Klein to the impersonal number: 24753. It was by this number that I was known until the day of my liberation, and it was this tattoo that I hated above all else.

Though I wanted nothing more than for it to rub off and fade into the past along with my horrific ordeal in the concentration camp, the tattoo stubbornly remained. Even as I rebuilt my life and my family in America, the numbers on my arm offered a constant reminder of what your Nazis had done to my family and my people.

Therefore, today, I am enclosing a check for $10. You see, the constant presence of these numbers eventually caused me to realize that they are actually lucky numbers, since they represent my survival and that of the Jewish people. After all, we survivors still walk the earth with our tattoos, but the Nazis have drifted away into dust and ash, only remembered as the villains of the world. I began to play these numbers in the lottery every day: 2, 4, 7, 24, 47, 53. It took 30 years, but it seems I was correct to regard them as lucky numbers, as I just won $8 million in the state lottery. I will be using this money to further the needs of my children and the Jewish people, both of whom are well and thriving.

The $10 is to reimburse you for the cost of tattooing these numbers on my arm, as I feel I owe you your part in my people's victory. Consider this a token of my appreciation.

Sincerely,
Yosef Klein

Rabbi Lieff then related how he had told the above story at a different event, and was later approached by a man who described a similar incident that occurred with his father, also a Holocaust survivor.

My father was in the hospital recently, where he was to undergo surgery. As he was being wheeled to the operating room, he suddenly became hysterical and began shouting: "No! I won't go! You can't take me there! No!"

My mother rushed to his side and tried to calm him, asking worriedly what had suddenly happened to cause such a dramatic reaction. My father pointed to the hospital band around his wrist.

"Is it too tight?" my mother asked.

"The numbers," explained my father in a stunned voice.

We looked, and unbelievably, the numbers on his wristband were the same as the ones tattooed on his arm by the Nazis decades ago!

"I can't go into surgery wearing these numbers," my father continued, his voice shaking. "These are evil numbers."

My mother was quiet for a moment, but then she leaned closer and said: "No, Chaim, these numbers are *lucky*. You see, the number before it died and the number after it died, but you won! You got to leave the Nazis behind, you have a life and a family of Torah Jews! These numbers are the best kind of *zechus* you could possibly bring with you to surgery."

My father calmed down when he heard this, and went into surgery with confidence and peace. The surgery was a success.

Rabbi Lieff concluded with one final, memorable tale:

A young *baal teshuvah* observed the custom of going to the *mikveh* every Rosh Hashanah. It was a custom that was both a meaningful and anxiety-ridden experience for him, as it was the only time of year that one indelible remnant of his past life might be revealed for all to see: a wraparound tattoo of a snake on his upper arm.

Generally, he was especially cautious to keep a towel slung casually over his tattoo until the moment of immersion, when he would cast it aside just long enough to dip in the water and then immediately reclaim it. For several years, he managed his pre-

Rosh Hashanah immersion without incident until one occasion, when he stumbled briefly on his way to the water and the towel slipped to the floor, revealing his tattoo for all the frum-from-birth attendees of the *mikveh* to see.

His face flushed in humiliation as a hush replaced the buzz of the crowded room. Some men pointed openly, while others averted their gaze.

"Look," rang out the unabashed voice of a child, "that man has a tattoo of a snake!"

The *baal teshuvah* cast his eyes to the floor, his face burning. But then another, stronger voice rang out:

"So, he has a tattoo? Big deal! So do I."

He looked up, and was startled to find that the voice emanated from Reb Asher, the venerable *gabbai* of the shul who had spent decades learning Torah on the same small bench. Could it be that such a *talmid chacham* could really have a tattoo as well? The shamefaced *baal teshuvah* didn't think so, but was still grateful for the *gabbai's* backing. The renewed buzz indicated that the chastened *mikveh*-goers had moved on from his tattoo. He completed his immersion quickly and then hurried to catch up with the *gabbai* outside the building.

"Listen, Reb Asher, I just wanted to thank you for sticking up for me at the *mikveh,* but I feel bad that you had to lie in order to do so."

The old man smiled. "It wasn't a lie."

When the other man's unbelieving half-smile didn't fade, Reb Asher drew up his sleeve.

"Oh," responded the *baal teshuvah* in an awed voice.

The tattooed number common to so many Holocaust survivors still stood out clearly on Reb Asher's forearm, and this tattoo was likewise a remnant of a past life.

"This tattoo," declared Reb Asher, "is a reminder of last generation's *churban*, when millions of our people fell to the Nazis. Your tattoo is a reminder of *this* generation's destruction, where millions of *neshamos* are also being consumed by various forces of the world.

But what is the difference between each of our *churbans*, really? We both survived! Let us both use our survival to rebuild and make a *kiddush Hashem* so we can serve Him in the best way possible."

We all go through challenges, and few of us emerge unscathed. In fact, many of us are scarred for life. The question remaining is: How will we regard those scars?

Certainly, the boy who decided to renew his commitment to the mitzvah of tefillin could have thrown in the towel at any time. Certainly, he could have regarded his past relationship with his father as an ordeal that would prevent him from going back to the person he once was. But instead, he used *his challenge to construct a new life; he rebuilt.*

A Holocaust survivor can certainly regard his own scar as a symbol of hopelessness and pain, of helplessness, as his world was destroyed around him. Or, he could use his unique marks to view himself as especially lucky, or to teach a young man of our own generation that those who survive, survive to rebuild. Scars left by our challenges need not be to our detriment. They can and should inspire us to greatness.

On the subject of scars, I have recently heard this story involving Rabbi Chaim Kanievsky — and unbelievable as it sounds — I have confirmed it to be true.

Baruch was simply running out of hope.

Sure, he had begun dating with a *shidduch* resume packed with details of his wonderful qualities. All of his rebbeim and friends could easily testify to his giving personality and his top-notch quality of learning. There was, however, one apparently insurmountable difficulty: the long, ugly scar trailing across Baruch's right cheek.

Baruch couldn't count the number of times he had winced at his own mirrored reflection and silently screamed: *Why, G-d? Why must I be so ugly?*

The story behind the scar was certainly not one of recklessness or thrill-seeking. It had been caused by a horrible attack that Baruch didn't like to think about. What he couldn't help but think about, however, was how freakish and unappealing it made him look, and how such a simple mark could be responsible for a five-year string of unsuccessful dates.

His *shadchan* had finally taken to admitting it outright to Baruch: the girls simply couldn't look past his deformity and see the sterling character behind it.

At the end of his rope, Baruch decided on impulse one day to grab a bus to Bnei Brak to speak to Rav Chaim Kanievsky. Perhaps a great *gadol's berachah* might sway the heavenly *beis din* in Baruch's favor and allow him to find his *bashert* at last.

When it was Baruch's turn to see Rav Chaim at last, he immediately poured out his pain and hurt to the *gadol*, describing the years of rejection that he was afraid were to be his permanent lot. Rav Chaim did indeed grant him a heartfelt *berachah* as well as a piece of unexpected advice:

"The next time you go out on a date, tell the story of your scar right away."

Baruch was puzzled by this advice. The story of his scar was not something he liked to dwell on, and certainly not the sort of conversation to initiate on a first date. Still, he resolved to follow Rav Chaim's words.

The next young woman he saw certainly seemed to possess the refined character and gentle sense of humor that Baruch liked, but her eyes traveled inexorably toward the scar on his cheek. Baruch steeled himself, and then waited for the right moment to bring it up. Soon there was a lull in their neutral conversation, and he seized the moment.

"I'm sure you must be wondering about the scar on my cheek. It isn't a story I like to tell, but I received it from a knife wielded by a murderous Arab in the *shuk*."

The girl leaned forward, her voice suddenly intensifying. "What happened?"

Baruch heaved a shaky sigh. "Well, I was walking through the *shuk* to get to the Kosel. People always used to do that years ago, since it was known to be relatively safe ground, usually crowded and patrolled by the police. This one time, though, it was sort of quiet. There had been some attacks against Jews recently, and I guess people had begun to fear the *shuk*. Still, it seemed pretty quiet and safe to me. There was also a small group of Jewish girls nearby, probably headed to the Kosel as well.

"Everything seemed fine, but then my attention was grabbed by the sound of screaming. I turned, and a large Arab wielding a butcher knife was closing in on the group of girls! Most of them scattered as he chased them, but one girl was backed into a corner, frozen and terrified. I quickly got behind the Arab and began to yell, "*Mishtarah, mishtarah,*" hoping to scare him off. He was startled at the noise behind him and, as he turned to face me, the remaining girl managed to slip away.

"He was set to flee, since the police were already on their way, but he wasn't going to let me get away with what I had done. He swiped the knife once across my face, slicing through my cheek, and fled as I collapsed to the ground.

"The hospital managed to sew the wound pretty well, but I was left with this permanent scar that I've lived with since."

Baruch heaved another sigh as he finished reliving the event, and was startled to find tears in the girl's eyes. It certainly wasn't a pleasant story, but this wasn't the reaction he had expected.

"I already knew that story," whispered the girl.

Baruch was confused. "How? Did you read the papers that day, or…?"

"I was the girl in the corner," she responded, her voice shaking. "I ran for my life that day, and I never looked back to find out who had saved me. For years, I've always wanted to thank the boy who saved my life, and suddenly here you are.

"You risked your life for me, and now I am finally able to say, thank you."

Through Hashem's intervention, one girl had found her hero, and one young man had found his *kallah*!

The scar that seemed like an unlucky curse turned out to be a lucky blessing. But of course, the word "luck" only means a revealed piece of the Master Plan — a plan that seems infinitely complex sometimes, but is nonetheless perfect in its detail.

I will conclude this segment with one more, telling story on the topic from Rabbi Yerachmiel Milstein.

He stopped by my house every six months or so in search of a modest contribution to support the immigrant village he helped build in Israel to absorb new arrivals from Russia. His excitable, high-pitched voice and happy, dancing eyes belied the deep furrows in his brow. Those were the lines that were painfully etched by decades of punishment at the hands of the communist authorities for the terrible crime of being an observant Jew in the Soviet Union during the 50's, 60's and early 70's.

It became a ritual. I'd ask the diminutive rabbi if he'd like a bite to eat. He would always counter in his Russian-accented Yiddish, "Perhaps just a glass of tea." My wife would serve him a steaming cup of dark orange brew along with a generous slice of homemade cake, both of which seemed to help straighten his sagging shoulders just a bit. Trudging door to door for small donations, he certainly didn't have time for a square meal.

He once looked up at me and smiled broadly. "Did you know there was such a thing as a Cantonist Shul?"

I remembered stories I had heard as a child, which described some of those dark but quite heroic days in Jewish history.

From 1825-1840, young Jewish boys, known as Cantonists, were kidnaped from their parents' homes and forcibly conscripted into the Russian army. These children, some as young as 8 years, were obligated to serve for 25 years. The authorities saw it as a corrective, forced assimilation of Jews into Russian society.

They were starved and beaten, in an attempt to turn them into "tough" Russian soldiers. Since they were Jews, they were subjected to scorn and abuse not only from their superiors, but from the other non-Jewish soldiers as well. In their malnourished states, the open cuts on their chests and backs, from repeated lashings, would turn septic and many who had heroically tried to remain alive succumbed to their wounds. It was an incredibly sad epoch in Russian-Jewish history.

To avoid this horrific fate, some parents actually had their sons' limbs amputated in the forests at the hands of local blacksmiths, and these sons — no longer able bodied — would thereby avoid conscription. Others would even commit suicide rather than be taken to the army.

Many young Jewish boys were forced into Czar Nicholas' army, and very few emerged alive as practicing Jews. Tragically, even the brave few survivors who secretly maintained their faith for 25 years found themselves unable to reintegrate into the Jewish community upon their return.

"The Cantonists actually did have a shul of their own," the wizened rabbi continued. "After all, they had nowhere else to go."

"My grandfather told me that he once attended the Cantonist Shul on Simchas Torah. These Cantonists could dance like Cossacks. They were huge, strong men, and the heavy Torah scrolls would seem like toothpicks in their arms. They effortlessly danced for hours on end. Though they were often boorish, coarse men (an inevitable result of their 25-year ordeal), they were nonetheless able to rejoice in their Judaism and celebrate the Torah. It was truly amazing."

He paused long enough to dip a sugar cube into the still-hot tea and placed the cube in his mouth, swallowing another long swig of the brew.

"Then, for the final *hakafah* (circuit around the synagogue's central lectern), the Cantonists, as if on cue, would suddenly remove their shirts in unison! With the Torahs held tightly to their bare skin, which was covered with the ugliest welts and scars you ever saw, they danced around even more energetically. Their smiles were now giving way to streams of tears as they looked out into the crowd of assembled Jews, as if to say, 'You may have studied and observed this Torah, but we gave our bodies and our lives for it. The Torah is at least as much ours as it is yours!' "

As he put the teacup down, he couldn't hide the tremor in his hand which caused a rattled meeting of cup to saucer.

Wiping away a tear with his napkin, he said, "In democratic America it is so easy. Yet so many say, 'It's so hard.' Go figure."

In Search of Peace

Who doesn't want mazal and berachah in their life? Often, when things seem to be quite the other way around, one might wonder: Why, Hashem? Why can't I have the berachah that so many of my friends have experienced? It may be possible that Hashem is asking you to rectify a misdeed that is holding back your berachah. In this story, Chaim Kranzman offers us insight into getting that berachah back.*

I had been married for quite a number of years already, and I was still not blessed with children.

All around me, friends who had started out around the same time I did, as young couples, were already animatedly discussing schools, bringing their sons to shul for *Avos U'banim* Motza'ei Shabbos programs, and hustling their families off to the bungalow colony for the hot summer months. And us? My wife and I still had the same quiet Shabbos table we had always had, and we tried unsuccessfully to mask our pain.

Every trip to visit friends was a separate agony and, for my wife, every Shabbos in shul was a source of sorrow. We were that one family on the block who were not part of the busy world of morning car pools, school plays, family functions, and PTA's. It was getting to the point where it was just too much for either of us to bear.

I had never been one for going to *gedolim* for *berachos*, but a friend of mine had been pushing me for a long time to seek out Rabbi Portugal, the Skulener Rebbe. He had a reputation for attracting all types of Jews to his door to lay their hearts open and receive blessing and comfort. At this despairing time in my life, I saw no further reason why I shouldn't be one of them.

So, the day arrived when I found myself standing in a long line of people awaiting their turn with the Rebbe. When my turn finally came, I presented my case in all its detail, hoping the Rebbe could say something to soothe the bitterness and anguish in my soul.

Instead of the words of *berachah* I had expected, the Rebbe looked at me steadily and said, "Where there is *machlokes*, there is no *berachah*."

Confused, I briefly repeated my story, wondering if the Rebbe had perhaps misunderstood my tale. After all, I had mentioned nothing about any *machlokes*. Once again, however, the Rebbe heard every word I had to say and then simply repeated his previous statement.

Dazed and somewhat disappointed, I spent hours that night pacing my dining room, trying to cast my mind as far back as I could to determine which *machlokes* the Rebbe could have been referring to. I had never been that contentious of a person, and I certainly had no memory of an out-and-out fistfight of any kind. Then, a bolt of lightning named "Yitzy Fishman"* struck my mind, and the memories flooded back.

Yitzchak Fishman and I had both been very popular in high school, each of us heading our own personal group of blindly devoted followers. There could not be two kings of one castle, and so Yitzy and I were natural enemies, each of us trying everything we could to make the other's life as miserable as possible. There were a lot of pranks, name-calling, and intimidation on both sides as we each struggled to assert dominance over the other. Of course, neither of us had won any kind of decisive victory by the time graduation came around, and I had only gained four years' worth of unfortunate memories of hostility.

Yitzy had approached me on the day of our graduation, somberly, and told me that he would never forgive me for what I had done to him. For my part, I only smirked arrogantly and replied that I returned the sentiment, that I was very glad to finally be rid of him altogether, and that I never wanted to see him again. That was the last we had ever seen or heard of each other.

Excitedly, I picked up the phone and managed, after a long wait, to reach the Skulener Rebbe. Briefly, I told him everything I had remembered and asked if this was the *machlokes* he had been referring to.

"I'm not a *navi*," the Rebbe replied. "All I can tell you is that where there is *machlokes* there cannot be *berachah*. Who knows? Perhaps this other man with whom you once had *machlokes* does not have any children either."

I thanked the Rebbe and ended the conversation. Right then, I began the difficult work of tracking someone whom I had once sworn never to see again. I knew I must somehow ask this man from my past for *mechilah*, and I knew it would be the most uncomfortable moment of my life.

It took numerous phone calls and long-distance area directories, but I finally found Yitzy Fishman. He had moved to Los Angeles several years ago and, at long last, I obtained his phone number and address. Still...after much deliberation, I knew that I would not pick up that phone. The only way to truly put the matter to rest was to fly to Los Angeles myself. If that's what was necessary to end my family's pain, that's what I would do.

The next day brought me to JFK to catch my plane. I spent the entirety of the flight davening that my mission should be successful; I had no idea what I would say to Yitzy when I saw him, but I prayed that Hashem would place the proper words in my mouth. Upon arrival at the airport, I rented a car and made my reluctant way to the home of a man who had once been my sworn enemy.

It was about 8 p.m. when I arrived at his front door, and every fiber of my being wished I could simply turn around. My feeling of dread had been growing throughout the entire drive to his house, but now I was literally shaking in fear. What kept me going was only the utter certainty that I would never forgive myself if I gave up now.

My final fears — or wild hopes — that I had found the wrong house dissolved when I read the Hebrew nameplate on the door. This was indeed Yitzy's house, and I was closer to him now than I had been in over a decade.

Swallowing and squeezing my eyes shut, I lifted my fist and knocked.

"Who's there?" called a man's deep voice, and my heart almost stopped. It was an older, more mellow-sounding tone, but it was most certainly Yitzy Fishman.

When I didn't answer for a time, the door opened slowly, and Yitzy's burly frame filled the doorway. He must have seen me through the peephole already, because his eyes were locked on mine and his jaw was tensed.

"Hi, Yitzy," I whispered, "I — "

"What are you doing on my property?" he shouted, fists slamming toward me in the air. "Get out of here this minute before I call the cops! I never want to see your face here again!"

"W-wait," I stammered, "let me just explain...I c-came from New York just to speak to you..."

"*I don't care where you came from!*" he thundered. "I want you out of my life! I thought I made that clear to you years ago!"

"Yitzy...please..." I sank slowly to the floor, my knees giving way, and I burst into bitter tears. The sight of this must have shocked and perhaps calmed Yitzy somewhat, because he unclenched his fists and softened his stance somewhat.

"Fine," he growled. "Say what you came here to say."

Sobbing, I poured my pain out onto his doorstep. I described how I had been married over 10 years and had not been granted children. I told him about my visit to the Skulener Rebbe, and about how I had been told that *machlokes* was withholding my *berachah*.

"I came here to ask for your forgiveness," I choked out. I finally raised my head, and was startled to notice tears glistening in Yitzy's eyes as well. One second he seemed about to pummel me, and the next...? Perhaps my story had made an impact? Tensely, I waited.

"I — " he gasped, his own eyes spilling over.

"What, Yitzy?"

"It's just that I...well, same here..."

My mouth dropped open. "You don't either..."

"I don't have any children either," he sobbed.

That same year, both my family and Yitzy's celebrated the births of baby boys. It was as though this *machlokes* was the stopper in the bottle of *berachah* Hashem intended for me; with the stopper removed, peace and mazal began to flow into my home at last.

I learned the hard way that *machlokes* is the most damaging force in the world. But perhaps my story can inspire others to forgive and forget and allow the *berachah* to flow into their homes and their lives.

Tears of Emunah

Life had gone dark for Mrs. Sarah Fernman* after the death of her child.

Friends and relatives streamed in from different states and countries to offer their help, their condolences, or just to lift her spirits with a friendly face, but it seemed that the tragedy had left her broken in a way that could not be fixed. Her other children needed her more than ever, but Sarah responded neither to them nor to her husband, Moshe, instead electing to remain in her room as long as possible, telling anyone who prodded her that her life was over.

This continued for weeks, until Sarah's family began to share in her utter despair, for it seemed that they had lost their mother as well.

One evening, Moshe decided that drastic actions were in order. He quickly devised a plan, and then approached his grieving wife where she sat on the couch, lost in her miserable musings.

"Sarah, listen to me. The Friedmans' wedding is tonight, and I'd like you to go to it. You have known the *kallah's* mother for so many years, and it's only right that you put in an appearance."

Sarah glanced up bleakly from her spot on the couch. "I can't, Moshe. I can't do it. You know that. How can I be happy at a time like this?"

Pain filled Moshe's eyes, and Sarah looked away hurriedly. "And how do you think this has been for me?" he replied, hoarsely. "I haven't just lost a child — I've lost the person I married, too! You've locked yourself in the house for weeks on end, you don't answer the phone, and you don't go out. No, this has gone on far too long! You just *have* to go to the wedding, whether you like it or not!"

Moshe left the room abruptly, and Sarah followed him with angry strides to the front door. "Why don't you understand, Moshe? I can't! I just...can't!"

He didn't offer a word in reply, simply opening the door and slipping outside. She hesitated, then quickly followed him. It was the first breath of fresh air she had had in weeks.

"Look, Moshe," she said placatingly, "I understand your concern. It's just...I can't imagine myself getting all dressed up, putting on makeup, pretending that nothing ever happened..." Tears began to drop from her eyes.

To her surprise, Moshe suddenly produced car keys from his pocket. "Sarah, you don't have to imagine it at all tonight...you just have to *do* it. Now, I left your *chasunah* clothing next door at the Bernsteins, and I'm giving you the car keys. I'm going back inside, and I don't want to see you back at this door until you've gone to that *chasunah*!"

Quick as a whip, Moshe slipped back in through the front door, and Sarah felt her mouth drop open as she heard the lock slide into place!

Did he just...how could *he?* Rage washed in waves over Sarah: the first emotion other than despondency that she had felt in a long while. She gestured furiously at Moshe, who stood smiling encouragingly at the window. He didn't seem to understand her. Finally, rejecting the alternative of creating a show for her neighbors, Sarah stalked off to the Bernsteins next door to get ready for a wedding she hadn't the slightest desire to attend.

At the *chasunah* itself, Sarah fought a losing battle to put on a good face. Music swirled all around the hall, and she found herself surrounded by friends and acquaintances she had not seen since the *shivah*, all of them delighted to see her out of the house and all of them kind and solicitous. Conscious of her loss, Sarah's friends and neighbors kept the conversation light and frivolous, but this simply had the opposite of a calming effect on Sarah.

How can I sit and discuss recipes and clothes when everything is meaningless in the grand scheme of things? I've lost my dear child,

Hashem! Sarah forced a smile and sipped her glass of water, trying to remember what the person next to her had just said instead of bursting into uncontrollable tears.

But the music swelled and the first dance began, and that was when Sarah's false smile froze into a painful mask. She watched, unbelievingly, as happy faces whirled around in a circle, the *kallah* joyous in the middle of it all. How could people be so happy like that? How could she, Sarah, ever care about anything else now that her baby was gone?

Suddenly it was simply too much, and Sarah fled from the room, the sobs beginning to tear out of her as she frantically tried the door of the ladies room, which was locked fast. She looked around desperately until she found a lone telephone booth in the corner of the lobby. She slid into it and slammed the door behind her, picked up the phone to pretend to make a phone call, and finally dissolved into uncontrollable weeping.

"Hashem," she cried, as though to someone on the other end of the line, "please find some way to get me out of here! I can't take this any more! It just hurts too much…I miss my baby, and I don't know what to do."

There was a sudden tapping at the door of the booth, and Sarah spun around to see a wizened old woman whom she had last spotted collecting *tzedakah* inside the ballroom.

"*Mein kindt,*" asked the old woman in soft Yiddish, "*far vus veinst du?*" ("My child, why are you crying?")

Sarah's deep shame at being caught hardened into anger. "Leave me alone," she snapped. "You don't understand the pain I'm going through, losing a child."

"I don't understand?" The old woman's voice was soft, but clearly reproving. "I, who lost 10 children to the Nazis during the war? Don't tell me that I don't understand!"

Sarah's heart skipped a beat as she felt her face redden. She softened her stance considerably. "And you never cried?" she challenged, albeit in a gentler tone.

"Of course I cried," the other woman assured her. "But I also learned to take advantage of my tears. Instead of only dwelling on *my* losses, I would say, '*Ribono Shel Olam*, do You see these tears? What happened to me has happened, but there are others who need Your help. Bring the Redemption to Your children, who still suffer every day.'"

Sarah found herself stepping out of the booth, and allowing the old woman to squeeze her hand reassuringly as she spoke. "No one should ever tell you that you have to stop crying," she declared.

"My husband wants me to stop," Sarah murmured.

"For yourself, yes. We cannot cry forever about the past. We should cry with *seichel*, with intelligence. We should cry for others."

The old woman gave Sarah's hand a final squeeze and then disappeared back into the crowds and the music from which she had materialized. Sarah felt emotion overwhelm her again, and she stepped quickly back into the safety of the phone booth, bursting into renewed tears. This time, however, she cried for every person she knew who was suffering and needed a *yeshuah*. She cried for all the people she didn't know, for all of *Klal Yisrael,* and begged Hashem to grant them all relief from their troubles and their pain.

When she rejoined the celebrants in the main ballroom, it was suddenly easy to dance. It didn't even seem to matter any more that she was still crying, because this time her tears were tears of joy and relief, tears of *emunah*; the pain that had dogged her every step since her loss was finally beginning to melt away, and in its place was a renewed realization of the beauty of the world and the One Who runs it.

Sarah would later recall this moment: "It's strange to say, but I've never felt so happy before in my life. When I joined that circle, I danced like I never danced before! Someone else's *simchah* turned into my own *simchah* as well."

The pain of losing a child had not gone away, but had been channeled into something more meaningful and more positive, something that allowed Sarah to heed her own experience and grow from it.

It was not happenstance that caused Sarah to meet an old Holocaust survivor, but rather something ordained from Above. It was a hidden message to Sarah, cautioning her not to surrender to her own pain and allow herself to die as well. Sarah met the old woman at just the right place and time. Perhaps it is fair to say that there really was *a Respondent at the other end of that line.*

A Match Made in Heaven

A father who is trying to marry off his daughter must do a great deal of research to make sure the boy is an appropriate match. It's a difficult task, but for Shmuel Reidmen, it was twice as difficult, because although the boy seemed just right for his daughter, he was all wrong for Shmuel. Now he was faced with the decision of his life.*

One of the most pressing topics in the Jewish world today is the challenge of *shidduchim.* As I approached this stage of my daughter Chaya's life, I took the task seriously, but I was confident that we would find her *bashert* without too much trouble. After all, she was smart, talented, and loved by her friends. *Shadchanim* were calling us regularly with prospects.

We just had to find the boy that met her criteria: someone with a commitment to learning, a big heart, and a personality to match. I knew there would be obstacles along the path to this perfect boy, but I never expected that the obstacle would be me.

The story began on a Friday afternoon. I was working at my office and my daughter was assisting me, as she had been since she returned from seminary. As we began winding up the week's business, Chaim Gold,* one of my best customers, walked through the door. My daughter very capably tended to his order, but Chaim didn't leave. Instead, he approached me and said quietly, "Shmuel, do you have a couple of minutes to discuss something?"

"Sure," I said. "What's on your mind?"

"Well, Shmuel, it's actually in regard to your daughter. I think that I have the perfect match for her. His name is Shaya Rosenberg.* He is originally from Canada and is now learning in one of the local yeshivahs. My son has brought him over a few times and I am really impressed with him. He seems to be a real *masmid* and a *mentch*. I have some information but can easily get you more. Do you want me to find out more so that you can look into it?"

While I appreciated his offer, we were already researching several excellent boys who were of the caliber our Chaya deserved. I told Chaim that we had a few active prospects at present. "Maybe if these don't work out, we'll get back to you," I concluded.

Chaim wasn't so easily discouraged. "Listen, Shmuel, I am telling you that this boy is top of the line, but if you don't want to look into it yet, I can't force you."

"I'm not trying to be overly picky, Chaim," I explained, sensing that he was a bit insulted. "It's just that Chaya is my oldest daughter and we really are trying to be very methodical and research each boy carefully. But listen, if you feel strongly about this boy, do some research and get back to us in a week or two, and we'll talk then."

After my discussion with Chaim, Chaya and I closed up shop and headed home.

As it was winter and Shabbos was early, the house was in high preparation mode when I arrived. I jumped right into the action, hauling the garbage out to the receptacle as my wife stood in the kitchen preparing the food.

Just as I walked out the door, I heard a shriek from the kitchen, followed by a loud thud. I dropped the garbage bag and ran to the kitchen to find my wife, Baila, collapsed onto a chair, writhing in pain.

"Baila! What happened? Are you okay?" I shouted. I could hear the panic in my own voice.

Barely able to speak, my wife groaned, "I've been feeling pain in my side all day, but it has now gotten so excruciating that I can't stand up. Please call Hatzalah."

The ambulance was there in seconds. The EMTs rushed her to the hospital, where her pain was diagnosed as stemming from a kidney stone. Although obviously an agonizing condition, it was not, *baruch Hashem,* life threatening. She would have to stay in the hospital over Shabbos, and I would stay with her.

Now we were faced with the necessity of obtaining Shabbos food at the hospital on very short notice. The *Bikur Cholim* pantry was stocked with snacks, but with less than an hour to go before Shabbos, it didn't seem possible to get any real food.

As I pondered this situation, what was surely an angel appeared at the door. He came in the form of a yeshivah *bachur* holding a shopping bag filled with food.

Knocking gently on the open door, he simply informed us, "I heard that you are going to be staying here for Shabbos. Please take this bag of Shabbos food. I'm sure you can use it."

I took the bag and looked inside. All the Shabbos basics were there: two challah rolls, a bottle of grape juice, a jar of gefilte fish, a package of cold cuts, a thermos of chicken soup, the works.

"Wow! This is amazing! Thank you so much, I really appreciate it," I said to the young man.

"Oh, it's really no big deal," he replied. "I do this every week. There's always someone who needs it."

I couldn't get over how kind this young man was, and what an amazing *chesed* he had done. Perhaps it seems strange to be so focused on food in the face of a major medical crisis, but once we had gotten matters under control I had become aware that I was very hungry. The thought of a Shabbos without Shabbos food was hard to face, but now, thanks to this young man, we didn't have to face it.

A few minutes later, I met another Jewish patient in the hall and asked him if he knew the *bachur* who brought the package.

"He's just an angel," the man replied. "He comes every week and brings Shabbos food to the Jewish patients. His first name is Shaya, and his last name is Rosen-something. He's from out of town, I think from Canada."

"Do you mean Rosenberg from Canada?" I asked.

"Yeah, I think that's his last name," the man confirmed.

I excused myself and dashed back to my wife's room. "All right," I told her. "Now I know exactly why we had to be here for Shabbos!"

Now it was her turn to look at me with concern.

"Why?"

"So that we could meet Chaya's future husband!" I stated with complete certainty.

I told my wife the entire story of how this very *bachur* had been mentioned to me for our daughter on that very day. "Obviously, Hashem is telling us that he's the one!" She looked at me again with concern and said, "Well...maybe. But maybe not."

I didn't waste any time getting back in touch with Chaim Gold. I found out which yeshivah Shaya attended and paid the *beis midrash* a visit as soon as I was able. There, not at all to my surprise, I found our prospective *chassan* deeply involved in his learning, exhibiting a zest and energy you could feel from across the room.

What else did I need to know? What more research did I need to do? This boy was placed before me by the Master *Shadchan* Himself. I saw who he was with my own eyes, and I was sure that he would make the perfect match for my Chaya.

I called up Chaim and gave him the go-ahead to set up a date. Two weeks later, the house was prepared to receive our special guest. At exactly 7 p.m., the bell rang. I opened the door and there stood Shaya.

"Come in!" I greeted him warmly. "Come sit down."

He joined my wife and me in the dining room for a little conversation. Starting a round of "Jewish geography," my wife asked, "Are you related to Mindy Rosenberg from Toronto? I have heard such amazing things about her. She is a real *baalas chesed* and is a good friend of my neighbor..."

Shaya politely broke in. "Rosenberg? I'm not related to any Rosenbergs. My last name is Rosenbaum. My family is from Montreal, and we don't have any relatives in Toronto."

"Your name is Rosenbaum?" I asked in surprise. "That's funny. I thought your name was Rosenberg. Sorry about the mistake. What is your father's name?"

"His name is Yitzchok," Shaya replied.

My stomach clenched and my face flushed at the sound of that name. It was one that I never wanted to hear again, a name associated with nothing but anger and disappointment.

Trying hard to bury the emotions churning inside me, I calmly excused myself. My wife followed me into the kitchen.

"What's the matter?" she asked me.

"Look, Shaya seems to be a great boy, but there is no way we could allow our daughter to even think about entering into the Rosenbaum family. Do you remember what Yitzchok did to me? He almost ruined my entire business. I would never do business with him again and I certainly can't imagine being family with him!"

My wife remained calm in the face of the storm brewing in my heart. "Listen, Shmuel, don't make a scene," she advised. "The boy is here already and you heard wonderful things about him. Don't ruin this for Chaya. Besides, maybe Chaya won't even be interested in this *shidduch* and we won't have to deal with it. So please, let's go back in there and send them off and let's see how things play out."

I took my wife's advice and returned to the dining room for a few more minutes of polite conversation. He went off with my daughter, and I spent the next few hours stewing in the steam of an old grievance.

As I could have predicted, when Chaya returned, she was nearly dancing with excitement. She had already gone out with a few other boys, and now she felt certain that she had finally found "the one."

"He's so kindhearted and his *middos* are so beautiful, and I know you saw for yourself what a *masmid* he is. He's perfect!" she declared.

I felt terrible about what I had to tell her, but sometimes the truth is painful. I just delivered the news simply and bluntly. "I'm sorry to tell you this, Chaya, but the *shidduch* is off."

"What? You mean they already got back to you and he doesn't want another date?" she asked, a look of puzzled disappointment clouding her face.

"No, I don't know what he is going to say," I informed her. "I just can't have you go out with a son of Yitzchok Rosenbaum. Trust me, this is not the type of father-in-law you want to have. Believe me, Chaya, this is for your own good!"

"But Tatty, please, give Shaya a chance! He isn't his father!"

"I'm sorry, Chaya, but the sooner you realize this isn't going forward, the sooner you'll get over it."

My daughter broke away from me, tears already spilling down her cheeks as she ran up the stairs to her room. I could hear her soft sobbing from where I stood, and my heart ached for her. Nevertheless, I knew I was doing the right thing.

When Shaya heard that we called off the *shidduch*, he too was crushed. He couldn't understand what had gone wrong, and of course we couldn't tell him. However, once he spoke to his parents about it, he understood that there had been a conflict. Still, he wondered, why couldn't we get past it?

The *shadchan* called and tried to convince me to change my mind, but after all the pain Yitzchok had put me through, forgiveness seemed impossible. Certainly, I was not about to let this man become the grandfather of my grandchildren and a permanent feature in my family's life.

I tried to get Chaya to consider some of the other fine prospects the *shadchan* had suggested. She, however, refused to hear of anyone else. One day, she sat down at the kitchen table and began revealing her thoughts on this entire episode.

"Tatty, I respect you very much, and I've always listened to your advice," my daughter told me. "But this time, it's my life we're talking about, and I think I should have a say in what goes on. I really think that breaking up this *shidduch* is a huge mistake. Shaya has all the qualities that I am looking for in a *shidduch*. You said so yourself.

"So I have been thinking about it for a long time, and I decided to call the *shadchan* back myself. How can I lose out on this boy just because you are not willing to forgive and forget? The incident with you and Shaya's father happened 10 years ago. Maybe he's changed. Maybe you don't even have all of the facts right. What if this is my *bashert* and I will be giving him up because of an old grudge?"

My daughter's words went straight to my heart. I was possibly destroying her happiness, all because I would not forgive and forget. Was that how far I was willing to take my *machlokes*? Even if it meant destroying my daughter's future?

After some deep soul-searching, I consented to her logic and gave my blessing for a second date. The couple went out and the rest was history.

Three weeks later, a meeting was set up between the two sides. With a fair amount of dread still roiling inside me, I prepared to meet Yitzchok for the first time in 10 years. But as he walked into my house carrying a huge bouquet of flowers for us, all my bad feelings melted away. We shook hands, embraced, and had a heart-felt conversation that resulted in a mutual decision to think of our children's good and heal our rift. A mazal tov was announced, and *baruch Hashem*, my daughter became a *kallah*.

As I look back at the story, I shudder to think that I was prepared to ruin my daughter's life just because of a grudge. Hashem showered me with blessing, and yet I was so very close to sending the *berachah* and my daughter's future right over a cliff. I saw how anger and baseless hatred can blind a person, and I am grateful that I learned this lesson. As a result of this realization, I now have a son-in-law and grandchildren I love with all my heart.

So please don't let *machlokes* blind you, because the one you will hurt the most is yourself. Bring shalom into your home, and Hashem will shower you, too, with blessing.

Amazingly, people can become caught up in machlokes to the point that they don't care what damage their actions will inflict. This story reminds me of another, told to me by a friend, about an episode that occurred on his block in Brooklyn.

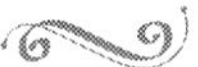

The Stern* family was getting ready to move from their home in Brooklyn to Lakewood. They had lived on the block for many years and they were well liked by everyone. Everyone, that is, except for the Friedmans.

The Friedmans had become involved in a conflict with the Sterns over a rather small matter. But that is the nature of *machlokes*: once it begins, it continues to grow and spiral out of control. So it was in this case, and as a result, the formerly close friends became locked in a cold war.

This state of affairs bothered my friend Mendy. He knew that the entire fight was based on nonsense. Things had simply gone too far for either side to back down, even though both families missed the friendship that had once existed between them.

Mendy decided that before the Sterns moved to Lakewood, he would try his best to make peace between the two parties. The question was, how? He had tried to talk to each party separately to arrange some sort of meeting, but his suggestion fell on deaf ears. Neither side would budge from its position. They were willing to keep the flames of conflict burning, just to avoid having to make any sort of apology.

Unwilling to admit defeat, Mendy searched for a strategy to get the two sides to forgive and forget. In a moment of inspiration, he recalled the technique of the great peacemaker Aharon HaKohen. Aharon would approach a person who was involved in conflict and tell him that the other party wanted to reconcile. Then he would go to the opposing party and tell him the same thing. With the dignity of each side thus protected, they would soon settle their differences.

"Well, if it worked for Aharon, it will work for me," Mendy assured himself.

The next day, he went to a local candy store and ordered two beautiful candy platters. To one platter, he affixed a card that read:

To the Friedman Family,

We are really sorry about all the fighting that has gone on between us. We believe that the time has come to make peace. Please accept this gift as a token of our desire to heal the rift.

May we continue to be friends and share in future simchos together.

With affection and caring,
The Sterns

Then Mendy composed the exact same note on behalf of the Friedmans and addressed it to the Sterns. He attached the second note to the other platter, and asked his children to deliver them both to the neighbors' homes.

"What is this?" Mrs. Stern remarked in surprise as she received her platter and read the card from "the Friedmans." At the Friedman's house, the reaction was the same. Overwhelmed by her neighbor's generous gesture, Mrs. Stern immediately went to the Friedman home and knocked on the door for the first time in years.

When Mrs. Friedman opened the door, Mrs. Stern was standing there, her eyes tearing with emotion.

"Rivky, thank you! Thank you so much for this wonderful gift — the candy, the thought, the offer to be friends again. I'm so happy..."

But her outpouring was interrupted. "Chana, what are you talking about? I'm the one who should be thanking you for reaching out to us!"

The sparks of friendship were reignited, and by the time the families figured out who had actually sent the platters, the flame was too strong to extinguish. Thousands of years after Aharon HaKohen paved the path of peace, his method was still working, mending the rifts and healing the hearts of *Klal Yisrael.*

The Love Behind the Mask

Reb Dovid Markstein relates how he experienced Hashem's unconditional love in the darkest of times*

It was Purim, a night when Jews worldwide celebrate our nation's miraculous delivery from Haman's nefarious schemes. It's a time when children don their adorable costumes, laughing with excitement and joy as they deliver *mishloach manos* to their friends and teachers. It was always my favorite time of year, and my wife and I would have given anything to be with our friends, families, and neighbors.

Instead of enjoying the usual happy scenario, we were spending our Purim in a hospital room at Philadelphia's CHOP (Children's Hospital of Pennsylvania), wondering what would become of our 3-year-old daughter, Miriam. Why was she running this mysterious fever? Why was she experiencing pains in her legs?

Our story, and Miriam's, really began on the first day of the month of Adar Aleph. Our heretofore healthy daughter had to be rushed to the hospital for emergency lifesaving surgery after which, at the advice of our pediatrician, she was transferred to CHOP for recuperation.

At that point, she developed severe complications from her surgery and it became clear that recuperation was going to take a lot longer than originally thought. As Purim was approaching and Miriam's condition appeared to be stabilizing, we requested that she be discharged from CHOP in time for the holiday and allowed to convalesce at home. We were quite excited by the prospect of going home to be reunited with our 4-year-old son, who was living with relatives, and letting our 6-month-old daughter sleep in her own crib. Most importantly, our 3-year-old daughter would finally be allowed to leave the hospital room where she had spent enough weeks to begin worrying that she had moved in for good. Yes, the prospect was exciting, but Hashem had other plans.

Purim that year fell on a Friday. On the Wednesday of that week, Miriam suddenly developed a fever. Because the original cause of her condition had never been identified, we had no way of knowing whether this fever indicated a danger to her life. Everyone was shocked and unnerved, and our excitement shifted into disappointment and despair.

The Fast of Esther was more worrying yet, as Miriam's doctor decided that day to replace her PICC line — an intravenous line leading toward her heart — in an effort to solve the problem. It was certainly not a pleasant procedure for our daughter, who had to be awake for the whole process. Our hopes for her imminent recovery were disintegrating before our eyes.

Purim night itself, Miriam was still running a high fever and began to complain about the mysterious pains in her legs. This was an especially worrisome symptom, since her legs had nothing to do with her condition. We called for an attending physician, but this latest development in our daughter's condition was unfortunately occurring the night before a legal holiday, and most of the staff had the night off or were in surgery. A nice but not particularly knowledgeable resident came to examine Miriam, but was unable to recommend any course of action. Finally a fellow, the next level of doctor in the hierarchy, breezed in to examine her and sourly told us that there was nothing that could be done for the moment. We were devastated, and our weariness was beginning to show.

"Look." I suddenly turned to my wife. "It's Purim, and we can't spend all our time being sad and depressed. It's the happiest day of the year, after all — a day when everything was as bleak as it ever looked until Hashem turned it all on its head and performed an amazing miracle. Let's just put everything aside for a moment and enjoy Purim. Maybe we'll make it the most amazing Purim this hospital has ever seen."

At the very moment I finished speaking, a Chinese-American nurse suddenly walked in. "Hello, I will be Miriam's nurse tonight. My name is Esther."

I felt a chill skitter up my spine as I turned to stare at my wife unbelievingly. Who would have guessed that our daughter's Purim night nurse would be a Chinese-American girl named Esther, of all things! It was an unmistakable message from our Father in Heaven. Just as the Persian Esther saved the Jews of Shushan, perhaps this Chinese-American Esther would be a messenger of salvation for us as well.

The next morning, Purim day, was the first time in six weeks that Miriam was allowed to put a morsel of food in her mouth: a shiny red lollipop. Her fever had completely gone and she was able to dress in her costume and join the Purim party that we had put together in the hospital's playroom. Purim did indeed turn out to be a pivotal point in our daughter's recovery. By the time she left the hospital, three weeks later, her condition had improved so dramatically that the nurses could not believe what they were seeing. Within several weeks of returning home, she was able to eat the same food as any other child, and today — thank G-d — she is completely recovered.

Words alone can never suffice to describe our overwhelming gratitude to Hashem for bringing about our daughter's recuperation and recovery. Purim is all about the revelation of hidden things, and for this briefest of moments, we were granted a peek behind the scenery. At a time when our pain and despondency had reached its lowest point, Hashem reached down and sent us a whisper of love, a quick kiss of endearment that says all that needs to be said:

Don't worry, I'm here. I'm holding your hand, and I'll guide you through it all.

Happily Ever After

Beauty is not something that always starts off beautiful. Many things in life seem difficult, even ugly, until, with time, they evolve into something that can only be thought of as beautiful. In hindsight, we are blessed to be able to look at the entire ordeal and see how all the pieces of the puzzle fit together. It is a shame that we cannot be granted this clarity while experiencing the problem, for then it would be the simplest thing to exclaim "gam zu l'tovah" in the face of adversity and pain. Often, the difference between happiness and misery is the ability to decide for oneself, "Shall I view this misfortune as the end of my life, or as an indication that Hashem wants to direct me along a different path?"

The following moving story was shared by Rabbi Yitzchak Leinerman, a noted mechanech and speaker. It is a case of exactly this difference in viewpoint.*

I was invited to attend a Shabbos event for about 500 people with one thing in common: they had all suffered from or had close family members suffering from cancer and other debilitating diseases. It was a Shabbos of *chizuk*, mutual understanding, and — for almost everyone there — some much-needed relaxation.

My purpose at the event was to give a lecture to inspire everyone together, as well as to provide individual *chizuk* to certain people, to inspire them personally.

I will be honest, though. There was one couple there that I studiously avoided. I had discovered their story, you see, and it was a story that I could not view as anything but completely horrific.

This couple's story began when they were newly engaged, with a bright, exciting future together to look forward to. It was exactly at this time in their lives, when everything seemed lined up neatly in a row, that the nightmare began.

It was a few weeks before the marriage when the groom noticed that his leg was causing him pain. He was a young man of reasonable health who did not have an alarmist personality, so he simply wrote it off as a torn ligament and decided to wait until after the wedding to have it checked out. His concern began to grow, however, when the pain persisted and increased to the point that he could no longer walk easily.

The day came, shortly before the wedding, when the pain grew so intense that he lost consciousness. In the midst of all the preparations, he was rushed to the hospital. Blood tests, X-rays, and examinations followed.

When the attending doctor emerged from looking at the X-rays, his face was grim. "I'm sorry to have to tell you this," he began, "but the problem with your leg is not a ligament, bone, or muscle."

"So what is it?" pressed the young man.

The doctor sighed. He was an ill-tempered man who liked his patients to reach conclusions on their own, but there was nothing left to say but the truth. "It's quite a bit more serious. It's a tumor."

"But I'm getting married in two weeks!" the young man blurted in a panic, shock and disbelief in his voice.

"Don't yell at me," snapped the doctor, "yell at the X-ray."

The young man was released from the hospital and returned home dejectedly, his mind swirling with all the information he had received about the ordeal he was to undergo in the next few weeks. Chemo, hospitals, pain, nausea...there was just no way that he could get married, now. His bright future seemed to darken as he realized that the wedding would have to be called off.

He called the bride and her family that night, and they were all deeply shocked and crushed by the news. The bride's parents conferred and came to a painful decision: the wedding must be called off. After all, why should their young daughter, at the prime of her life, be subjected to such a difficult burden? Clearly, Hashem did not wish this *shidduch* to be, and certainly He would find their daughter another, healthier groom. It was the hardest decision of their lives, but there didn't seem to be another choice.

The following morning, though, chaos was unleashed when the bride walked into the kitchen to find her mother on the phone, first with the band and then with the hall, trying to arrange cancellations.

"Ma, what are you doing?" exclaimed the girl.

"I'm canceling the hall and the band."

"Why?!"

"You know why." Her mother's voice was pained.

The girl's voice hardened. "No, I don't know why! I don't know about you, but I'm going to my wedding and leaving with my husband. Don't cancel anything."

Before her mother's astonished eyes, the girl retrieved the phone, called back the band and the hall, and told them not to cancel the wedding. "If anyone says otherwise," she ordered, "don't listen to them. People are playing a prank on me and trying to ruin my life."

The girl's next stop was at the doctor of her *chassan*, where she demanded to know if he would possibly lose his ability to walk again. In his usual brusque manner, the doctor responded that he saw no reason why that should happen. This satisfied the girl, and both sets of amazed parents were then informed that the wedding was indeed going forward.

And indeed it did; many people said afterward that they had never witnessed such a mixture of joy and tears as the groom was escorted to and from the *chupah* in a wheelchair. Emotions were already running high, and so the dancing was memorable and extraordinary; everyone wanted a part in this unique *simchah*.

It was a week after the wedding, after the last of the *sheva berachos* had wound to a close, that the new couple went together for additional X-rays. The news then was the very worst kind of surprise that either of them could have imagined: the tumor had caused the bone to partially disintegrate, and there was simply no choice but to operate on the cancerous leg and begin chemotherapy immediately.

The pain and the tears on both sides were indescribable, but there was no other course of action to be considered. The newly married man had surgery on his leg, and the couple's promising fresh start turned into the realization of their darkest fears, as he lost his ability to walk.

Knowing this story as I did, I simply turned the other way whenever I saw this young man with his young wife pushing him around in his wheelchair. I felt fear flutter in my stomach when I pictured talking to them, imagining I would say the wrong thing and communicate the depression I felt when I considered their tale. It would be foolish of me to try to give them *chizuk*; I was sure that I was more likely to just say the wrong thing.

But Hashem had other plans for me. It was already Motza'ei Shabbos when I turned around and discovered that the young couple, wheelchair and all, had somehow managed to slip behind me unnoticed.

"Why are you avoiding me?" asked the young man, point-blank.

Put completely on the spot like that, I found myself opening my mouth and coming out with the undressed truth. "Because I'm afraid that I will simply burst into tears instead of talking to you."

"Does that give you the right to ignore me?" he demanded.

I thought for a moment, and then cast my eyes down. "No, it doesn't."

And so they shared their tale with me from their own firsthand experiences, each one filling in the details that the other forgot, and sure enough, I found my face soaked with tears by the time their story was completed. "Thank you," I whispered, shamefacedly. "I should have done this a long while ago. I'm truly sorry for both of you."

There was a confused pause from the couple. "Why?" asked the wife, finally. "Did you not see the miracle?"

"No," I answered, truthfully. The whole reason I had avoided them was that I saw only tragedy!

"The doctors were wrong," she continued, in a tone that indicated she was explaining the obvious. "They said they wouldn't have to operate, but then they did. If I had known the truth when I asked the first time, I don't know if I would have gone ahead with the wedding. Hashem saved me from rejecting my intended husband!"

I was floored. I stood there, staring at this young woman, who wasn't even half my age, and trying to understand the amazing way that she saw the world. In my own head, I couldn't imagine that she would have seen anything good at all in her situation. If anything, I imagined that she would be furious at being forever burdened with a wheelchair-bound husband because of an impatient doctor's erroneous prognosis!

Instead, her message was completely different. She marveled at how beautifully Hashem had directed her life and helped her make the right decision. She rejoiced at this decision, for it allowed her to be together with the young man whom she was intended to marry, regardless of his condition!

"I tell you," Rabbi Leinerman concluded, "if you think I cried when I heard their story, you should have seen me afterward..."

A strong young woman taught a seasoned lecturer a life lesson. To this day, whenever a difficult situation eats at him and he feels ready to explode, Rabbi Leinerman stops for a moment and takes time to dwell on the fact that it is up to him to decide if this occurrence is a life-ruining tragedy or simply a nudge from Hashem onto a different and better path.

No one in the world is entitled to make that crucial decision for you. The lens through which you view your life is entirely up to you. Choose the right one and, like this noble young woman, you may just merit to live happily ever after.

It is an established fact that the Jewish world's most difficult questions inevitably find their way to the great Rav Chaim Kanievsky in Bnei Brak. Human beings who arrive at his door bent under the weight of their broken hearts seem to leave lighter of step and uplifted by his kind words and fervent blessings.

On one particular day, a very unique *din Torah* found its way to the *gadol's* home. An engaged couple walked in with two sets of parents in tow — not an uncommon sight. After all, many young couples customarily flock to Rav Chaim for *berachos* before beginning the new chapter of their lives. But this particular couple had something quite different to discuss.

Three weeks before the intended wedding, it had come to light that the *chassan* had contracted a very serious illness. There were numerous treatments necessary to even give the young man a chance to recover, and the success of these treatments would not guarantee that he would walk away a healthy person. The *chassan* came before Rav Chaim with the claim that his *kallah* must not be subjected to the pain and difficulties that lay ahead of him. If it was Hashem's will that he face these trials, the young man contended, then it was best that he face them alone. Painful as it would be for them both, the wedding simply must be called off.

The *kallah's* response was equally firm. If Hashem had seen it fit to visit this illness upon her *chassan after* they had become engaged, it was clearly His will that she help him get through it. She maintained that the *chassan* was incorrect in assuming that he was meant to suffer through it alone, and that she would not allow him to do so. Hashem was testing her, she declared, in order to determine whether she was really an *eizer kenegdo.* She fully intended not to leave his side in order to pass this test.

All eyes turned toward the great sage; emotions ran high in the room as both *chassan* and *kallah* wiped tears from their faces.

"You should not separate," Rav Chaim spoke. "Indeed, the wedding must go on as planned and with the help of Hashem, you will build a *bayis ne'eman b'Yisrael.*"

The *chassan* and *kallah* both heaved tremendous sighs of relief and thanked Rav Chaim. The parents wished each other hearty congratulations, and true *simchah* filled the room as they all celebrated for a few minutes. Finally, wreathed in smiles, the party that had come to settle this strange dispute left together.

When all was quiet, one of the members of Rav Chaim's inner circle spoke up in amazement. "How did you reach a *p'sak* on such a difficult case? On what was the decision based?"

Rav Chaim answered, "It's a clear midrash (*Bereishis* 33:1). We learn that Alexander of Macedonia once visited the king of Kotzei while the latter was presiding over a case that had come before him. One man had bought a parcel of land from the other and, once the sale was complete, the buyer had found a great treasure that had been hidden on the land. The seller insisted that the treasure rightfully belonged to the buyer of the land, since he had sold the land and everything in it. The buyer maintained that the treasure was still the seller's, since he (the buyer) had expressed intention only to buy land, not treasure.

"The king weighed the situation, and then asked one of the men if he had a son. When that man replied that he did, the king asked the second man if he had a daughter. This, too, turned out to be the case. 'Let this one's son marry that one's daughter,' ruled the king, 'and let the treasure be a wedding present for both of them.'

"When Alexander heard this decision, he informed the king that he would have done differently: he would have commanded that both the buyer and the seller be put to death and the treasure absorbed into the king's treasury.

" 'Does the sun shine on your land,' responded the king, 'and do your trees bear fruit? If they do, it is not in the merit of your people, but in the merit of the animals found there. In a land where there is cruelty, there can be no blessing.' "

Rav Chaim further explained: "We learn from this midrash that when one Jew thinks only of the welfare of another Jew and is *mevater* on his own desires, he will never lose out. When the king saw how each man thought only of the other one's well-being, he came up with a ruling to benefit them both. So too, in this case, our *chassan* and *kallah* can stand only to gain from their *shidduch*."

The marriage proceeded as planned, and the chassan did indeed recover from his illness. And yes, they lived happily ever after.

Chapter 2:
Time for Change

There are times in our lives when certain circumstances or occurrences drive home the message that it is no longer enough to complacently accept the status quo. It is time to change, to set a new course in life because we want to, not because we must. Deep within ourselves, we recognize that these changes will bring about the happiness and the fulfillment that we are lacking.

The Alter of Slabodka once said, "Teshuvah iz nit besser veren, nar anderish veren." ("Repentance is not about becoming better; it's about becoming different.") In this chapter, we will meet some special individuals who plotted a new course for themselves and radically changed direction. Change is never an easy thing, but then, no one ever said becoming great is supposed to be easy.

Forty Seconds

In our physical, materialistic lives, true inspiration is hard to come by. But there are times—those rare instances that are never forgotten—when Hashem strikes your heart with a lightning bolt of inspiration; the world is temporarily illuminated for a few brief seconds, and it's as though a window into the heavens was thrown open. Suddenly, you know what you have to do, and you are certain that G-d is there, leading you gently along the way.

But these moments are fleeting, and it becomes our challenge to seize them when they come. We might use inspiration to make life-altering decisions that change us for the better, or, more commonly, we might allow the magic moment to lapse until its impact is forgotten. In the unfortunate cases where we choose the latter, we may never know what we almost had until it's too late. In this powerful story related by Rabbi Zecharia Wallerstein during a pre-Rosh Hashanah lecture, we will meet a young woman who was presented with just this kind of moment, and we will see how she dealt with it.

Miriam grew up in a traditional Jewish home in Chicago, Illinois. Her parents were not at all religious, though they did find it important to maintain their relationship with their local Reform temple and send Miriam to the temple's day school.

Miriam's Jewish education therefore consisted mostly of Hebrew songs and basic Bible stories, for that was the extent of the school's Judaic connection. Though several Orthodox teachers were employed there, they were under strict orders to refrain from discussing practical application of Torah and mitzvos in their classes. So worried were the school authorities about the possibility of Orthodox influence that they included a specific clause in these teachers' contracts that prohibited them from inviting students for Shabbos meals.

All these precautions notwithstanding, Miriam still managed to develop a close relationship with Mrs. Weiss, her beloved fifth-grade teacher. Mrs. Weiss saw something in Miriam that led her to believe that this student was special; her *neshamah* might be reached. Even at the risk of her job, Mrs. Weiss could not help following her impulse to invite Miriam to her home for Shabbos.

Miriam's parents consented to the invitation, and so it was that Miriam arrived at her teacher's home just before it was time to light the Shabbos candles. Mrs. Weiss, clad in her Shabbos finery and looking quite different from the way she did on an average school day, smiled warmly at her student and beckoned her closer.

"Come listen to the blessing over the candles," she said.

Miriam approached timidly, her face a question. Briefly, Mrs. Weiss explained the reason that women light Shabbos candles, emphasizing that it was a special gift from Hashem to Jewish women.

"One day, when you have children of your own, you can light candles, too," Mrs. Weiss told Miriam.

"Can I light them now?" Miriam asked hesitantly.

Her teacher smiled. "You don't have to light them, Miriam. I will light them for you, for now."

"But, Mrs. Weiss," Miriam protested, "this might be the only time I ever get a chance to do this. We don't do it at home. Can I please light them now?"

Mrs. Weiss relented, setting up two more candles and quickly showing Miriam exactly what to do. Then, the two of them lit the candles, waved their hands in front of them, and covered their faces, as is the custom. Slowly, in a word-by-word repetition, Miriam recited the *berachah* with her teacher.

"The custom now is to pray to Hashem for anything you desire," Mrs. Weiss explained, softly. "It is a very special moment when a woman lights candles, for Hashem is waiting to hear your voice."

So Miriam prayed in front of the candles, and she did indeed feel something indescribably special around her and within her, something she wished would last forever.

Life for Miriam continued exactly as her parents had planned it. After elementary school, she attended a public high school and then, before Miriam could turn around, it was already time for college. Memories of dear Mrs. Weiss from fifth grade had long faded into the mists of time, and Miriam's life remained devoid of anything noticeably Jewish. So divorced was she from her spiritual roots that she felt not a single twinge of discomfort at the prospect of attending a private college. In fact, so as not to make any waves, Miriam became known as Mary—just another of many in a prestigious secular college.

Mary was actually quite popular in her new school, and was succeeding greatly in her studies as well. She blended in seamlessly with her new social group, studying alongside them, playing sports alongside them, and of course, never failing to be on time for the daily classes. The college years flew by, and soon Mary was looking forward to graduation, for she had met a handsome Italian boy named Vinnie, and was eager to settle down and start a family.

The wedding plans were soon solidified, and Mary agreed to be married in a beautiful church in a ceremony presided over by Vinnie's family priest. If any misgivings existed in light of her Jewish background, Mary certainly wasn't conscious of them.

On the day of her wedding, there was a giddiness in the air as Mary's friends pulled up in a limousine to bring her to the church.

This was the day she had waited for all her life! Dressed in her wedding gown, Mary slid into her seat in the limo and basked in her friends' admiration.

"Wait," one of the girls interjected. "I don't want to forget... Mary, we have a surprise for you."

"What is it?" Mary asked.

"We'll show you, but you have to close your eyes."

Mary did so obligingly, and she felt the weight of something being slipped around her neck.

"Okay, you can look!" they shouted.

Opening her eyes, she saw her friends nodding approvingly at the shining, golden necklace with the diamond-studded cross now resting over her heart.

Time seemed to stop...

Much later, Miriam would say that something must have happened in Heaven at that moment. All she knew for sure was that a part of her she barely understood was screaming at the sight of that large cross glinting in the sunlight. "No! No! No!" cried her soul. She imagines that these screams flew up, beyond our world, piercing the heavens and landing right at the foot of G-d's Throne of Glory.

"What is the meaning of this screaming neshamah?" the melachim asked.

"That one belongs to me, now," responded the Satan dismissively. "She was once Yours, but she threw it all away and now she's on her way to marry a non-Jew."

"One minute," interjected a small voice. It belonged to a little white angel. "Not so fast. I speak on her behalf."

"Who are you?" thundered the Satan.

"I am the angel that was created when Miriam lit Shabbos candles at her teacher's house. She did a mitzvah."

The angels in the Heavenly Court looked at one another in confusion, and then brought the matter to G-d Himself.

"Tell the court how long it took for Miriam to perform that mitzvah," G-d said.

"Forty seconds," stated the white angel.

"Then this is her judgment: She will be given 40 seconds at this point of her life to change her mind. She merits this chance because of the wholehearted mitzvah that she performed."

Back in the limousine, Mary's friends were staring at her expectantly. "Well?" one of them finally said.

Mary shook herself and smiled, running a manicured fingernail along the glittering cross that lay upon her heart. "Thank you! It's just beautiful."

The conversation restarted where it had left off, and Mary forgot the temporary unease that the gift had generated. After all, everyone gets a little jumpy before their wedding.

She settled back to stare out the window, just as the limo glided to a halt at a red light.

Just a few feet away from the limo, but in a different world entirely, five Bais Yaakov girls from Brooklyn were lost in the streets of Chicago. They had traveled in for Shabbos, as there was a Shabbaton that weekend, where girls from all over America were arriving to attend the function of a well-known *kiruv* organization that had touched so many lives. Separated from their group and growing increasingly nervous, the five girls had just noticed the shiny limo that was stopped right in front of them, as well as the eye-catching bride who was peering out the window, a jeweled cross around her neck.

The girls quickly approached the limo; there wasn't a lot of time before the light would change.

"Excuse me," one of the girls called. "Would you give us some directions? We aren't from around here."

The bride looked at them, and something subtle seemed to change in her expression. "You girls are Jewish, aren't you?"

"Yes..." responded the girl who had spoken, uneasily.

"So am I," responded the bride in the window, a small smile arriving on her lips as though by accident. "I know where you're probably going. To an Orthodox temple, right? I can show you where it is—I used to go there a long time ago when it was a Reform temple. Today is the Sabbath, and you must be going there to pray, right?"

All five awestruck girls nodded unbelievingly; a couple of pairs of eyes traveled inexorably toward the gleaming cross around their fellow Jew's neck.

Just then the light turned green, but the bride had already called for the driver to pull over.

"We're going to help these girls find their temple," Mary instructed the driver. "We're early, we have plenty of time, and this is a confusing neighborhood that they shouldn't navigate alone. Let's please just take the limo and lead them to where they have to go."

"You're on your way to get married," grumbled one of her friends.

"It's only a few blocks away," Mary said firmly.

The limo went slowly down the block as the Bais Yaakov girls trailed behind it, lost in feverish discussion.

"If she's Jewish, we can't just let her go to that wedding," hissed one of the girls.

"How on earth do you think we could stop her?" another girl muttered resignedly.

"I don't know," returned the first girl, "but how on earth can we let a Jewish girl marry a non-Jew?"

After a lot more urgent whispering that lasted right up until the limo halted in front of a shul, the girls decided on a plan.

They approached the limo with friendly smiles, thanking the bride profusely for her help and for going so far out of her way.

"But as long as you're here," one girl added as though it were an afterthought, "why not come inside with us and get a blessing from the rabbi for your wedding day? You did say you were Jewish, after all."

The bride's mouth dropped open. "An Orthodox rabbi would give *me* a blessing?" she asked in disbelief.

"Of course," reassured the other girl, "but you have to come inside."

Ignoring loud sounds of protest and indignation from within the car, the bride appeared to be mulling it over. "You know," she said at last, "that's actually a really nice idea. It would be a very holy thing to do, to get a blessing from a rabbi on the day of my wedding."

She leaned her head toward the front of the limo to confer with the driver, and then engaged in a brief, though heated, whispering match with her friends. Finally, the limo door opened to reveal the bride in her full wedding regalia, surrounded by several surly-looking girls in evening finery. Their glances at the Bais Yaakov girls were not friendly.

"Just one thing," one of the Jewish girls added hastily. "You'd have to remove that necklace before entering the synagogue. Out of respect, you understand."

"Oh, yes," agreed the bride instantly, "of course I understand."

"I can't believe you, Mary!" whined the girl who had first presented the necklace as she snatched her gift back. "First we go out of our way to help people that we never met before, and now you're going to get a blessing from a *rabbi*? Have you completely forgotten where you're supposed to be going, today?"

"It'll only be a few minutes," muttered Mary absently. Her mind was focused more on the unusual sense of liberation she felt after removing the necklace. As though her soul could breathe easier...

Inside the shul, Mary followed her new friends to the women's section, where they handed her a Hebrew prayer book with an English translation, informing her that it would be a few minutes before the rabbi would be available.

There was some minor commotion among the assembled women at the completely unexpected appearance of a clearly irreligious girl in a full bridal gown. Luckily, an older woman—the rabbi's wife, Mary learned—had taken in the situation and she immediately hushed the other congregants back to their prayers.

Feeling achingly self-conscious, Mary gingerly seated herself in a nearby chair and waited for the service to conclude.

Just then, from her view on the balcony, Mary noticed a young boy—probably no older than 8 or 9—don a prayer shawl and begin singing a song from the spot that the cantor had just occupied. It was a beautiful song—one of the girls told her it was called *Anim Zemiros*—and something about it entranced her and caused her to momentarily forget her discomfort as the melody soared across the temple. There was something incredibly touching about it, something that filled her with a sense of longing.

Then it was clearly the end of the service, for Mary noticed the men rising and removing their prayer shawls and replacing their books. Her new friends led her downstairs to the rabbi, where she shyly explained about her Jewish roots and asked for his blessing that her marriage would bring only good fortune.

The rabbi regarded Mary quietly for a moment. "Tell me," he said at last. "Do you know anything about your Jewish roots? Are you truly willing to put it all aside without having ever explored it?"

Mary shrugged. "I never really had a chance, rabbi. I didn't practice Judaism as a child, and then I went to a totally secular college."

"Well," the rabbi responded slowly, "would you consider postponing the wedding for a little while, just to learn some more about your heritage? My wife and I would be happy to help out however we can."

Mary's head swam. "Are you serious, rabbi? You've never met me, but you and your wife would teach me about my Jewish roots?"

"We absolutely would," the rabbi responded with a smile. "We're here for you if you're willing to have us."

Maybe it was her slow, pensive walk, or maybe it was the look on her face, but Mary's friends knew immediately that there was something wrong.

"Don't tell me you're not going to marry Vinnie anymore!" shouted one girl from the window of the idling limousine.

Mary looked up at them, and it was as though she were seeing different people with a different pair of eyes. Sure, these were the girls she had gone to school with and spent countless hours with, but suddenly the whole length and breadth of that shared experience seemed to pale in comparison to the fire in her soul. Suddenly, she had no desire to re-enter that car; no desire even to reclaim the gift the occupants of the car had in their possession.

"I felt something in that synagogue," she said simply. "I'm not going with you today. I'm not doing it."

"What about Vinnie?" shouted the other girl over the sound of the others' shrieking. "He thinks he's getting married today!"

Resolution hardened Mary's tone. "Then *you* marry him. I'm done."

"Fine, Mary. Then we're done with *you*. Have a nice life. Let's get out of here, girls!"

The limousine peeled off without further ado, leaving Mary in front of the shul in her wedding gown, confusion and fear battling pride and relief in her gulping sobs.

Miriam grew very close to the rabbi and his wife, who took her under their wing and nurtured her growth in Judaism and its practices. Slowly, Miriam began to attend shul and keep Shabbos and, after some time had elapsed, she was fully observant was ready to travel to Israel and study in a seminary for *baalei teshuvah*.

From there, everything began to fall into place for the newly minted *baalas teshuvah*. Two years after her arrival in Israel, Miriam was introduced to a wonderful, spirited young man whose religious background was similar to hers, and the two were soon standing under the *chuppah*, where Miriam finally had the wedding G-d had intended for her.

Miriam's husband became a "Reb Are'le Chassid" not long after they married; these Chassidim are distinct in Meah Shearim with their large white yarmulkes and long robes. The couple soon welcomed several beautiful children into the world, and Miriam's heart and soul were finally fulfilled.

A fascinating tale, to be sure, but it doesn't end here.

Rabbi Wallerstein adds:

"How do I know this story? A teacher in my school who attended seminary in Israel actually ate at Miriam's house one Shabbos! It was part of a program in her seminary in which they would learn about all different types of Jews by eating at their houses every Shabbos. That particular Shabbos, it was time to learn about 'Reb Are'le Chassidim.'

"Well, they arrived at that woman's home, and had no idea that she had a past of any kind. She looked like any other Chassidishe woman from Meah Shearim—she was very welcoming and kind. When her husband went to shul, she motioned to the girls to wait for her on the couch for a few minutes, and then when she would come down, she would light the candles.

"A few minutes later, she reappeared...wearing a wedding gown. The girls tried not to show their surprise as she swept over to the candles and lit them, remaining there for 45 minutes as she swayed back and forth, davening with all her heart and reading the names of people who needed *yeshuos* of every kind. The girls were puzzled, of course, but for all they knew, it might have just been a *minhag* of Reb Are'le Chassidim.

"However, after she finished davening, she sat down and told the fascinated girls the story you just heard. When the story was finished, Miriam still had one last thought to add.

" 'I know that it was in the *zechus* of those candles I lit in fifth grade that I was given that one chance to do *teshuvah*. I know it was the angel created by that one mitzvah that earned me that brief 40-second window before the red light would change and the limo would speed away. That's why I made up my mind that I would commemorate the day I found G-d by wearing what I was wearing when I found Him.' "

The car stopped for 40 seconds. Go outside and count how long your average red light lasts, and it will be about that length of time. Is it not

incredible that 40 seconds decided whether Mary would marry Vinnie and be lost to Judaism forever, or whether she would marry a Chassid and live a life of Torah and mitzvos in Meah Shearim? Forty seconds can be the difference between the highest and lowest levels of spirituality. Forty seconds changed Miriam's entire life.

Yes, there are moments of clarity and inspiration, but sometimes those moments can last only 40 seconds or perhaps even less! No matter how long the magic moment, it is always just long enough for you to earn your place in history. The decision is always yours to make: choose wisely.

Never Forget

I had the good fortune of being present at a Motza'ei Shabbos shiur delivered by Rabbi Kalman Krohn of Lakewood, N.J., in which he discussed how the actions we perform here on earth have a ripple effect that reaches the heavens themselves. He related the following story to illustrate this point; it is my belief that this story does indeed shake heaven and earth—and it makes a powerful impression on the reader, as well.

Baruch Charnmen* was devastated to discover that the stomach pains he had been experiencing were indicative of a very serious disease: one that required an immediate operation. He was put in touch with the UK's Dr. Raymond Stone,* an irreligious Jew who was one of the country's most sought-after doctors.

At the consultation, Dr. Stone expressed confidence that he would be able to successfully operate, but with one caveat.

"I have a personal request," the eminent doctor announced to the surprised young man. "I would like you to take care of me as I will take care of you. I would like you to teach me about Judaism, because I never really had a chance to learn a lot about it."

Baruch readily agreed to the deal and with that promise secured, he went under the knife shortly afterward. The operation was a resounding success, and Baruch was delighted at his new lease on life. His hospital room was soon filled with his parents, relatives, and friends, all of them rejoicing at the *refuah* granted by Hashem through His *shliach*. Dr. Stone was happy as well, of course, but he was also biding his time until his patient's recovery was complete.

When a few days had gone by, Dr. Stone visited his charge. "I've kept my end of the deal," he said with a pleasant smile, "and I think it's time for you to keep yours. You said you would help me with my Judaism."

Baruch considered this for a few moments. Where did one begin? "I'd like to share a story with you, if that's okay," he said, finally.

"Of course," agreed the doctor.

"My father used to tell this tale," Baruch began. "I've always seen it as a good example of what it means to be a dedicated Jew, and I hope it helps your connection to Judaism as it has helped mine."

David Mayer* was a fixture in the shul; the elderly man was the resident *talmid chacham*, meticulous in his observance of mitzvos and never failing to treat his fellow man with dignity and kindness. It didn't take long for the casual observer to conclude that David Mayer was a man who had a special relationship with his Creator. There was, however, the very curious matter of *Bircas Kohanim*.

As you know, the end of Yom Tov davening usually brings the shul's Kohanim to the front of the room where they stand, their faces and outstretched arms wrapped in their talleisim, and pronounce the special blessing of Kohanim to their fellow Jews in shul. With its soft, beautiful melody and heartfelt words, *Bircas Kohanim* is one of the highlights of any holiday davening. Generally, every last person attending shul makes sure to be there to receive the blessing of the Kohanim.

Everyone except David Mayer, as it turned out.

You see, it began when a certain fellow in shul happened to notice the venerable old man exiting the shul the moment before the Kohanim were going to begin. This was curious enough for a man who barely ever budged from his spot, but of course, it would not be impossible that he needed some air or the men's room at that exact moment. At first, the observer disregarded this anomaly. But the following day, when Mr. Mayer left the room at the exact same moment, there was no denying the oddity.

Why would a man of Mr. Mayer's stature not have the patience to be there for Bircas Kohanim? It doesn't make sense? He was puzzled.

The matter grew even more urgently noticeable the following Yom Tov, when the elderly man repeated the same performance. There was no further denying that his actions were calculated and deliberate. But *why?* Deeply troubled, the observer felt that there was no other option but to present his findings to the Rav of the shul. Perhaps the Rav could put his mind at ease.

As it happened, the Rav himself had never noticed this peculiar behavior on the part of his congregant, as he made sure to keep his eyes closed when the *berachah* was about to be recited. Still, the information disturbed him and he resolved to put an end to the mystery. He invited David Mayer to his home for a Shabbos meal. The old man agreed quickly enough; he was living on his own, after all, and his Shabbos table could sometimes be lonely.

The meal was highly enjoyable, partly due to David Mayer's incisive *divrei Torah*, his sharp wit, and his deep singing voice. Following bentching, when the two were alone at the table, the Rav decided to take advantage of the mutual feeling of mellow camaraderie.

"Reb David," he commented, "I must tell you how impressed I have been by the way you daven. People notice, and it's a *kiddush Hashem* of the highest order."

The old man waved a dismissive hand. "Please, don't be too impressed. I'm just another Jew who davens."

The Rav smiled. "You're quite a humble man, Reb David. Everyone in shul has only the greatest respect for the way you conduct yourself during the *tefillah*. I was actually wondering if I might ask you a question concerning your davening."

"Of course," Mr. Mayer responded interestedly. "What is it?"

"Well," the Rav leaned back as though to take the forwardness from his next words, "I have recently spoken with another individual from our shul who expressed surprise that a man of your stature would leave davening so early."

"Early?" Mr. Mayer's face registered his confusion. "I'm usually there until well after the last *Kaddish*, actually."

"I'm talking," the Rav explained softly, "about when you leave before *Bircas Kohanim*."

The old man's face froze into a strange grimace, and then he began flushing rapidly. To the Rav's alarm, Mr. Mayer's hands were suddenly shaking and his body jerking with discomfort.

"Reb David?" the Rav asked worriedly. "Are you all right?"

"I —" the old man managed through a sheen of perspiration. "I just...didn't realize that...anyone had noticed."

The Rav hurried to bring the old man a glass of water, which Mr. Mayer drank gratefully. After a minute or two, he composed himself somewhat.

"I'm sorry for my reaction," he said after a while. "I wasn't ready for that question at all."

Guilt pangs gnawed at the Rav's chest. "Look, if it's a difficult subject, I'm sorry I brought it up. You don't have to talk about it."

"No." The old man sighed. "No, I think it's about time to say something about it. May I perhaps have a bit of schnapps to calm my nerves?"

When the schnapps had been brought out, Mr. Mayer took several sips and calmed down further. "Tell me," he said abruptly, "are you a survivor of the war?"

The Rav shook his head.

"Well, I am," the other man said, simply. He rolled up his sleeve to display the numbers that are often an indelible reminder to Holocaust survivors of the hell they witnessed.

"I saw it all," Mr. Mayer said quietly. "I saw my brothers die in torturous pain and I watched my best friends die in Auschwitz. They simply refused to do what the Nazis wanted and give up. It was their bodies that died, but never their spirits.

"I had a group of friends in my barrack. We all shared the same determination to keep a spark of *Yiddishkeit* alive despite it all. On Shabbos, we davened together right under the Nazis' noses. We put aside morsels of food for our meals and we sang *Shalom Aleichem* and made *Kiddush*. We liked to imagine that we were back in our homes for just a little bit of time each week. Sometimes, we even sang *zemiros* if we were feeling daring enough. It helped heal us, Rabbi.

"The unofficial leader and the oldest member of our group was Yaakov. He was the sort of man who was a leader by nature, and he became our acting Rav. He made *Kiddush* every week, and he was the one honored to say a *d'var Torah* at our 'Shabbos meal.' He gave us the strength to keep fighting.

"Well, when Pesach time came around, Yaakov made the decision that there was no way we would allow ourselves to eat bread. No, we were going to trade our rations for flour and bake matzos like the good old days. We were going to have a Seder.

"We laughed at him. Oh, how we laughed! Baking matzos in Auschwitz? Celebrating our 'freedom' in that hell? But Yaakov was completely serious, and it wasn't long before we had bartered our rations enough to obtain two matzos' worth of flour. We baked our matzos on top of a furnace. Somehow, Yaakov even managed to get his hands on some grapes and he used them for our '*arba kosos*.' *Maror*, we didn't need. We had enough of that every day.

"When Pesach night came...well, it was amazing! We actually felt a little of that freedom. Our souls took nourishment from the words of the Haggadah, which Yaakov recited by heart. The question of why this night was different from all others took on a meaning it never had before; indeed, this night was really very different! We may have been sitting on the floor with a few pieces of matzah, but our hearts swelled with *emunah*.

"But then, at the height of our joy, an SS guard burst into the room, shouting and swearing at the top of his voice. Before we knew what was happening, he was among us, striking at us senselessly with his club and demanding to know who the leader of this event was.

"'Tell me who it is,' he shouted, 'or I will kill all of you right here!'

"Well, Rabbi, there was no way I was about to let that beast kill Yaakov. This was a bullet I was willing to take. So I stood up. 'I'm the leader,' I said. 'Please leave the rest of them alone. I made them do this.'

"The Nazi hit me in the face so hard that I literally saw stars, and pushed me to the ground, where he put his gun to my head. 'I'm going to kill you, but I'm going to do it tomorrow, when the whole camp can see. We will teach you how to celebrate a Jewish holiday!'

"He barked a laugh and stomped out of the room.

"At roll call the next morning, I knew my end was near. I came prepared to meet my Maker, knowing full well that I would not be returning from this gathering. I would be called to die. I stood at attention until my name was called, at which point I was told to come to the front. Whispering the words of *Vidui*, I followed instructions.

"I stood up straight as the SS guard who had caught us shouted about how I was going to die for my terrible crimes, and how it would be a lesson to anyone else who tried to flout the rules. I just closed my eyes and waited for the bullet. I was at peace.

"But then a voice rang out, '*NO! Don't kill him!*' My concentration broke, and I saw Yaakov running toward me. 'I am the one you want!' he was shouting. 'I am the leader of the group! You're killing the wrong man!'

"I felt my heart clench with horror, and I shouted back, with all my might, 'No, I'm the leader! I'm the one you want!' I ran over to Yaakov, desperately trying to force him to return to his roll-call position, but he fiercely refused, and the Nazis watched us argue for a while, obviously enjoying themselves.

"Finally, they decided that they would kill the older one and make the younger one watch at close range. The verdict was a crushing blow: Yaakov was going to die. Yaakov, our Rav and our leader. There was nothing more I could do.

"With a heavy heart, I watched them bring Yaakov to the front of the crowd. The guard asked him in a bored voice if he had any last requests.

"'Yes, I do.' Yaakov's voice was firm and unafraid. 'I want to talk to my people for two minutes.'

"They granted this to him, and everyone held their breath, waiting to hear what Yaakov's last words would be. Yaakov turned to face everyone, his face determined, and then he did the strangest thing I have ever seen.

"Raising his hands toward the crowd, Yaakov began to sway with his arms outstretched. He then sang in a beautiful voice:

"'*Yivarechecha...Hashem...V'yishmerecha...*'

"'*Ya'eir...Hashem...Vi'chuneka...*'

"Yaakov moved his hands as though to embrace the whole crowd as he sang, and we all silently mouthed the words of the age-old blessing along with him. Rabbi, I didn't even know he was a Kohen, but here he was, *duchening,* and I had never heard such a beautiful *duchening* in my life. I felt the tears choke me as I watched, and I knew I would never be the same person after witnessing this saddest yet greatest *kiddush Hashem* ever.

"With the last words of Yaakov's *berachah*, he lowered his hands, his face already at peace in another place. Everyone jumped once with the sudden snap of a gunshot, and Yaakov's body crumpled to the ground. A couple of guards leaped forward to drag the corpse away, and I was left standing there, feeling like my mouth was full of ashes and my heart had been torn from my body.

"How could Hashem let Yaakov die? I was crushed like you could never imagine. Such a great person like Yaakov, who had risked his life over and over again to keep Torah and mitzvos! Well, if this was what being a Jew was all about...that was when I decided, in the middle of my darkest depression, that I was through with being religious. You have to understand, Rabbi, that it just made no sense.

"Somehow, I survived the next few months in the camp until we were liberated at last. I was finally a free man. And, as a free man, I resolved to hold fast to what I had decided. No more religion, no more praying—I was through! The very first week after liberation, I decided that I would deliberately violate Shabbos, just to prove to myself that it was all over for me. But then, as Shabbos drew closer, my mind kept displaying that image of Yaakov, hands outstretched, completely at peace at the last moments of his life. I felt compelled to keep Shabbos that week, and so I did.

"After Shabbos, though, I tried to eat my first nonkosher sandwich. It was just a sandwich, after all. But I *couldn't,* because there was Yaakov again, his image begging me to remain firm in my *emunah* even after everything I had seen. His image appeared a third time when my relationship with a non-Jewish girl was making its way toward marriage. Once again, I couldn't go through with my plans. It was time to acknowledge that I just couldn't betray the memory of Yaakov, and so I threw myself back into *Yiddishkeit* with a passion, and I never looked back again!"

With tears in his eyes, David Mayer concluded, "Every Yom Tov, when it's time for *Bircas Kohanim*, I'm overwhelmed by the past. Yaakov's image comes to me again. I see his last *duchening* again, and then I know I have to leave the shul, because as long as I live, I never want to forget that *Bircas Kohanim*. I want the taste of it to remain. That's why I go outside and I envision that moment again and I cry. I cry for my family who were lost to me, I cry for my people...but most of all, I cry for Yaakov."

"If you want to do something truly meaningful," said Baruch to Dr. Stone, "try to make it to synagogue when the Kohanim are reciting their blessing, and picture the man who had the strength to pronounce that blessing as the last thing he ever said. Perhaps it will do for your faith what it did for David Mayer's."

I am reminded of another powerful incident that occurred several years ago, in Boro Park.

Every year, during the *aseres yemei teshuvah*, there is a grand gathering in Boro Park for the boys of all the local *chadarim*. Hundreds of children from all over the New York area converge in a large hall for the purpose of reciting *Tehillim*. In order to merit special mercy and blessing from Hashem, children of Chassidishe, Litvishe, and Sefardi backgrounds alike unite for this massive exhibition of *kiddush Hashem*.

The hundreds of chairs that are set up in the hall are meant for the children, as it is a children's event. Adults are asked to remain nearby in a different location so as to better accommodate the true stars of the show.

And so it was at one of these gatherings that a rebbi happened to notice an elderly man sitting in one of the front rows of seats reserved for children. Although he felt sorry for the gentleman, the rebbi simply could not allow him to take one of the children's seats. It simply wouldn't be right. Hesitantly, he approached the old man and tapped him gently on the shoulder.

"Excuse me," he said, "but these seats here are reserved for the children. There are seats for adults elsewhere."

The old man frowned. "No, no, you don't understand. I have to sit here."

The rebbi sighed. "Look, I understand that you want a good seat, but these seats are really, truly, meant *only* for the kids. It's their event. Come and let me show you to a different place."

"Please leave me be," the old man pleaded.

The rebbi raised his voice slightly. "Listen, I can't make any exceptions. I'm asking you to please get up and I'll take you to where the adults are sitting..."

He trailed off in confusion as he noticed that the old man had begun to tremble. Slowly, shakily, the old man reached into his pocket and produced a deeply creased, yellowed paper. Unfolding the paper, he showed the rebbi the old photo of two children that was hidden within it.

"These were my two boys," the elderly man said softly. "Meir and Yossi were taken from me during the war and killed in the Nazis' camps. They never had the opportunity to go to events like these. For the last 60 years, I think of them every day, and so I make it my business to be there whenever there's a children's event.

"So please," he concluded, his voice breaking, "let me sit here, where I'm sure the *neshamos* of my two precious boys have come to join the other children here today. Let me stay in the presence of my children."

The rebbi's knees felt weak; he was struck dumb with awe. Of course, he extended his permission for the old man to remain where he was. He watched with an aching heart as the old Holocaust survivor cried and recited *Tehillim* along with the hundreds of young boys, holding the aged photo of his own lost children before him.

It was an image that the rebbi would never forget: a loving father who could never, ever forget to think of his children.

Wake Up, Yitzi!

In this story, Yitzi shares his experiences being a teenager in today's world. In a life that kept threatening to veer out of control, Yitzi managed to grab the wheel and jerk it back in the right direction. This is a story to be learned from.

I grew up in a very close-knit, Torah-true home. For many years, my greatest role model was my father, and there was simply nothing I wanted more than to make him proud. I strove to do just that, and it seemed like there was a bright future ahead of me. My parents were proud of my dedication to *Yiddishkeit*, and they had high hopes for my growth in learning.

Unfortunately, my entry into high school was when things began to go wrong. For some reason, I just couldn't seem to find my way in the learning. It wasn't that I couldn't follow it, or even that it was too difficult for me; I simply lost my interest. Taken aback, my rebbeim tried as best they could to get through to me, but by then, it was as though a wall had formed around my *neshamah*. Gradually, I began to seek means and friends outside of the yeshivah to fill that sense of need that boredom made so pressing. While I still dressed like a yeshivah *bachur* on the outside, it was more or less only a costume; I felt truly excited and comfortable only with the new life I was forming for myself on the streets.

Dumbfounded by my actions, my parents tried pressuring me to abandon my new ways, perhaps thinking that all I needed was a little discipline to push me back into the yeshivah mold. This backfired completely. Their attempts to assume a tough stance and stay on top of me only made me angrier and more bitter. A rift formed between us, and I drifted farther and farther away from Torah Judaism, with the help of my newfound friends.

For a long while I was completely unreachable, but then, at age 17, I could no longer ignore the sense of spiritual freefall that was leaving me depressed. My soul was aching. I wanted to be a good person, and I wanted people to be proud of me. I found another yeshivah where there were others like me, young men who had lived a rough-and-tumble existence on the streets and now wanted to regain their spiritual footing. My rebbi there was a wonderful man who really believed in me and accepted me for who I was instead of what others expected me to be. His trust and his faith helped me grow, and slowly my feelings of anguish and emptiness began to subside.

Although I was happier now, it was no easy feat to completely rid myself of my former life. I began to wish that Hashem Himself would send me a clear sign that He wanted me back, some indication that my *avodah* and my Torah were something precious to Him. Short of that, all I knew was that my life in the streets had been exciting, and I sometimes felt that my recommitment to Torah and mitzvos was preventing me from ever feeling as excited again.

Well, those messages came last summer.

In order to clear my head, I used to borrow my parents' car and joyride around the mountains, savoring the fresh mountain air and the uninhibited freedom of the road. Behind that wheel, I felt as though anything were possible.

And so it was, as I was cruising down Route 52 on my way to Woodbourne, the wind whipping pleasantly in my face as the music blasted, my pleasure was rudely cut short by a speeding sports car that entered suddenly onto the highway, cutting me off so sharply that I had to push the brakes to the floor.

Now, I don't have to tell you that I was upset; we've all been cut off sometime or another. But I was young, daring, and angry, and so I made the decision that I would speed up to cut this sports car off in return—there could only be one king of the road! As Route 52 was narrow, with only one lane in each direction, I had to veer into the opposing lane to accomplish this. I figured there wouldn't be much of a problem, as I and my nemesis were the only two cars on the road.

I pressed on the gas pedal, and as I pulled slowly alongside the other car, aiming to cut him off from his left, he responded by gunning his own accelerator, keeping himself too far ahead of me to let me get in front of him. We both kept at an even 75 mph—he in his lane and me in the opposing one—neither willing to yield the other an inch. It was about then that I noticed a car on the horizon of my lane, heading right toward me. It seemed like the battle of wills had to end now, as I simply couldn't pass the sports car.

I released my accelerator and touched the brake, trying to slow down enough to fall in behind the speeding sports car. But, as I slowed down, so did he, and my passage into the correct lane remained blocked! Frantically, I accelerated again, hoping that perhaps he meant to let me get ahead of him: no such luck. He sped up as well, and the oncoming car was now only a short distance from me. With a sudden clench of my chest, I realized that I was rushing headlong into a probably fatal accident.

The decision was upon me quicker than I was ready for it: I could either veer into the correct lane and hit the sports car to avoid a head-on collision, or I could stay where I was and let the inevitable collision happen. With only a little over 10 seconds to impact, I suddenly saw another option. I desperately veered to the left, jumping onto the shoulder of the opposing lane to avoid the screeching car that was about to rush into me. To my horror, the oncoming car had decided on the same strategy, and he veered to his right, which meant he was on a direct collision course with me!

With my life flashing before my eyes, I made my last move, cutting the wheel viciously to my right to send myself hurtling at the sports car. At least, I told myself, it wouldn't be a head-on impact. Perhaps we would survive. I screamed in horror as I jumped into the right lane, closing my eyes against the inevitable crushing impact, the screech of brakes, and the scraping of metal on metal...

To my shock, the sports car was gone, speeding far ahead as my car hit the lane and began to swerve out of control. I slammed on the brakes and slowly, after a panicked few seconds, I managed to come to a stop. My pulse racing with adrenaline, I pulled onto the shoulder and shakily climbed out of the car, every fiber of my being buzzing with the realization that I should have been dead just then. Clearly, Hashem hadn't intended that to happen.

Over the next few days, I began to think a little more seriously about my mortality. I realized that life is not an eternal gift, and that my continued existence was only through G-d's grace. My davening took on new meaning after my experience; I decided that life wasn't only about me enjoying it; it was about leading the fulfilling existence for which Hashem had spared my life.

Still, it is the nature of man to forget, and my burst of inspiration soon faded. Though I returned to yeshivah after that summer with the intention of turning over a new leaf, I found myself drifting slowly and unmistakably back into my old habits and routines. The month of Elul may have been in the air, but I was having a difficult time heeding its call. Then, in a very tragic way, Hashem called my name once again.

A good friend of mine was diagnosed with an aggressive cancer; the situation was deteriorating very quickly, and the prognosis was not good. Devastated, I couldn't stop wondering why Hashem would see it fit to take such a young person this way. With fresh resolve, I decided that I would not let this opportunity pass me by. I poured my heart out to my Creator, weeping profusely in a way that I had never done before, even on Yom Kippur. Every *tefillah* was an opportunity for me to petition Hashem anew, to beg Him to hear me, to answer me, to save my good friend.

To my sorrow, it was not meant to be. My good friend died, and I spent his *shivah* as crushed and despairing as any member of his family. After the *shivah*, however, I felt a change within me. As though waking up from a deep slumber, I finally heard Hashem's message to me, amid all this despair. *Yitzi, life is short. You must take advantage of every moment. You must not waste your days.* With a burning determination, I attacked my learning as I never had before. I am sure that, from his place in Gan Eden, my friend rejoiced in the change he had wrought.

I had what was certainly the best *z'man* of my life that winter. Even as the days grew dark and cold, a fire burned within me as I felt the success and enjoyment of my learning growing every day. I wasn't quite there yet, but I was closer than I had ever been.

Perhaps my final lesson came about as springtime arrived and it was time for Pesach preparations. As Yom Tov drew closer, I scoured my room for *chametz*, removing some half-empty boxes of cereal and snacks and putting whatever remnants I found into a small box. As I was feeling around in my drawer for any hidden *chametz*, I chanced upon a small plastic bag full of memories.

Stunned, I riffled through old pictures and letters from several years ago, all of them exchanges of some kind between myself and my friends from the past. It was then that I realized why part of me was still holding fast to a time that was long gone; I understood what I had to do to prove to myself that I was truly ready to change.

I took the bagful of memories of my former self to the yard of the dormitory, scraped together small bits of wood, and formed a little bonfire. *Chazal* teach us that *chametz* represents the Evil Inclination. The symbolic burning of *chametz* is meant to represent the purging of stubborn evils in one's heart. With that in mind, I tossed my little package of sins into the flames and watched in satisfaction as my own personal *biur chametz* took place.

As I watched the flames, I felt that the last remnants of the stains upon my soul were being purged, and I allowed myself a moment of appreciation for how far I had come. I had finally gathered the courage to drag myself that last inch over the finish line and show Hashem that I was willing to be the person He wanted me to be. I felt a renewed confidence that I would not let Him down anymore, nor would I let my parents down, nor—most importantly—my own self. Smiling, my eyes damp, I imagined Hashem beaming down proudly on me. *I'm proud of you, Yitzi. You've finally heard Me calling you and heeded that call. You've come such a long way...but I always waited for you.*

Sometimes, it takes a while for a person to know himself. The day I truly changed for the better was the day when I finally realized how precious my life was, and how precious my family, my friends, and my rebbeim really are, as well. Pursuing a life of pleasure may have looked attractive and glittery from the outside, but from within it was only artificial and meaningless. In my return to the values of my soul, I have found true satisfaction and happiness at last.

Therefore, if I could offer you some advice, it would be this: don't get caught up in the constant search for fun. If it's true pleasure you seek, you need only dig a little deeper into your soul to find that everything you need has been there all along, just waiting for you to discover its worth. Remember that life is not forever.

Make the most of it; I can promise that you won't regret it.

Shabbat Shalom

Rabbi Duvi Bensoussan relates a powerful story that demonstrates clearly just how far Hashem will go to help His children who are willing to make just a small leap of faith.

It was holiday season, and Jack Manter* was elated about his newest shipment of fine jewelry. With all sorts of glittering, beautifully worked gold necklaces and rings—many tastefully studded with diamonds—he was well prepared for a highly profitable Saturday and Sunday.

Jack was a Jewish resident of Brooklyn, but he wasn't particularly observant. Although he would attend synagogue on holidays and the High Holy Days, there was just no way he could conceive of being a Shabbos observer. The way Jack saw things, there was a tremendous inner strength necessary to surrender the most profitable day of the week, and this was a strength he simply did not possess. Shabbos was an intriguing concept, but not one that he could picture as his reality.

Saturday arrived, and Jack peered out the window of his home and watched somewhat guiltily as his friends and neighbors walked to shul, clad in their best clothes, with their children close at hand. He was planning to go to work, but he did not wish that to be common knowledge among his religious neighbors. When the coast was clear, Jack quietly slipped into his car and sped off. Business was business, after all, and today was a big day.

Sure enough, there was already a long, impatient line of customers by the time Jack arrived to open his store. In no time at all, the small jewelry shop was packed with people eager to find and purchase the perfect holiday gift.

The day wore on and as the flow of customers reached a lull, Jack was heartened to see another customer arrive: a tall man in a thin trenchcoat, already holding his credit card at the ready. Jack ignored the prickle of unease he felt as this man asked—in a somewhat agitated voice—to see his best stuff. Any customer was a good customer, and this one looked ready to spend a lot.

The strange man grew more anxious as he repeatedly asked Jack to bring out more and more items for him to examine. No item seemed expensive enough for this man to purchase for his wife's birthday. Jack felt at a loss, his best jewelry displayed before him, as the man's agitation suddenly reached a boiling point.

As if in a dream, Jack suddenly noticed that a gun had appeared from under the trenchcoat and was now pointed at his head.

"Put everything in this bag or you will die," growled the man, producing a cloth bag with his other hand.

Jack stood frozen, awash in a sense of unreality. Fear gnawed at him, but he was in a state of shock and could not bring his body to move.

"I don't have time for this!" screamed the gunman. "Put the jewels in the bag, or I pull the trigger and do it myself!"

Every limb of his body locked in place, Jack suddenly thought of his wife, his children, and all the twists and turns of his life that had led to this moment. Though he was trembling uncontrollably, his body still refused to move. Instinctively, he began whispering a stammering prayer to G-d.

"I-I know it's Shabbos, Hashem, but p-please help me. I know I shouldn't be here, but You're the only One W-Who can save me now. Help me!"

The madman's voice rose even further, but now there was an edge of hysteria in it. "Who are you talking to? What's going on? Is there someone in this store I don't know about? Tell me!"

"N-no," Jack managed. "It's only me."

But the robber glanced around wildly, perhaps convinced that the police were somehow able to see him, and then he slammed a handful of jewelry into his bag and hurried from the store.

Jack's stiff limbs seemed to melt like butter, and he collapsed into his chair, taking a few minutes to simply breathe. When he had managed to relax a bit, he summoned the police and then began to gather his belongings together.

"I'm going home for Shabbos," he announced to the only One Who could hear him.

When the police had gone, Jack locked the store securely and immediately went home. Hashem had spared his life, and he was going to repay the favor.

When he showed up in shul later that Shabbos, his neighbors greeted him with surprised smiles and raised eyebrows. "What are you doing here, Jack?" they asked. "It isn't Yom Kippur!"

But when he continued to attend shul the following Shabbos and then the one after that, their whispers became more pleasant and respectful. Jack was assigned a good seat and given *aliyos*. He began to relish the peace of the seventh day, as well as the meals he now enjoyed together with his family.

But time has a way of reducing the impact of events, and it wasn't even a year before he began to experience gnawing doubts. *Do you have any idea how much money you've lost because you're not working on Saturdays? How do you ever plan on making up the deficit?*

The small voices in the back of his mind were constant and urgent; Jack's resolve slowly weakened to the point where he knew he would take action. The biggest weekend was on the horizon once again as holiday season approached. He had calculated that it was possible to make as much in that weekend as he did all year, and there simply didn't seem to be any further excuses holding him back.

Jack told himself that he wouldn't let his family down, and that he would be sure to keep the *following* Shabbos to the letter, but this was simply an opportunity that he would be insane to pass up.

Still, to soothe the agitated strains of his conscience, he decided that he would not desecrate Shabbos directly. In fact, all he would do is show jewelry to his customers, while a non-Jew would be given the responsibility of handling all money and financial dealings. To sweeten the deal a little further, Jack resolved to take the train to work rather than drive. He would even bring a small bag with grape juice, challah rolls, pastrami, and pickles, so he could still make *Kiddush* and have a tasty Shabbos meal!

On the anticipated day, Jack arrived at his shop, Shabbos meal in hand, together with his new hire, Max, who was to take care of all monetary transactions. Sure enough, huge profits seemed in the making as customers streamed in and out of the store. Max handled every credit card, check, and dollar bill that was given in payment, and Jack was pleased to realize that today was shaping up to be the best day of business in a very long while.

At about 1 p.m., Jack decided to have his Shabbos meal. Turning to Max, he explained that he would be taking his lunch break now and that Max would have to manage in his absence. Max readily agreed, and Jack happily left the store to go sit down at a nearby café, where he had obtained permission to eat his own food. In a quiet corner of the room, he washed for his bread, made *Kiddush,* and even sang a Shabbos song or two as he enjoyed his meal.

After a pleasant half-hour had elapsed, Jack headed back down the block to return to work. He was stopped in his tracks at the sight of flashing lights and the sound of sirens in front of his store!

Feeling his heart sink, Jack hurried over to the roped-off area that was now flooded with policemen. As his worried gaze took in the scene, he almost stopped breathing when he noticed a man being led away from the scene in handcuffs. It was the same man who had robbed him at this time a year before! He could never mistake that anxious, contorted face.

Peering into the store itself, panic fluttering in his chest, Jack was shocked to the core. Max lay dead at the counter, a pool of blood spread around the floor. Jack's mouth was suddenly dry as a bone.

"Sir, is this your establishment?"

Jack barely glanced at the policeman who had approached him and he nodded shakily. "What happened?" he managed.

"You were very lucky," the policeman replied, shaking his head in wonder. "We've been after this guy for a really long time, because his modus operandi is to kill anyone who witnesses his crimes. We believe that he returned to your store today for you, since you were there when he robbed you last year. Unfortunately for your employee, this lunatic must have mistaken him for you and he was just shot without a word."

Overcome, Jack dropped to his knees and covered his face with his hands as tears coursed down his cheeks. "Hashem," he murmured, "I only kept Shabbos for a little while, and yet You saw fit to save my life. You saved me even though I had barely taken a step in the right direction. I promise You that I will never violate Your Shabbos again!"

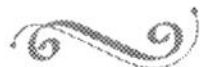

Rabbi Bensoussan adds: That is the power of G-d's love, and how far He will go to inspire change in even one Jew. He is like a father whose son has broken off contact with him. That father will do anything — from letters, phone calls, messages, and even messengers — to convey his love, anything to attain even a moment's conversation with his son.

So does our heavenly Father, Hashem, call out to us through whatever means possible. Let us give Him the recognition He deserves and, in return, we can always be assured of His never-ending love.

Forgive Me

There is no one for whom teshuvah does not apply. In every Jewish heart, no matter how blackened with soot, there is a pure spark of holiness that can still be reached given the right circumstances. Rabbi Duvi Bensoussan relates a story that he heard from a rebbi in Jerusalem.

There was a certain rebbi in Yeshivah Ateres Yisrael in Jerusalem who was known to be a *tzaddik* of the highest caliber. This rebbi would regularly go door-to-door at all hours of the day and night to collect money for impoverished widows and orphans. Before each holiday, he would happily distribute this money, along with food and clothing, to those who needed it. Given his sterling reputation, he was often entrusted with large sums of money from people who were confident that it would be put to good use. Unfortunately, word of this fact made its way to the wrong ears.

It was a few nights before Rosh Hashanah one year when the rebbi sat up late at his dining-room table, engrossed in a *sefer*. Gradually, he became aware of strange noises at the door, as if the lock were being tampered with. In one terrible moment, three hooded men burst into the room. One grabbed him roughly by his collar and leaned close to his face.

"Where is the money?" the hooded man demanded in a cold, flat tone. "Don't bother denying that you have it. We *know* you do. Now, where is it?"

Although he was shaking with pain and fright, the rebbi resolved that he would not divulge this information. That money belonged to orphans and widows, and it wasn't his to give away. With trembling lips, he said as much to the men who loomed over him.

The man closest to him demanded, "Do you not understand

what's going on here, rabbi? This is no game. Give us the money, or we will kill you!"

The other two men branched off and began to ransack the room as the third stood guard over the rebbi.

The rebbi's wife, who stood trembling in the corner of the room, pleaded with her husband, "Just give them the money!"

"I can't," whispered the rebbi. "It's not mine to give."

At that statement, the man standing over him fell upon him savagely, beating him mercilessly with his fists and kicking him with his feet. The barbaric pummeling continued, until blood soaked the face of the rebbi and pooled around his body.

"Now tell me where the money is," the robber said, breathless with rage. "If you don't tell me, I'll finish you off right here."

Heaving what felt like his last breath, almost vomiting with pain, the rebbi forced out, "I...won't...give you...the money."

The brute muttered a curse and slipped a knife out of his pocket, brutally stabbing the rebbi in the stomach. The rebbi threw back his head and howled with the pain; he was feeling his consciousness dimming. No matter...the money would not go to these animals ransacking his room.

"You don't understand," he wheezed, "I *can't* give it to you. It's for the orphans and widows, and they won't have anything to eat for Yom Tov without this money."

"Rabbi," the robber pronounced in utter bewilderment, the rage slipping from his voice, "do you not understand? We are going to *kill* you!"

The rebbi summoned up a reserve of strength he didn't know he had, and raised his arms to open his shirt and pull aside the *tzitzis* over his chest. "Go ahead, then," he murmured. "I will not give you the money of orphans and widows. It belongs to them, not to you."

The hooded man sank to his knees suddenly, still holding the bloody knife in one hand. Shaking his head violently as though to clear it, he appeared to be conducting a vicious battle in his own mind.

Suddenly, he rose to face the two other men who were already approaching the rebbi in anticipation of "ending it." Screaming like a man possessed, he shoved them across the room with both his hands.

"*No!*" he howled. Sinking back into a crouch once again, his knife clattering to the floor, he lifted the blood-soaked rabbi into his arms. "What have I done?" he wailed. "Oh, G-d, what have I done?"

Shocked and bewildered, the remaining two robbers fled the scene immediately through a window, eager to put distance between themselves and their suddenly insane comrade.

The remaining robber carried the rabbi gently down the stairs and secured him in the back of his getaway car, peeling off his mask to reveal that he was crying profusely. As he started the car and began driving to the hospital, his shoulders heaved with his sobs.

"You are the greatest *tzaddik* I have ever seen in my life," he wept. "I have never seen this kind of purity…you are an angel. How could I have done this to you? How could I? I'm so, so sorry…"

Jamming his car into a spot in front of the emergency room, the rebbi's would-be killer gently lifted his victim from the backseat and raced into the building. "Somebody help this man!" he screamed. "This rabbi is about to die!"

A stretcher was produced immediately, and the rabbi placed upon it.

The robber leaned in close to the rebbi, his eyes bloodshot with tears. "Please forgive me," he whispered fervently. "I never meant to hurt a *tzaddik*."

The rebbi's eyes fluttered open. "You did *teshuvah*. I heard you. I forgive you. All is forgiven."

The robber clasped the rebbi's hand in wordless gratitude and then turned on his heel to flee, never to be seen again.

Rabbi Bensoussan exhorts:

This man swung from one extreme to another in moments: murderous thief to baal teshuvah in a heartbeat. When you think about it, we are that robber. We tear our neshamos apart throughout the year with our sins and our filth, and then we hurry to shul on Yom Kippur to cry and beg Hashem to forgive us for our destruction of the spirit that He entrusted with us. And, like a medic in the emergency room, G-d cleans and bandages our wounds so that we can survive another year to rectify our mistakes.

Like the rabbi who forgave, our Father will always embrace us with love despite our shortcomings. Our job is to seek out this love and humble ourselves enough to ask for it. If we truly mean it, we will not be turned away.

Dear Chaya...

In this story, a teacher named Chaya, once a counselor at a girls' camp, shares her account of how powerful an effect our words can have upon our children, our students, or anyone else who looks to us for the answers to life. Devorah was one such person in Chaya's life, and Chaya has never forgotten her. After reading this story, you won't forget her, either.

As a camp counselor, I was often privileged to deal with many wonderful young girls. Most of them were clearly the products of Torah homes, who had come to camp to enjoy a summer of fun, learning, and unforgettable experiences. Occasionally, though, I was called upon to deal with a challenge: a girl who was not following the rules or the spirit of camp and who was beginning to have a negative effect upon others. In such situations, I tried my utmost to connect with the troubled girl in order to understand where she was coming from and what she wanted out of her summer. I hoped that in this way I could form enough of a friendship to direct the girl along the right path.

Devorah was one of these diamonds in the rough. She was a funny, lively girl who was very pop-culture savvy and who demonstrated many rough edges. As I got to know her, I would discuss all sorts of topics relevant to a Jewish girl her age and attempt to offer her some clarity and guidance. I really hoped that my words somehow penetrated her *neshamah*, though her outward behavior indicated nothing of the kind. Still, perhaps a minuscule seed had been planted.

Summer drew to an eventual close, and I bid Devorah a heartfelt goodbye. One day, I prayed, this lively young girl would reach her potential.

Three years had passed since that summer with Devorah, and the entire experience had been pushed to the back of my memory in the face of concerns with school, exams, friends, and seminaries. Then, one day, I received a bone-chilling letter in the mail that brought my memories of Devorah flooding back over me. This letter would change my life and the life of my future students, but at the first glance, it simply filled me with sadness.

Dear Chaya,

You're probably shocked to get this letter from me. It's been three years since I've seen you last, and you probably thought you would never get a letter from me. I'm sure you remember who I am, though.

To be honest, I liked you very much as a person, but I never accepted the stuff you told us campers. I thought of you as a religious fanatic, even though you were always nice to me on a personal level. Still, I just never wanted to hear about Judaism. I can still picture the hurt on your face when you walked into the bunkhouse and caught me reading a magazine that was "not for a bas Yisrael." I don't know if you remember this, but you sat down with me, held my hand tightly, and just looked so sad as you tried your best to convince me to change. Well, Chaya, it's not easy to change. It takes a lot of willpower and determination, but most of all, you have to "want" it.

I want you to know that things have changed an awful lot since then. Yes, I'm still like I was three years ago, but my hand is outstretched to you again, though in a very different way. This time, I want you to look at me with happiness and be really proud of me.

You see, I just survived a terrible accident. I'm lying here in the hospital, paralyzed on the right side of my body. I can't really move, and I can't even talk well, but my other hand can still write, and it is this hand I extend to you. The doctors say that mine is a lost cause, and there is no hope for full recovery. But they're wrong.

In a certain way, I'm recovering now more than I ever have. I'm not sad anymore, because I learned an important lesson. Oh, I learned it the hard way, but I still learned. You see, now I am all but motionless, but I think of the days when I could laugh, talk, sing, dance, play, daven, do mitzvos, help people, and thank Hashem for every moment of life He gave me…but I lie here and cry as I think of what I did with those happy days.

I dirtied my ears, I polluted my eyes, I pursued and eagerly absorbed countless images, music, books, and movies that had no place in my life. My mouth, which I now realize is the most precious tool Hashem gave us, was used for unclean language and songs that I never should have indulged in.

I still see that sad look on your face, Chaya. I still see you sitting on my bed with tears in your eyes. I still see your disappointment. But how can my motionless mouth atone for what it said? How can my unresponsive body correct all the countless actions it did to ruin my precious neshamah? Even though the doctors keep repeating that there is no possibility of recovery, the clamoring of my soul says differently. I can feel it shouting, and I just know that there's a way to fix what I've done.

Last night, I thought of it.

I want you to tell people my story. I want them to know what I've done with my life, so they don't miss their opportunity to keep the same thing from happening to them. Tell them that as long as they can move, sing, dance, walk, play, and listen, they must use these gifts in the correct manner. Don't waste time, and make sure to always thank Hashem for what He's given you. Use your precious time to clean your neshamah and help others do the same.

I know how important it must seem to be as cool and as "in" as others; I was one of those people myself. But look at me now: stiff and motionless. See to it that others get this message as well.

I want people to take the precious body that Hashem has given to them and return it untarnished by sin, like a brightly polished diamond.

That's the only kind of recovery I can ask for.

Love, Devorah

The previous story reminds me of one told by Rav Sholom Schwadron, the famous Jerusalem maggid. It seems that the Chofetz Chaim once delivered a powerful message to his students...

There was a commotion in the yeshivah of Radin, for the Chofetz Chaim had asked that his *talmidim* gather at his home on Friday night at 2 a.m. While it wasn't unusual for the *talmidim* to hear a *shiur* from their rebbi on Friday nights, this time the Chofetz Chaim had specified that he was going to tell them an important secret! The strangeness of this request led many people to believe that the great *tzaddik* was about to reveal the date of Mashiach's arrival. Understandably, no one in yeshivah slept at all that Friday night, prior to the 2 a.m. *shiur*.

Well in advance of the appointed time, the Chofetz Chaim's small house filled with people. The mood was somber, and everyone was silent as the set time arrived and the great sage made his slow way to his seat. Into the awed silence, the Chofetz Chaim spoke a few quite familiar words.

"*Elokai, neshamah she'nasata bi tehorah hi.*" ("My G-d, the soul that You have bestowed upon me is pure.")

Pausing for a moment, the rosh yeshivah then went on to translate the words into Yiddish. After a moment, he continued on to the next sentence of the prayer, and then proceeded in that manner until the entire paragraph had been broken down and translated into Yiddish. The assembled crowd listened intently, but none could say what message the great man was trying to convey.

"The *tefillah* doesn't say," the Chofetz Chaim explained with quiet intensity, "that Hashem will return "a" *neshamah* to us at the End of Days; it says he will return "*our*" *neshamah*, the same exact one that we gave to Him will be given back to us. If we returned it pure, we will receive a pure *neshamah*. If we gave it to Him dirty and defiled, it will be returned in just the same condition.

"Is that not frightening? If we did not treat our *neshamos* properly in this world, we will face the embarrassment and disgrace of having an unclean *neshamah* at *techiyas hameisim*. All of the greatest people—Moshe, Aharon HaKohen, the Avos—will be there to greet us with their souls sparkling brightly, and there we will be with our defiled *neshamos*!"

After reiterating this point several times in a tone of utter awe and amazement, the Chofetz Chaim fell silent. This was his great secret, and it was one that everyone in that room would remember for the rest of his life.

Chapter 3:
Judgment Day

Whose heart does not beat a little faster when Rosh Hashanah arrives? Within us all, there is a realization—however muted—that on that Day of Judgment, our deeds are being scrutinized and weighed on a Heavenly scale. On that Day of Judgment, we pray that we are inscribed in the Book of Life as we raise our hearts and voices to pronounce Hashem our King and let the sound of the shofar clear our minds of their clutter. We feel awake in a way that is not duplicated on any other day of the year; we truly know of Hashem's kingship and we pray that, among the deeds that lay before Him, He might discover our love, our sacrifice, and our unfettered devotion.

The people we will meet in this chapter have internalized this realization and have become inspired by it. Ultimately, they were raised to heights they never dreamed they could reach.

Avinu Malkeinu. Yes, He is our King, but first and foremost He is our Father, and He loves us more than we can ever know.

Forget Me Not

Rabbi Duvi Bensoussan relates a personal account of an experience that happened to him years ago, on Erev Rosh Hashanah, in which he witnessed firsthand the incredible hashgachah pratis (Divine intervention) with which Hashem rewards those who do His will. Incidents like the following, where one clearly sees G-d's hand in the world, serve as a clear reminder of His constant presence throughout the bitterness of galus.

The yeshivah that I attended in Israel, Yeshivas Itri, was located right near the Arab village of Beis Lechem. In that village, living right among the Arabs, was a legendary Jew-hater named Tzvika, who hated the boys of the nearby yeshivah with intense loathing.

Tzvika was a secular Jew who had sought to distance himself as much as possible from his religious birthright. Married to an Arab woman and the father of a Muslim family, the proximity of our yeshivah was a constant thorn in his side that he would likely have given anything to be rid of. My fellow *bachurim* and I would shiver when he would fix us with a murderous glare whenever he happened to pass by. If ever a person had wished to drive the Jews into the sea, it was surely Tzvika!

One year, a while before Rosh Hashanah, I decided to commit myself to the age-old *segulah* of davening at the Kosel every day for 40 days. The belief is that if one continues pounding on the Heavenly Gates for that long, that person will be granted his or her request, whether it is deserved or not. I was personally acquainted with many friends who had seen unbelievable *yeshuos* after trying this *segulah*, and so I resolved to go through with it myself.

Well, I made solid progress for 37 days before I realized that I had made a terrible miscalculation. Day 40 of my *segulah*, which I had previously calculated to be the day of Erev Rosh Hashanah, was in fact going to fall on the first day of Yom Tov itself! The Kosel was an hour-and-a-half walk from my yeshivah, and surely I would not obtain permission to go out that far; we were required to remain in the yeshivah on Rosh Hashanah.

Crushed, I brought my dilemma to my rebbi to ask his advice. I didn't want to disobey the yeshivah's rules, but I was just so close to attaining my goal!

My rebbi considered the situation for a minute, and then said, "Why don't you go to the Kosel on Erev Rosh Hashanah and then stay there until after Maariv? The halachic day begins after *shekiah*, as you know, so that night will be counted as your 40th day, and then you can walk back to yeshivah. That much I'm sure we can let you do, so that you can finish your *segulah*."

Overjoyed, I thanked my rebbi. I was going to complete my 40 days after all!

Erev Rosh Hashanah arrived, and I was immediately swept up in the fever of preparations for Yom Tov. As I hurried from place to place, I didn't realize that time was moving along quickly, and that my window of time to catch a bus to the Old City was rapidly narrowing. Eventually, I glanced at my watch and did a shocked double take. Was my watch broken, or was it truly only 45 minutes to Yom Tov? There would be only one more bus going toward the Kosel that day, and I had to be on it! Hastily, I pulled on my hat and jacket and ran up the steep hill to the bus stop as quickly as I could. At last, wheezing breathlessly, I staggered over to the stop with a little over a minute to spare. I had made it.

Sure enough, I had barely caught my breath before the bus was pulling up to the stop. I was the only one waiting there and, as the doors opened, I noticed out of the corner of my eye that the driver had a strange, crooked smirk on his face.

The bus did not come to a complete stop, but rather began rolling slowly alongside me, the doors still hanging open. I hurried along next to the bus, certain that it would soon come to a halt. Instead, the bus driver seemed to be giving his vehicle a burst of acceleration just as I was about to board, sending me sprinting frantically toward the doors that still remained invitingly open. This game continued for a minute before I glanced up at the face of the driver and froze. Tzvika!

He was grinning at me mockingly, his eyes glinting with amusement as he continued teasing one of the black-hatted young men that he hated so fervently. He laughed harshly, clearly enjoying his game.

"*Nu, yalla!*" he barked at me. "*Ratz!*" ("Well, come on! Run!")

I needed to get on that bus, and so I had no choice but to comply. I began running faster and faster as Tzvika glided alongside of me, his laughter ringing in my ears as I struggled to catch hold of those open doors. Adrenaline pumped within me as my feet pounded at the street. I had to make my 40th day, I just *had* to, and I wasn't going to let Tzvika ruin it for me! With one last, desperate burst of speed, I took a running jump for the door; my fingertips just brushed it, but I fell short and crashed to the ground, my bus fare scattering everywhere as the bus slammed its doors and sped off.

I climbed painfully to my feet, my heart pounding with frustration and anger, and I felt a sudden rush of despair. *Please, Hashem! I wanted so badly to go to the Kosel for the 40th day. Don't let me down now! I'm so close!* But I had just lost half my change, and I didn't even have enough money to board another bus. Yom Tov was drawing rapidly closer, and I just didn't know what to do.

Suddenly, a voice behind me asked, in Hebrew, "Excuse me, is there another bus to the Kosel?"

I turned, and there was an elderly man just arriving from the direction of my yeshivah, wearing the traditional white suit that some of the older residents of Jerusalem donned for Rosh Hashanah.

"I don't think so," I told him, sadly. "The one that just came was the last."

He frowned. "No, I don't think it was. There's supposed to be another bus coming."

I sighed. "Well, even if there is, I'm not going on it."

"Why not?"

I explained briefly about having dropped my change without going into embarrassing detail about what Tzvika the *rasha* had done to me. I then began walking away, figuring that Hashem simply did not want me to reach the Kosel for reasons of His own.

"Don't worry," the old man called after me. "I'll just have them punch my bus card an extra time for you."

Hope rising within me again, I thanked the old man profusely. It looked like I might just make it to the Kosel after all! Moments later, another bus did indeed pull up to the bus stop. I boarded it with a smile, grateful to Hashem for saving the day. I cheerfully took my seat, as of yet unaware that my adventure hadn't ended quite yet.

At first, the ride toward the Old City went along smoothly enough, the bus driver stopping every so often to accept a few more passengers. Then, as we reached the center of town, I was astonished to notice that the bus veered to the left, away from the Kosel plaza, rather than staying to the right! Panic stricken, I ran to the front of the bus and demanded to know why the driver wasn't taking the correct route. At first, he insisted that he *had* gone the right away but then, as I explained what I had just noticed, he suddenly slapped his forehead in anguish.

"*Oy vavoy,* you're right! I usually drive a different route, and I make this turn every day. I forgot that I'm supposed to be going to the Old City!"

Feeling panic bubble up inside me, I pleaded with the driver to please turn the bus around and return to the correct route. Briefly,

I explained the *segulah* I was involved in, and how today was to be my 40th day.

The driver apologized profusely and then proceeded to make a sharp turn onto a narrow side street with the intention of using it as a shortcut back to the right area. I was nervous enough as it was, but the driver seemed perfectly at ease as he accelerated confidently down a street that barely seemed wide enough to fit a car.

Suddenly, there it was. Parked carelessly in the exact middle of the street was a silver Volvo; our path was effectively blocked! We were at a standstill in the middle of a street that the driver couldn't even back up on, and I began praying silently as the driver leaned on his horn vigorously. *Hashem, please! I have to make it! I just have to!*

The frustrated driver leaped down from his bus and began knocking on the doors of the nearby houses, angrily demanding to know whose car was blocking the street. A couple of enterprising young passengers left the bus as well with the intention of physically lifting and relocating the offending vehicle. My heart began to sink.

Finally, a middle-aged woman came rushing toward the scene, yelling "*Slichah! Slichah!*" as she hurried to move her car. The passengers all returned to the bus, along with the driver, and we were soon able to reach the main road that led down into the Old City.

We were back on route, and it was 10 minutes to *shekiah*.

"Hurry," I urged the driver, who was already barreling down the road at what was almost certainly an unsafe speed. "We don't have much time left."

Just as we were reaching the Old City at last, the bus ground to a screeching halt. Ahead of us was the dismaying sight of numerous pulsating lights and the eerie wailing of sirens. There was no choice but to let us off the bus right there, as there would certainly be no clear passage anytime soon.

Thanking the driver profusely, I hopped off the bus with the rest of the passengers and started toward the site of what must have been quite an accident. As I arrived at the scene, I was astonished to see an Egged bus turned on its side, surrounded by policemen. Then, with a jolt of horror, I saw a screaming man leap out of the overturned bus, his body shrouded in flames! He collapsed onto the ground, writhing with agony as policemen swatted at him desperately with jackets and blankets, trying to douse the fire. It seemed to be doing little good; the harder they swatted, the more ferociously the flames seemed to burn, and the louder and shriller the man's screams became.

I moved closer, hypnotized by the unearthly sight, and it was then that I received another shock as I identified the face of the man who was burning to death before my eyes: Tzvika.

Suddenly faint, I realized which bus it was that had overturned on the road, and that I was supposed to be on that bus. Ambulances had arrived, and wounded people were being pulled from the wreckage, many of them having suffered burns as well. I felt weak in my knees, shaking with emotion as words burst suddenly into my mind.

Hinei, Yom Hadin hagadol v'hanora! (Behold, the great and awesome Day of Judgment is upon us!)

This particularly severe judgment could easily have been mine, had Hashem not sent a *rasha* as His agent to spare me. Far from trying to make my life difficult, my devoted Father had been there all along, orchestrating events so that I stayed alive while a *rasha* hurried off to his judgment. Perhaps, in my frustration, I had forgotten the presence of Hashem, but there could be no clearer reminder that He had never forgotten me.

That Rosh Hashanah remains one that will never leave my memory.

We must take the time to prepare ourselves to receive this awesome day with the proper attitude. Let us show Hashem that we constantly think of Him, and in return, may we merit to receive His blessing and His assurance that He constantly thinks of us, as well.

Joey's Big Day

Rabbi Zecharia Wallerstein has inspired and affected the lives of thousands through his organization, Ohr Naava, and through his popular lectures. In a pre-Rosh Hashanah lecture given in Los Angeles, Rabbi Wallerstein related an incredible story that will no doubt serve as food for thought in the days before the Yamim Noraim, the High Holy Days.

Years ago, as a boy in summer camp, my rebbi decided to tell me a story.

It wasn't that he had planned it that way; all of us boys were seated haphazardly around a picnic table in the fresh summer air, and our rebbi was certainly doing his very best to impart some *Chumash* and *Mishnayos*.

The learning rebbi himself was a young man named Yossi who also did double duty as a counselor. He was an athlete of note, and few of the competing camps stood much of a chance when Yossi strode out onto the basketball court. Perhaps it was this aspect of my rebbi that I was dwelling on as my mind drifted from the *sefer* to the open space of the park and its many athletic possibilities. Instead of learning as I should have been, or playing ball as I wished I could, I was occupying my time by focusing the heat of the sun through a magnifying glass and scorching as many innocent leaves and bugs as I could find.

Well, that was about when my rebbi lost patience with me and decided to try another tack.

"Wallerstein," he boomed, standing up suddenly and causing me to jump, "the problem here is that you don't understand how precious every word of the Torah is. Believe me, if you had understood that, you would put away that magnifying glass as quickly as possible and you'd be looking inside in no time. I know you're treating this like a game because you're in camp, but it's no game."

He began pacing, and we all focused with renewed interest on this shift in our agenda.

"I want to tell you boys a story," Yossi said, finally. "It's an amazing story, and it's one that I know to be true, since I know the person it happened to."

I settled in to listen. I had no trouble putting away my magnifying glass for a story, after all!

This is the story Yossi told:

There was once a young boy named Joey. Though he grew up in an irreligious home, his parents sent him to a Jewish day school, where he developed a strong, lasting relationship with his eighth-grade rebbi.

Even after Joey moved on to high school, where he became famous for his skills on the basketball court, he kept a Rosh Hashanah tradition of joining his rebbi for *Kiddush* before the shofar-blowing. By 12th grade, Joey was team captain and basketball was clearly going to be his future career.

One year, Joey showed up at his rebbi's door with an apologetic look on his face. "*Chag Same'ach*, rebbi," he said. "I'm sorry, but I only came by to join you for *Kiddush*. I won't be staying for the shofar."

"Why not?" exclaimed his rebbi.

"The big game is today," Joey explained urgently. "The college scouts are going to be there, and I'm the most valuable person on the team! If they can just see me play, I might finally be on the right track to the NBA. I can't give up this opportunity just to hear a shofar."

The rebbi looked sad, but he nodded slowly. "Okay, Joey, if that's how you want it. But won't you join me for some cake and soda, and give me 15 minutes of your time?"

Joey agreed to this, and waited at the dining-room table as his rebbi went into the kitchen to bring the food.

A little while later, desperate not to lose any time at all, Joey had hopped on his bike and was already pedaling as fast as he could down the street, his heart pounding as he hurried to meet his team at the big game. Maybe it was his mind wandering, dreaming of his glamorous future in professional basketball, but Joey didn't notice the car until it was almost on top of him, its brakes squealing horribly and its horn blaring until he could hear nothing else.

Then there was a terrible impact, and Joey felt himself pummeled into the concrete as his bike was mangled under the wheels of the car.

At first everything was quiet, but then Joey heard the screaming start as all the onlookers rushed to see the boy who had been struck.

"Help!" they were wailing, *"that boy was hit! Someone call an ambulance!"*

One person standing above Joey was shaking his head sadly. "There's nothing we can do anymore, I think. Look at him. The kid's already long gone."

"It's no big deal," Joey called. "I wasn't hit that hard. Come on, help me up, I've got a game to get to."

But, oddly, nobody seemed to hear him. Time went by, and Joey was suddenly aware of paramedics placing him on a stretcher, hefting him into the ambulance.

"What's going on here?" Joey yelled once again. "I'm fine! I feel fine! I've got a very, very important game to get to and you need to let me go, okay? Why isn't anyone talking to me?"

None of the paramedics so much as looked at him, except one who winced and folded his arms sadly. "It's so sad, a kid this young. We'll take him to the hospital, but it's already too late. Poor kid."

Joey's mind was racing. Why wasn't anyone talking to him? Why didn't anyone seem to hear him when he spoke? In a flash, he knew: it was all a gigantic prank! Obviously, the opposing team wanted to put him out of commission so they hired someone to bump him with a car and then hired a fake ambulance to take him away!

"Okay, the fun's over!" shouted Joey. "What a great joke! Now take me off this stretcher and let me get to my game! You won't stop me this easily!"

But again, no one responded. No one in the hospital seemed to hear him either, and Joey was puzzled and frightened. What was going on, exactly? He screamed as loud as he could when a sad-looking nurse covered his face with a sheet, but he felt a rush of relief when he heard the doctor summoning his mother to his bedside. Finally, someone who would be able to hear him.

Yet, when the doctor raised the sheet from Joey's face, all the boy's mother did was stifle a scream with her hands and begin crying uncontrollably.

"Joey, Joey," she cried. "My boy! My dear son! How could this happen to you? *Why did this happen to you?"*

"I'm still here, Mom!" Joey shouted, tears in his own voice. "Tell them to let me go! I'm still here!"

His father arrived soon afterward and sank into a chair immediately, crying bitterly, and that's when Joey began to realize that something was very, very wrong. He stopped screaming, watching numbly as some religious Jews came by to prepare his body for burial. The world around him was suddenly foggy, as though it wasn't really there at all, and soon everything grew dark altogether.

When the lights came on again, Joey was in a bright room that seemed to go on forever. A gigantic scale was before him, and Joey was frightened at the sight of it. Without knowing how he knew, Joey realized he was no longer in the world of the living.

A being appeared in the room then, a tall, cloaked figure whose face was hidden. Somehow, Joey knew it was a *malach*—an angel of G-d. He felt his knees go weak with terror.

"*Hinei Yom Hadin!*" the angel boomed. "Your Judgment Day is here, Yosef ben Dovid."

Joey could barely lift his head in his fright. "B-but it can't be," he stammered. "I was just going to a game!"

"The time for games has ended, Yosef ben Dovid. The world you knew is now only the past."

"What will happen to me now?" Joey squeaked.

"You will soon see," the angel declared.

Joey suddenly noticed an imposing table that had not been there before, and seated at the table were three sharp-eyed men with flowing white beards who were wearing talleisim.

"We are your *beis din*, Yosef ben Dovid," one of the men said. "We are here to judge your life."

"How can..." Joey began, but his next words died in his mouth as the most ferocious-looking being he had ever seen, a powerful angel clad in black, strode into the room.

"I am your prosecutor, Yosef ben Dovid. I am your Evil Inclination and I am the Angel of Death. You will soon belong to me."

Joey had never before felt as afraid as he felt now, as though his entire body would melt from fear.

Then another angel entered, one of the purest white, and smiled at Joey with a kindness that filled him with hope and longing.

"I am your defender, Yosef ben Dovid. Soon, your fate will be in *my* hands."

The Angel of Death shifted restlessly. "Let all the sins of Yosef ben Dovid come before the court and climb onto the scale!" it roared.

Suddenly, angels as black as the night began streaming into the room, piling themselves onto one side of the huge scale. Strangely, some of them seemed to be missing heads or feet. Joey stared, and the defending angel saw him staring.

"The deformed angels were created by the sins that weren't wholehearted," it explained gently. "These are the ones that you either didn't think about or didn't run to do. They weigh less than a full sin."

Joey took some comfort from these words, but then he swallowed as he saw how many thousands of angels were weighing down the sin side of the scale. Suddenly, the presence of half-hearted sins didn't seem to matter.

The Angel of Death pointed triumphantly at the scale as Joey trembled. "Do you see, Yosef ben Dovid? Do you see now that you will be mine? Let me show you where you will be going."

"I don't want to see it," Joey whispered. But the black-garbed angel waved a hand, and a dark pit yawned open before him. Joey could hear horrific screams of pain and despair, and he convulsed with trembling. Nothing had ever scared him as much as this dark pit!

"You belong to me, Yosef ben Dovid!" boomed the evil angel.

"Not yet," interrupted the defending angel. "Let all of the mitzvos performed by Yosef ben Dovid come onto the scale!"

Joey felt a little more encouraged as streams of pure, white-garbed angels streamed into the room and assumed their own places on the opposing side of the scale. Still, it soon became clear that they did not even come close to outweighing the thousands of evil angels on the other side. Once again, Joey felt despair.

"Let there be *din*," announced the prosecuting angel. "Look at the scale! He must come with me!"

"What is your response?" the *beis din* asked the defending angel.

The defending angel stepped forward. "The Sages have taught that *machshavah k'maaseh,* that the thought of mitzvos is regarded as action. Therefore, it is only fair to count all the times Yosef ben Dovid *meant* to do the right thing. For instance, did you know that he often wanted to keep the Shabbos, but was forced to desecrate it by his irreligious family?"

"You are correct," decided the *beis din*. "Let all thoughts of good deeds come forward!"

Thousands more pure angels poured into the room, settling into the scale and tipping it further, further, further yet, until...a hush fell over the courtroom, and Joey felt his heart leap within him.

"The scale is exactly even," murmured voices in the room, awe-struck. "Never before has this happened, not since the beginning of time!"

"Wait," called the defending angel, "there's one more coming!"

Joey turned, and he gaped. One last, lone angel had entered the room to stand beside him, and it appeared to be dressed half in black and half in white!

A furious argument erupted, the prosecuting angel shouting that the new arrival belonged on his side while the defending angel maintained that it belonged just as much on his. Finally, quiet fell over the room as the judges stood.

"Let Yosef ben Dovid determine the nature of this angel," declared the *beis din*.

Joey swallowed hard and looked at the strange angel. "What do you represent?" he asked in a small voice.

"I am the shofar-blowing you were supposed to go hear today," the angel replied.

Immediately, the prosecuting angel stepped forward in triumph. "You see, you are mine, Yosef ben Dovid! You didn't go to hear the shofar because you decided to go to your game. You will come with me to Gehinnom."

"NO!" shouted Joey, falling to his knees in despair. "The angel is also white, not just black! I *wanted to go! I wanted to go to shofar, but there was the big game! It isn't fair!"*

But the Angel of Death swooped over to stand beside him. "No, Yosef ben Dovid, this is as fair as can be! You made the wrong decision, and you're now in *my* power. Come with me!"

Joey felt a searing pain on his back as the angel sank his claws into it.

"NO!" he screamed again, squeezing his eyes shut and shaking his head vigorously. *"I won't come! No!"*

"Joey, what's going on? Why are you screaming?"

Joey's eyes snapped open, and his eighth-grade rebbi was patting his back nervously. Joey clutched his rebbi's hands in panic.

"Don't let them take me, rebbi! It isn't fair! I'll be good!"

"What are you talking about, Joey?" The rebbi looked completely bewildered. "Don't you know where you are? You dozed off here in my dining room while I was getting some cake and grape juice for the *Kiddush*, and suddenly I come back to see you thrashing around, shouting about something being black and white...is everything okay?"

Joey sank back into the couch, feeling the tears begin to flow. "It was a dream, rebbi," he said in disbelief. "It was all a dream."

"It must have been quite a dream," the rebbi said with a wry smile. "Look, I was just about to tell you that I took a little longer in the kitchen than I thought, so maybe you'd better get going very soon if you want to make that game."

The boy sat bold upright. "The game? Oh, no, rebbi, I can't go to the game. No, that was the wrong decision on my part."

Briefly, Joey told his incredible dream to his rebbi, describing the courtroom, the angels and, most importantly, the one angel that failed to save him. They had plenty to talk about, but that was all right, because Joey had plenty of time to talk as he and his rebbi walked to shul to hear the shofar together.

The summer sun was still high in the sky and the rolling baseball fields still beckoned, but for once, we kids all sat quietly with our learning rebbi as our minds tried to work through everything we had just heard. But Yossi wasn't finished.

"Boys, I just want to add that I know what happened to Joey so well because Joey is me. After that fateful Rosh Hashanah, I became a full-fledged *baal teshuvah* and I put my dreams of professional basketball to the side in favor of a much brighter future as an observant Jew. I couldn't have been given a better lesson on the power and importance of every precious mitzvah we do. Every word of Gemara, *Chumash* or *Mishnayos* that we learn creates a bright angel, even here at camp. And you never know which angel might come back to protect you someday and tip the scales in your favor on Judgment Day.

"So don't take it lightly. Take it from me, boys: it's all real. Very, very real."

"This," concluded Rabbi Wallerstein, "was the story that I heard that day, and a story I will never forget."

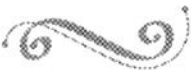

We can never know which mitzvah might be the scale-tipper for us, for our families or for all of the Jewish people. We should cherish each mitzvah as the golden opportunity it is, and we should regard our own scales, on Judgment Day, as perfectly even. But perhaps that little white malach that you created with a small mitzvah — one that you could have easily passed up — might be all that scale needs to tip in your favor. Remember this story, and remember to cherish the opportunities that Hashem has given us.

The Choice Is Yours

The following story was related by Rabbi Kalman Krohn, who had gone to Israel a few years ago with the express purpose of saving a teen who was teetering on the edge of dropping religious Judaism completely, having surrounded himself with irreligious friends who were having a very strong influence on him. With G-d's help, Rabbi Krohn managed to get hold of the young man and he wasted no time in bringing him to various Rabbanim and gedolim for advice and chizuk. One particularly memorable visit was to the house of Rav Yisroel Grossman.

Before entering Rav Grossman's home, I told Zev* to be at his ease. Rav Grossman was well known for being a sweet, soft-spoken man who would surely concentrate on strengthening a young man such as Zev, rather than rebuking him.

When we entered, Rav Grossman was sitting in an armchair, looking quite weak.

"I've come here with a *bachur* who needs *chizuk*," I told the Rav. "He is a good boy who has strayed from a Torah lifestyle under the influence of bad friends. He's trying to change, and I've brought him here to speak to you."

The great Rav lifted his head to examine Zev with a kindly but intent gaze, and then suddenly he spoke, his voice far stronger and more determined than I had expected.

"Zev, you are now standing with the clock at one minute to 12. You are standing in judgment and not just for a verdict of life or death—no, this is a harsher, nearly unimaginable judgment. You might attain a *netzach netzachim* (an eternity) of joy so profound that the entire depth of experience in our world cannot compare, or you might attain the deepest level of Gehinnom, where you will be afflicted with the kind of pain that nothing in our world can parallel.

"That is your choice now, Zev. Happiness or despair: Gan Eden or Gehinnom!"

I was taken aback greatly, as was Zev, who stood reeling at the onslaught of vivid descriptions and powerful words. For reasons known only to him, Rav Grossman had evidently decided to slip off the kid gloves for this task.

"There are two tactics used by the Evil Inclination to bring man to sin," the Rav continued relentlessly. "One is the desire of young men to view unclean images, and the other is to plunge a person so deep into sin that his entire spiritual future is lost to him. It is as though he is removed from the world.

"That is the fire afflicting you, Zev. Do you know who presides in judgment over you right now? You do! You, and only you, can make the choices that affect the outcome of this judgment. Your friends are not helping you, you must understand; they are killing you! You think that you have a good relationship with them, but what they are offering you is poison chocolate."

The great Rav paused for a moment to catch his breath. It was clear that this encounter was affecting him just as deeply as it was affecting Zev, who looked as shaky and as close to tears as I had ever seen him.

After a minute of weighty silence, Rav Grossman continued, in a softer tone.

"I think I should share a story with you. Years ago, I spent a Shabbos outside Yerushalayim with my family. I was very accustomed to the peace and quiet of a Yerushalmi Shabbos, and so I was shocked when my Friday-night walk with my son was interrupted by loud, pounding disco music and the sharp smell of alcohol.

"Young men and women wandered the streets near a club, drinking, dancing, and shouting terrible things. I was devastated that Jews would behave in such a manner, and I walked past them in sadness. After all, what could I do?

"My son, however, was set on doing *something*. 'Come, Tatty,' he urged. 'We must go to the mayor's house and complain.'

" 'I've heard about this particular mayor,' I told him. 'He is not a friendly man. He carries a gun, and if we wake him in the middle of the night, who's to say he won't use it?'

"My son wasn't swayed by this. 'Then I'll walk in front of you, Tatty,' he said. 'If he gets angry enough to shoot, I will be the one who gets shot.'

"When I realized how much my son wanted to do this, I agreed to accompany him to the mayor's home. It was 2 a.m. by the time we arrived there, and it took a lot of bravery to actually knock at that door. No one answered, but as I turned to leave, my son began to shout, 'Mr. Mayor! Please wake up!'

"Startled out of his bed by the noise, the mayor answered the door in his pajamas, half-asleep. 'What's the meaning of this?' he growled. 'Do you know what time it is?'

" 'There's a fire in your city,' my son answered. 'Not a regular fire, but a spiritual one, where people are playing loud music and violating Shabbos right in the middle of town. Please put a stop to this before it's too late."

"The mayor's face turned purple. 'This is why you woke me up?' he roared. Just then, his wife came to the door and did a double take when she saw me.

" 'Dani, don't you realize who you're shouting at?' she asked the enraged mayor. 'This is Rabbi Grossman. He is a special rabbi, and you must be nice to him.'

" 'Look,' my son offered, 'I just want to speak to them and explain that it's Shabbos. I want you there only because it's dangerous, and without your presence I might be attacked.'

"At the further urging of his wife, the mayor finally agreed to accompany us. As we walked together down the street—two *charedi* men and an irreligious mayor—the mayor had calmed down enough to talk. He told us how he had grown up in a religious home but had later become secular. He told us how his daughter had married an Indian and lost contact with him 10 years ago, and how his son had needed a leg amputated because of a soccer injury, and had blamed his father for not being at the hospital to prevent the amputation.

" 'He curses me whenever he sees me,' the mayor told us. 'Public or private, it doesn't make a difference. He blames me for the loss of his leg, and he tells me he wishes I would die an unnatural death. Nowadays, he's so depressed that he doesn't talk to anyone, even me.

" 'When I went to a nephew's bar mitzvah a few weeks ago, I felt like a mourner among celebrants. I was surrounded by my *charedi* family, and I listened to them happily discussing a piece of Torah as I sat there like a dummy. There was so much laughter and happiness in that room, and I realized that I had traded it all in for Gehinnom.'

" 'My brother and I had a chance to speak in another room for a little bit, and he shook his head sadly, bemoaning the fact that I could not share in the *nachas* that he had from his family. Looking into my eyes, he said: *This nachas is already lost to you in this world. Imagine the Next World! Oy! Oy!* And rabbi, every *oy* cut deeper into my heart until I realized that I had lost everything. I hadn't made the right choices, and now it was too late to fix my life!' "

Rav Grossman leaned forward, his eyes searing into Zev's. "Now *I* tell you: Zev, look at my life. I have over a hundred grandchildren and many great-grandchildren. Everyone fights over the honor of helping us, and each one wants to learn with me, walk with me, and shower me with all the *nachas* they can. One of my sons is in the kitchen right this minute, helping his mother. Another of my sons has 16 children and a large business, yet he always finds time to help us. He comes here in the morning to make breakfast for us and sometimes even at night to make sure we're sleeping comfortably.

"That's me, Zev. How about you? Who is going to marry you, and how will you raise your children? How do you think your sons and daughters will treat you if you raise them in your ways? Will you have *nachas* like me, or will you feel alone and lost, like the mayor of that town?"

Zev's eyes were filmed with tears, and his voice was whispery and choked. "I…I want to do better, I do! I want to do the right things, but it's just so hard, when everything is *there*, right in front of me…"

"You think you have everything," Rav Grossman sighed, "but you have nothing. Unfortunately, you are afraid of losing all that nothing. Do you think your 'friends' would have only kind words to say if I asked them what they thought about you? If you don't think so, then how can you trust them to advise you about your life?

"Make an accounting of what you would lose by doing *teshuvah*, and what you would gain. You will see clearly that the brief enjoyment of a sin pales in comparison with the eternal light of a mitzvah. Your surface relationships with your 'friends' pale in comparison with the lasting friendship of rebbeim and *chavrusos*. By not doing *teshuvah*, the only one who ends up losing everything is you."

There was a heavy silence in the small room as Rabbi Grossman leaned back to catch his breath and let his words sink in. Zev was quiet, his pale face set as he conducted what must have been an explosive inner conflict. Imagine what it must be like for this young man to try convincing his physical, materialistic self to surrender its demands in favor of caring for his soul. Right before me, I saw the battle of every Jew playing out on this young man's face.

Sounds of happy conversation and clatters from inside the kitchen informed me that Rav Grossman's son really was assisting his mother in arranging some items. I took a moment to marvel at the simple beauty of this home as Rav Grossman began to speak once more.

"There is a story in the Gemara about a man named Yosef Meshisa, who lived in the times of the *churban Beis HaMikdash* and had shrugged off the yoke of Torah observance. When the Romans sacked Jerusalem at last, even they were wary of entering the *Beis HaMikdash*. They decided that a Jew should go in first, and that Jew would be permitted to keep whatever he took out. Yosef Meshisa offered his services, and walked out of the *Beis HaMikdash* with the Menorah in hand.

"When the Romans saw the majesty of this Menorah, they refused to let him keep it, declaring that it was an object befitting a king, not a commoner. They ordered him to go back in and choose another item. This time, Yosef refused. The Romans tried offering him incentives, in an effort to get him to go back in. But he refused. Again and again. Furious, they threatened him with torture until death if he did not comply, and yet Yosef resisted.

"As the Romans brutally tortured him, Yosef cried out, 'Woe unto me that I angered my Master once. I will not anger Him again!'

"Imagine, Zev, a man that had sunken to such depths that he had no trouble trying to take items from his people's own *Beis*

HaMikdash as personal loot...and yet he did *teshuvah* in those last moments of his life. He was killed *al kiddush Hashem*, and he earned his place in the World to Come before it was too late.

"I want you to daven hard, and I want you to beg Hashem to help you make the right choices. Beg Him to help you break free. As I told you when you came in, now is your judgment day; you are the judge and I'm telling you to choose life! The choice is always yours."

Rav Grossman sighed, and suddenly seemed to sink back into his chair. When he spoke again, his voice was what I had remembered it to be: soft and kind.

"I am an old man, Zev. I don't know when my time will come, but I know that they will ask me if I did everything in my power to turn you back to the right path, and I will proudly answer, 'Yes, I did everything I could.'

"The rest of your journey is up to you."

Turning to me, the Rav asked how I knew Zev, and I explained that I had come to Israel because I had heard he was in trouble. The Rav was visibly moved, and he raised his hands upward to proclaim, "*Ana Hashem, hoshia nah...Ana Hashem, hatzlichah na...*"

Rising from his chair, Rav Grossman approached the shaken Zev and embraced him, kissing him warmly on the top of his head. He closed his eyes and pronounced a heartfelt *berachah* that Zev should merit to do *teshuvah* as soon as possible.

Zev never forgot his encounter with Rav Grossman, even though he still had a long distance to go and many difficult choices to make. But now, he also had in his spiritual arsenal the confidence that he had the power to overcome the obstacles facing him.

It was a long journey indeed, but Zev ultimately separated himself from his dangerous peer group and turned his life around.

We all have big decisions to make in our lives, and we sometimes feel so daunted by them that we forget the gift that Hashem has given us:

the power to shape our own destiny. Our job is to look at the big picture and fight with all we have to do what's right.

Why? Because it's worth it.

To Merit Miracles

The following story was related by Rabbi Duvi Bensoussan at a Brooklyn seudas hoda'ah held in his honor.

There is no way that I can properly express the feelings of gratitude that I have toward Hashem for the unbelievable miracle that He performed on my behalf.

I will never forget the night when the car I was driving tumbled off the Garden State Parkway, swiping a tree and barreling over the barrier in a 104-foot freefall to the ground below. Not a scrap of that car remained intact; the entire body and all its components were completely totaled. All passersby who witnessed the accident had no doubts in their minds that the poor driver of that car could not possibly have lived. The police who arrived at the scene were just as sure of my death as the witnesses were; in fact, it took 20 minutes before any officer even bothered to peer into the remains of the car. Perhaps they were in no hurry to view what I'm sure they expected to find.

I will always remember the dumbfounded reaction of the police officer who found me alive and well, though lightly injured. "You're alive?" he gasped, his eyes gazing in wonder. And—thank G-d many times over—indeed I was. The tow-truck driver who came to remove the wreckage testified, in amazement, that he had never seen anyone walk away from this sort of catastrophe. Absolutely nothing of the car was intact, save myself…and one other thing.

When my brother went to see if anything was salvageable from the wreck, he found tiny shards of thick plastic that he soon identified as remnants of a batch of CD's of lectures that I had given to the *Sefardic* community in Brooklyn. They were to be distributed in my hometown of Lakewood, New Jersey. Of that batch, *one CD* remained as mysteriously unharmed as myself: it was entitled "Protected by Our Bulletproof Vest," and in it I spoke about the mitzvah of *tzitzis*. My eyes filled with tears when I heard the title of the surviving CD, as I was certain that its *zechus* had saved me that night.

Several weeks after the accident, when I had recovered somewhat from the sheer trauma of it all, I decided to return to the area where my miracle had taken place. It is hard to describe the emotion of reliving a moment where I had nearly lost my life. As I approached the exact spot where my car had left the parkway, I found the tree that I had hit and stared in astonishment at the sheer scale of the drop I had taken. One hundred and four feet… the fact that I survived a terrifying plunge like that could be seen as nothing short of an open miracle. I felt as though this spot were sacred ground, a place where Hashem had shown me His kindness and His love like never before. As I mused over the spiritual closeness I felt there, I thought of a story I had once heard about a young boy during World War II.

Thirteen-year-old Yoel Hirsch* had heard the rumors. While many people claimed that the trains into which the Jews of the neighboring towns had been loaded were merely bound for industrial areas where the newcomers could live and work in relative peace, Yoel and his family suspected differently. There were such things as death camps, word on the street informed them, and it was to these prisons that the Jews were being conveyed. They were not headed toward calm and prosperity; they were headed to almost certain death with a barely significant chance of survival.

Before this monstrous juggernaut called World War II had swept onto the scene, Yoel had led a fairly carefree life. He was a good student in his small *cheder*, and outside he was a popular playmate for a group of friends with whom he spent a lot of his time. One hobby and talent of Yoel's was building things, and it was a highlight of his life when he and his father went together one day to build the treehouse of Yoel's dreams in a forest not far from their home. This treehouse became the boy's secret escape, where he could always go to relax, to read, to sing songs to himself, or to simply be alone. The greatest part of it all was that one had to climb pretty high in order to reach this spot, which was no difficult feat at all for the nimble Yoel. Within this little sanctuary, he felt like the leader of his personal kingdom.

But Yoel's life changed forever when the Nazis finally arrived in his town. He awoke one morning to the sound of terrified shouts: "The Nazis are coming! The Nazis are coming!"

Heavily armed Germans in smart uniforms and jackboots flowed through the streets of the small Jewish town in a deadly wave, peppering gunfire indiscriminately into the terrified, screaming crowds as they ordered all Jews into the town square. From his vantage point at a small window, Yoel realized that the Nazis were arraying themselves, several soldiers to a street corner, in such a way that there would soon be no avenue of escape. Panicked, he ran to share this news with his father, who was busy helping Yoel's mother and baby brother prepare to leave.

"Papa!" Yoel cried, his eyes wide with terror, "what are we going to do?"

The older man leaned down so that he was eye to eye with his beloved son. "Listen to me, Yoel. There isn't any time to talk about this. Jump out the back window and run to the forest. Don't look back. Perhaps you will be safe there."

"I can't leave you, Papa!" Yoel began sobbing with fear. "I want to stay here with you!"

But his beloved father's eyes were determined. "This isn't the time to think about me. I have to stay to protect Mama and the baby. You run, now, and hopefully everything will be okay, soon."

Yoel gulped. "I-I can't..."

The older man squeezed his son's shoulders. "*Run, Yoel! Run! Go!*"

Shaking with fright, Yoel quickly kissed his parents goodbye and sprang gracefully out the back window. This was his element, this dashing around. This was what he knew best. Though a constant flow of tears stung his eyes, Yoel slipped easily under the radar of the Nazi guards and flew into the safety of the forest he loved, to the only place that felt as much like home as his home itself: the treehouse.

The familiar branches seemed to embrace Yoel in welcome as he scrambled up the big tree and into his makeshift "palace" high in its branches. When he was finally safe, his heart no longer racing desperately, Yoel burst into fresh tears.

"Hashem," he cried, "what's going to happen to me? What's going to happen to Papa, to Mama, and to everyone? Oh, Hashem..." He trailed off into frantic sobs; there didn't seem to be any words left.

Yoel forced himself to stop crying after some time, as he didn't want the Nazis to hear. Even in the safety of his treehouse, the boy was frightened to the core of his being. He jumped with every gunshot; squeezed his eyes closed with every horrific, distant scream. His town was once a peaceful place, and it was almost impossible to believe the evil sounds emanating from it.

Yoel remained in the tree for two entire days without venturing down for food and water. After that time, when the last snatches of German conversation had faded away and the last gunshots had long been fired, Yoel finally returned to his town.

Otherworldly devastation greeted him; only a ghost town remained. Smashed glass and scattered belongings were strewn everywhere, and the air seemed to ring with the deafening lack of the ordinary, everyday sounds of his hometown. No men prayed in the torched shul; no children crowded the tables of his small *cheder*; no life at all remained to greet the frightened young boy.

Yoel's home appeared to have been turned upside down and shaken before being righted. Any vestige of hope he may have held that he would find his beloved father waiting for him there died almost immediately after he stepped into the house. There was no one among the living in there. There was food and water, though, and Yoel filled a small sack with as much as he could carry. His body was ready to give out after its two-day deprivation, and it was with a flash of gratitude to Hashem that Yoel broke his fast.

Finally, now strengthened, Yoel decided that he would escape again to the forest. Perhaps the Nazis would return to the town for the ones who had been lucky enough to avoid them.

Slipping nimbly back into the forest again, Yoel was shocked and then pleasantly surprised to find an old school friend of his waiting for him, along with a few other people from his town who had somehow evaded the Nazi death machine. At least now, he was no longer alone. For the remainder of the war, Yoel and this small group of survivors were a family. They stayed in the deep forest for a long time, living off the land and whatever other food they could get their hands on until the welcome news finally reached their ears: the war was over, and the Nazis had been scattered and defeated.

Everyone went their separate ways to seek word of what had become of their families. Yoel learned, to his deep sorrow, that his entire family had been killed. On that day, Yoel cried as he had never cried before, for he was now truly alone in the world. He would never sit at the Shabbos table with his dear family again, and he would never again feel the warm embrace of his beloved father. All that remained were memories.

Yoel resolved that the blood-soaked earth of Poland would no longer be his home. As soon as he got his belongings together, he joined other refugees and made his way to Israel.

In his new home on a religious kibbutz, Yoel was soon introduced to Sarah, a young Holocaust survivor from his old town who shared his dream of rebuilding a lost world. The two married in a small, beautiful *chasunah* that brightened the hearts of everyone present. At last, Jewish youth were actualizing the eternity of the Jewish nation. Soon, the Jewish people would be strong once more.

Unfortunately, this particular dream did not end up being simple to attain. After several years of marriage, Yoel and Sarah still had not been blessed with children. It was an acute pain in Yoel's heart when he thought of how much he had lost, and how it now seemed he was being denied a happy future as well as a happy past. With so many relatives lost, who would ever carry the name of his father, or his mother? Though Yoel paid many visits to rabbanim and performed various proven *segulos*, there was no change in his heartbreaking situation. The years began to slip by, and Yoel and Sarah's prayers remained unanswered.

One summer, Yoel and Sarah decided to travel. Sarah had mentioned to Yoel how much she wanted to go back to Poland to pray at the graves of *tzaddikim*. Although Yoel had resolved never to set foot in that country again, he relented when he saw how much this trip meant to Sarah. Perhaps it *was* time to relive the past and come to terms with the present. It wasn't long before the tickets had been purchased, and the two Holocaust survivors were on their way to the land that had not provided a safe haven for them and their families.

To Yoel's shock, the streets of his old hometown had not changed too much. But for the fact that there wasn't a single Jew in sight, it could have easily been the same place that Yoel had called home so many years before. Even his own former home stood in much the way it previously had, though repaired and repainted. Painful memories stung Yoel's mind as he remembered the happy years he had spent in that small house and the horrible circumstances of his departure.

Standing at her husband's side, lost in her own reverie, Sarah suddenly asked, "Yoel, what about that treehouse you've told me so much about? Do you suppose it still exists?"

Yoel was excited by the thought of the treehouse. "You know what? I'm certain of it! Let's go check it out."

"Do you remember where it is?" asked Sarah dubiously, falling into step with Yoel.

"There are some things in life one never forgets," her husband answered resolutely. "That treehouse is one of them."

The two walked through the forest together, down the unchanged paths that Yoel had trodden so many times before. This forest had been his home at a time when nothing else could be. At last, after that turn *here* and that small path *there*, Yoel stood at the base of the tree in whose branches he had spent so many happy days of his childhood. Tears glistened in his eyes.

"Here it is," he said, softly.

Just visible, if one strained his eyes to see the highest boughs of the great tree, were the sturdy wooden slats of the construct once lovingly created by a happy-go-lucky boy and his adored father. Yoel felt a closeness to Hashem here that he had never felt before. Here, his prayers were answered, and here he had felt the unmistakable embrace of G-d as he was spared from certain death.

That was when Yoel had an epiphany. *Here* was the place he should have come to daven all this time! Hashem had heard him here once, and perhaps He would listen again. Tears spilling over his face, Yoel began swaying gently as he davened to Hashem from the depths of his soul, as he had so many years ago. This time, his fervent prayers were for something different.

You saved me once, Hashem. Please, my dear Father, save me one more time. Bless me with children.

Yoel couldn't explain why, but somehow he felt that, this time, his words had reached their mark.

Ten months later, his suspicions were proven correct when Sarah gave birth to a beautiful, healthy baby boy.

Rabbi Bensoussan adds: When I stood at that tree on the side of the Garden State Parkway, I felt like Yoel must have felt when he returned to visit his treehouse. I felt so close to Hashem in that precise spot; I felt such a rush of love and gratitude that I simply had *to pray. I cried as I poured my heart out to Hashem there, and I prayed for my family, my friends, and the wonderful people in my shul."*

May Hashem hear all of our tefillos as though they were offered in the same way, and may He bring our people the Redemption we so sorely need.

It is interesting to note that the Torah's description of Yitzchak entreating Hashem to grant Rivkah children is worded as follows (*Bereishis* 25:21): *Yitzchak entreated G-d opposite his wife, for she was barren. Hashem allowed Himself to be thus entreated, and his wife Rivkah conceived.*

What was it about this specific prayer that brought Hashem to relent? Why, after 20 years of marriage does the Torah acknowledge this seemingly ordinary prayer as the *tefillah* that finally did it? Surely this wasn't the first such entreaty!

The answer can be found in *Targum Yonasan ben Uziel's* expounding of this verse. He writes that Yitzchak traveled to pray on Har HaMoriah, where his father had once bound him to be sacrificed. This was a place of tremendous personal merit, and it was therefore a place that Yitzchak felt would spell an answer to his prayers. On that mountain, Yitzchak willingly gave himself up to be sacrificed, and on that mountain he was finally answered. The special connection with Hashem that Yitzchak had experienced in that place was what made his prayer so uniquely potent.

Throughout the centuries, the Jewish people have never needed to look farther than *Akeidas Yitzchak* for a merit that our prayers be answered. On Rosh Hashanah itself, we recount the Torah's description of the sacrifice, and we sound a ram's horn in remembrance of the ram that ultimately replaced Yitzchak.

It is said that Yitzchak's decision to allow himself to be brought as an offering for the sake of Hashem is what injected the spark in the Jewish soul that facilitated the many more Yitzchaks through the ages: those who willingly surrendered their lives for *kiddush Hashem* and in whose immense merit we might ask to be remembered by Hashem.

The following story is reprinted with permission from Rabbi Yerachmiel Milstein. In this tale, we see an awe-inspiring example of that great, eternal merit of Yitzchak's sacrifice.

There's a synagogue near my office where I often "shoe-horn" Minchah into my usually over-programmed day. During the winter months, when Minchah is prayed in the late afternoon, corralling a quorum of 10 men for Minchah can be quite difficult, as most men—like me—are still at their places of work, far from the residential neighborhood in which this particular synagogue and my office are located.

This past winter, New York experienced its umpteenth snowstorm and on this particular day a thin coating of ice was added for good measure. At precisely 15 minutes before sunset, I left my office as usual and made my treacherous two-minute foot journey to the synagogue, praying that somehow nine other men would be similarly inspired.

Braving the ice-encrusted steps leading down to the shul, I nearly slid into the open door and stumbled into an almost empty room. The rabbi was there, and like a telemarketer selling prime property to the unemployed, he was working the phone trying to coax one or two reticent Jews into braving the elements and joining us. Another gentleman was there, one of the reliable regulars with whom I would occasionally chat as, on more than one occasion, we were waiting for the room to fill. He looked at me and, commenting about the weather, invited me to sit down and get comfortable for the duration.

"You know, I never asked you where you're from," I started, "although I'd recognize a Hungarian accent anywhere."

"Budapest," he replied with a sweep of his hand.

"So you must have come over after '56," I said, judging him to be a man of about 60 who, like so many Jewish people I knew growing up in New York, had made his way to the United States as a child in the aftermath of the Hungarian revolution.

"No," he smiled, "I got one of these." With that he rolled up his sleeve and showed me a blue-green tattoo with European-style numbers. As if to explain my confusion he added kindly, "I'm a little older than I look: already in the 70's."

His young face still gave me pause. "You must have been among the youngest survivors. How did you make it?"

"Only with miracles. Without miracles nobody survived." A man of uncommon good looks, he pointed to the upper bridge of his nose which had the slightest bump and two small scars on either side. "I once made the mistake of being too starved and physically exhausted to stand up quickly enough for a vicious SS officer, so he gave me this present at the end of a particularly vicious beating. He stomped on my face with his perfectly shined, cleated boots. It was plain *mazal* that he only caused cosmetic damage. Had he blinded me I would have been shot dead on the spot, because there was no room in Auschwitz for anybody who couldn't work. No. Nobody survived without miracles."

I marveled at his easy demeanor in speaking about a topic that had silenced most of the Holocaust survivors I knew, and I thought this a rare opportunity to learn more about the man and his experiences. "I hope I'm not causing you too much anxiety by dredging up the past, but what other miracles did you experience?"

Smiling broadly he said in a mixture of English and Yiddish, "Too much to count. Even the first moment I set foot in the camp, Mengele—*yimach shemo!* (may his name be erased!)—was making his infamous selection of those he deemed healthy enough to work, herding them off to one side. Those who were too young, too weak, or too diseased to work were shoved to the other side, to die. Although I was just 14, G-d put an idea in my head so that when that devil asked my age, I straightened my shoulders as high as they would go and loudly shouted, '16!' Only later did I learn that this was the exact minimum age of survival."

It was quiet for about a minute as he seemed to lose himself in his thoughts and become all but oblivious to my eager stare.

Speaking more slowly and deliberately than before, he said in a voice barely more than a whisper, "In the end we were skeletons. They starved us and worked us so hard that we were just bones. We couldn't lift. We couldn't run. It was the most we could do to schlep ourselves off the floor in the morning. From working the gas-chamber detail, my bunkmates and I knew that it was only a matter of days before we would be 'sent to the showers' to be disposed of as well. On the day the Nazis decided to execute us we left the barracks without so much as a whimper. We had long expected this. But when we entered the room next to the gas chamber and were asked to undress, it all sank bitterly in. We were a bunch of young men, children really, who were supposed to be worked to death, and when that didn't come soon enough for the Nazis, we had to then be grotesquely killed by gas."

Tears welled up in my friend's eyes and began to build in mine as well.

"My friends, who seemed lifeless moments before, started to scream hysterically and to throw temper tantrums on the floor. Another just went insane. But me, I had this feeling that I didn't want to die like that. I thought about my religious upbringing and remembered my beloved rebbi, who had taught me the first letters of the Hebrew alphabet and remained my rebbi until after my Bar Mitzvah. I wondered what he would have said to me at this moment."

His tears had overrun their banks and were now gracefully gliding down his chiseled cheekbones.

" 'You are not the worthless scum you are being made to be, but precious Jewish children who are being killed because of their special connection to G-d. This makes you as holy as any sacrifice brought on the altar of the Holy Temple.' I could almost hear my rebbi's soft voice talking to me.

" 'You are as holy as any human can get. Although Jews do not believe in human sacrifice, still, G-d has decided that today you are a human sacrifice.'

"So I thought, what would be a fitting prayer for a human sacrifice? I called out to anyone who would listen, 'Hey, has anybody got a *siddur* (prayerbook)?' Oddly enough, a tattered book appeared. Sensing the end might be very near, I opened it quickly to the *Akeidah*, the part of the Torah many recite daily where God commands Abraham to take the life of his son Isaac as a human sacrifice. And with more feeling than ever, I began to recite the last prayer of my short life."

I don't remember at which point the rabbi gave up and got off the phone to become drawn into our conversation, but his eyes were as wide as mine as my friend began to recite the words of the *Akeidah* by heart. With his beautiful voice and melodious Hungarian accent, the words became a powerfully moving song.

"And they came to the place of which God had spoken to him, and Abraham built the altar there and arranged the wood, and he bound Isaac his son and placed him on the altar upon the wood. And Abraham stretched forth his hand and took the knife, to slaughter his son. And an angel of God called to him from heaven and said, 'Abraham! Abraham!' And he said, 'Here I am.' And he said, 'Do not stretch forth your hand to the lad, nor do the slightest thing to him, for now I know that you are a G-d-fearing man, and you did not withhold your son, your only one, from Me.' "

Narrowing his eyes to no more than a sliver he said, "As soon as I said these words, a commotion broke out, with SS officers rushing into the room yelling, 'Get dressed quickly!' and we were ushered out of the room with great haste. They told us the Americans were coming and that the Nazi cowards had enough trouble disposing of all the bodies that were already dead. They couldn't afford to create any more bodies and as such we were better off alive to them."

He sighed deeply, "No, my friend, without a miracle nobody survived."

Rosh Hashanah in Auschwitz

The following story was related by the Veitzener Rav, Rabbi Tzvi Hirsch Meisels zt"l. Rabbi Meisels was a renowned Rav in Veitzen, Hungary before World War II. After miraculously surviving the war, Rabbi Meisels came to America and reestablished himself in Chicago, where he became one of that community's most prominent and beloved rabbanim.

This story is an account of his experiences in Auschwitz in the year 1944. The story was culled from the preface of the sefer called "Mekadshei Hashem."

Although Holocaust stories can be frightening or depressing, I found myself completely uplifted by the courageous deeds and rock-solid emunah displayed by the heroes of these stories, and I believe you will be uplifted as well.

These were people who never gave up their faith, even in the face of cruelty and seemingly meaningless death. I felt it was important that these stories should be told to our generation so that we too can be inspired to live lives of kiddush Hashem.

I was especially honored to have spent time interviewing Rabbi Zalman Leib Meisels, Rav in Seagate, who experienced and survived Auschwitz alongside his illustrious father. He enlightened me as to what it meant to live with faith in the death camps.

What better way to prepare for the Yom Hadin than to learn of our brethren's preparations for the Days of Awe in those days of darkness.

1,400 Youngsters Condemned to Death

"Everyone out! All boys out!" screamed the Nazi guards as they tore through the men's barracks of Auschwitz on Erev Rosh Hashanah 1944. They pummeled and kicked any obstruction, searching for boys 18 and younger who might be hiding.

The boys streamed out of the barracks, chased by the guards who barked at them like dogs. The adults—many of them fathers of the boys who were being rounded up—wandered about in helpless fear. What now?

Soon, 1,600 boys were marched out to an open field behind the barracks My 14-year-old son Zalman Leib had miraculously escaped.

Suddenly, the head Nazi officer in the camp appeared on the scene. He ordered that a pole with a crossbar on top be erected. The young men looked on in fear, wondering what new torture awaited them.

When the pole was in place, the officer issued his command: "All children will pass single file beneath the crossbar. If your head touches the bar, then you may return to your barracks. If your head does not touch the bar, then you are to remain on the side as you will be brought to a different barracks."

The boys realized immediately that those whose head did not touch the bar were destined for the gas chambers. In a desperate effort to touch the bar, many boys tried to stand on their tiptoes as they passed beneath it. Soon, however, the SS guard noticed their ploy and responded by slamming his club down on the head of those who attempted it, sending them crumpling to the ground in a pool of blood. They were quickly carted away to the gas chamber to finish the job.

When the selection process ended, there were 1,400 children

left standing on the field. They were marched to an isolated barracks which was guarded by the kapos. There they were to remain without food or drink until the next day—Rosh Hashanah—when they would be taken to the gas chambers.

Bargaining for Life

The following day, the first day of Rosh Hashanah, a rumor spread throughout the camp that the boys were going to be gassed that evening. Horrified fathers, relatives, and friends of the captive boys paced the periphery of the sealed barracks all day, hoping that somehow their beloved child would be released before the fateful hour.

The kapos who were guarding the barracks turned a deaf ear to the cries and pleading of the fathers on behalf of their sons. Under the best of circumstances, the kapos were generally cruel and corrupt. In this situation, their lack of mercy was bolstered by the reality that, should the head count fall short when the Nazis came to retrieve their captives, the kapos themselves would have to die in the place of the missing boys.

Nevertheless, for some families, all was not lost. There were still people in the camp who had money, valuables, and jewelry hidden for just such a time of need. They offered the kapos small fortunes in exchange for their son's lives. Eventually, the kapos found a way to capitalize on the situation without risking their own lives. For the right price, they would simply commandeer another boy—one who had been left free—to replace the ransomed boy. Once the replacement was safely locked in the barracks, the kapo would let the ransomed boy go.

Many of the fathers were willing to redeem their sons even if it meant that another boy would be taken in their sons' places. The haggling over the price of the ransom went on throughout the entire day of Rosh Hashanah. The kapos had the time to hold out for a high price because the SS-men were not around to interfere. They stayed at the main gate of Auschwitz, while the Jewish kapos fulfilled their orders inside the camp.

But there were many men of great reason who did not want to redeem their sons at the cost of another child's life. The eyes have never seen, the ears have never heard, and the world will never forget this wondrous act of the sanctification of Hashem's Name. Their dedication to the ways of the Torah, even at a time of great pain and suffering, was without parallel to anything I had ever witnessed.

A Father's Sacrifice

On that fateful day, I was approached by an unassuming Yid from Oberland.

"Rebbe," he said, "my only son, my beloved child, is in the barracks of the doomed boys. I have the money to redeem him, but I know for a fact that the kapos will grab another boy to replace my son. I am asking you for a halachic ruling. Am I allowed to buy my son's freedom? Please answer me, and I shall do whatever you decide."

When I heard his question, I was seized with trepidation. This was a life-and-death question that I wasn't sure I could answer. I responded, "My dear friend, how can you expect me to answer this difficult question under the present circumstances? Look, even during the times of the *Beis HaMikdash*, such a serious question of life and death was decided by the great Sages of the *Sanhedrin*. I am here in Auschwitz, where I have no *sefer* on halachah, no rabbis to confer with, and to make things worse, I don't have a clear mind due to our suffering."

Reflecting on the question, the following thoughts went through my mind: If the kapos would first release the ransomed boy and then capture another boy as a replacement, I could possibly argue in favor of letting the father pay for his son's release, for there was a possibility that another boy would not actually be seized. After all, the kapos were Jews, and as such, they were forbidden to seize a boy and cause his death. In fact murder is one of the three cardinal sins for which one must be willing to give up his life rather than transgress. One could not be absolutely sure that the *kapos* would indeed snatch another boy; perhaps at the last moment their Jewish conscience would not allow them to violate this grave prohibition. If such a possibility existed, the father would be allowed to buy his son's freedom.

Unfortunately, I knew from similar cases that the kapos would first secure a replacement and only then would they release the ransomed individual. If they first released the ransomed child and then were unable to seize a substitute, there would be no guarantee that they would have the correct head count. Because there was no doubt that another child would have to be seized before this father's son would be released, I could find no reason to allow the father to ransom his son.

These were my thoughts, but I did not render a decision.

The poor father begged me, crying bitterly. "Rebbe," he pleaded, "you must decide this burning question for me while I still have a chance to save my only child."

"My beloved Yid," I implored him "please don't ask me to decide on this question because I have no *sefarim* here in the camp to help me decide what is right."

But the Yid persisted. "Rebbe, does that mean that you do not permit me to redeem my only child? If so, I willingly accept your ruling."

"My dear friend," I countered, "I did not say that I don't permit you to redeem your child. I cannot rule either way. Do whatever you feel you ought to do, as if you had never asked me at all."

Seeing that I could not be swayed, he passionately cried out "I did what the Torah demands of me. I asked a *shailah* of a Rav, the only Rav I could find. If you cannot permit me to redeem my child, that tells me that you are not sure whether halachah permits it. For if you had no qualms about permitting me to do it, you would have told me so. I assume that your refusal to commit one way or another can be interpreted as a halachic ruling that I am not allowed to ransom my son.

"I abide by that ruling, even though it means that my only son will be burned in the fires of the crematorium. I will do nothing to free him because that is what the Torah ordains."

I begged him not to think of my words as a ruling but rather to imagine that he had never asked me the question in the first place. Sobbing profusely, he repeated his heartbreaking words and he kept his promise to do nothing to ransom his son. All of that Rosh Hashanah day, he walked around expressing his joy at having merited to sacrifice his only son to G-d. Although he could have redeemed him, he did not; he understood that the Torah does not sanction it. He prayed that his sacrifice would be as sacred to G-d as was the *Akeidah* of Yitzchak, our forefather, which also occurred on Rosh Hashanah.

Think about the righteousness of this simple Yid. I am convinced that his words made a tremendous impact on the heavenly realm, and that Hashem gathered all of the heavenly hosts and ministering angels to announce proudly, "Look at what a marvelous human being I have created in My world!" As it says: *Yisrael in whom I take glory* (*Yeshayah* 49:3).

Shofar Blowing in Auschwitz

Miraculously I had obtained a shofar through one of the transports that had just arrived in the camp. All day I went from barracks to barracks blowing the shofar for my Jewish brethren. This was fraught with great danger; if I had been caught by the kapos, I would have been killed on the spot. But through Hashem's great mercy, I merited the ability to blow the full 100 shofar blasts about 20 times that day. The sound of the shofar uplifted the broken spirits of the inmates. At the very least, they possessed the knowledge that they had the merit to fulfill the mitzvah of *tekias shofar.*

When the 1,400 boys in the isolated barracks found out that I had a shofar, they pleaded that I come to blow the shofar for them. They wanted to have the merit of this precious mitzvah during their last moments before they were killed *al kiddush Hashem.*

I did not know what to do. Entering the barracks was extremely dangerous, for the Nazis could show up at any moment. If I were found among the boys, there was no doubt that I too would be taken to the gas chambers. The kapos would never allow me to escape. I stood there, weighing my decision, unsure as to whether I was permitted to risk my life to blow the shofar for the boys.

"Rebbe, Rebbe!" they cried. "For Hashem's sake, have pity on us and grant us the merit of hearing the shofar in our final hour."

Despite the power of their words, my doubts were reinforced by my son, Zalman Leib, who was with me and begged me not to put my life at risk.

"Haven't you blown the shofar 20 times already? Isn't that enough?" he argued. Listening to his heartfelt plea, I realized that he was right. On the other hand, the cries of those children tugged at my soul.

Overcome with pity, I thought that perhaps this great mitzvah would protect them at this critical time. Hearing their cries, other people implored me to go in and blow the shofar for them, assuring me that due to the merit of the mitzvah I would come out unscathed.

I decided that come what may, I could not turn the boys down. I started haggling with the kapos, who stubbornly refused to allow me into the barracks. At last, in exchange for a sizeable sum of money that was raised on the spot, they gave in. They warned me to listen for the sound of the bell at the main gate, for that was the signal that the Nazis were entering the campgrounds.

I agreed to their stipulations and entered the barracks. I stationed my son Zalman Leib outside, to keep an eye on the road and to let me know immediately if he saw the SS officers approaching the main gate. I told him to interrupt me even if I were in the middle of blowing the shofar.

To tell the truth, my decision did not go in accordance with halachah. I knew full well that endangering your life for the mitzvah of shofar is forbidden. But my decision at that moment was based solely on the fact that my life had little value at that time. Who in Auschwitz was able to know how many days he had left to live? We had seen with our own eyes that every single day, they killed and burned hundreds and thousands of people. We watched people simply drop dead of exhaustion due to the intense labor. And the dead lay at our feet like sheaves of wheat after the harvest. We saw no value in human life anymore. This was the crux of my argument for acceding to the boys' request. I risked my life only because I knew that in truth, my life had very little value.

My Sermon Before Shofar Blowing

There is not a writer or a poet in the entire world who can portray my feelings as I entered the sealed barracks. It was only due to a miracle of G-d that my heart didn't burst in anguish when I saw before me the teary-eyed children, heard their cries and screams that reached the heart of heaven. And they all pressed forward to kiss my hand and my clothing and they cried these simple but heart-wrenching words:

"Rebbe, Rebbe! Oh! Mercy! Have mercy!"

These were words that no ear had ever heard before. Many of these boys were my former *talmidim* and congregants. When I began reciting the verse "*Min Hameitzar, from the straits did I call Hashem,*" they interrupted and begged me to say a few words before the shofar service. Too agitated by their overwhelming sorrow, I was unable to move my lips or force my tongue to speak. In addition I was afraid of the delay. It was getting late, the sun was setting and the SS men could arrive at any moment.

But the boys would not let me continue, and at last I relented. I began by discussing the verse *"Tik'u bachodesh shofar bakese. . .. blow the shofar on the new moon, on the holiday of concealment."*

I explained that truly, Hashem's design and purpose for our suffering was at this moment hidden and concealed from us. "We don't know what happened to our families, and we don't know what our fate is either. But we are not to despair, as it says in the Gemara *(Berachos 10a)* that even if a sharp sword is placed on someone's neck he should not refrain from praying for mercy."

Then I explained the verse in *Tehillim* (121:1): *I raise my eyes to the mountains, from where will come my help? My help is from Hashem, Maker of heaven and earth.* Why does Hashem have to be identified as *"Maker of heaven and earth"*? Why must we raise our eyes to the mountains?

I explained to the children that there are times when a person is besieged on all sides. "All he can see are frightening mountains that threaten to swallow him up and he realizes that there is no logical or natural way that he can be saved. And although he firmly believes that the enemies of *Klal Yisrael* will be defeated eventually, this does not help him in his present predicament, because he knows that his life is hanging by a thread.

"David HaMelech seeks to strengthen this person by reminding him to keep trusting in Hashem, Who created heaven and earth in a split second, as it says, *By the word of Hashem the heavens were made* (*Tehillim* 33:6). Just as G-d created the world in a split second, so too He can save a human being, even if the sharp edge of the sword is resting on his neck. That is why it says, *I will raise my eyes to the mountains.*

"My accursed enemies, who besiege me like huge mountains, close in on me from every side. From where will my help come?

My help hinges on seconds. The answer is, *My help is from Hashem, Maker of heaven and earth.*

"I trust that He who created the heaven and earth in an instant will send His salvation from His holy sanctuary immediately."

Final Words

I cannot hold back the words. I tell this story so that future generations will know the great *mesirus nefesh* and the fervently holy words that I heard from these young boys shortly before they were taken to their death.

After the blowing of the shofar, as I was about to leave, one boy stood before me and cried out in great anguish: "Dearest of friends, the Rebbe has strengthened us by telling us that even when a sharp sword is upon our throats we should not despair of mercy. But I say to you, we can hope for the best, but we must prepare for the worst. For the sake of Hashem, my brothers, let us not forget in our last moments to cry out *Shema Yisrael* with sincere devotion."

With heartrending voices and burning passion, they cried out, "*Shema Yisrael.*" Then another boy stepped forward and said, "We are not going to give the Rebbe a *yasher koach* for his great *mesirus nefesh* in providing us with our last mitzvah, that of *tekias shofar.* But all of us bless you that in this merit, Hashem Yisbarach will help that the Rebbe will merit leaving this place alive and well." All the boys answered in thundering unison, "Amen!"

As I was leaving, a few boys came over to me and asked if I could get them a morsel of bread so that they could also fulfill the mitzvah of *seudas* Rosh Hashanah during their last moments. From the time they had been locked up, a full 24 hours, they had not tasted any food or drink; they were aware that according to halachah, one was forbidden to fast on Rosh Hashanah. To my great sorrow, there was no way for me to fulfill their wishes and re-enter the barracks. That bitter day was a fast day for them. From the midst of that fast day they were taken to the crematoria.

It is interesting to note that in *Midrash Rabbah Esther* (9:4) we find a startling precedent for the sacrifice of these 1,400 children: Having set up the gallows, Haman found Mordechai in the *beis midrash,* surrounded by crying children, wearing sackcloth and learning Torah. Haman counted 22,000 children. He locked them up, placed guards over them, and said, "Tomorrow, first I'll kill all these children, and then I'll hang Mordechai."

The children's mothers brought them bread and water and told them, "Children, eat and drink before you die tomorrow, so that you will not die in hunger."

The children responded by placing their hands on their holy books, swearing, "By the life of our rebbi Mordechai, we will neither eat nor drink. We want to die fasting!"

Recalling the events of that woeful Rosh Hashanah, I cannot help but admire the courage and strength of those young boys in sanctifying G-d's Name. It truly was a reenactment of the *Akeidas Yitzchak* that happened on that day. The self-sacrifice evident in Avraham Avinu's willingness to offer up his only son was reawakened in the readiness of those boys to give up their lives *al kiddush Hashem* in such a lofty and sublime manner.

May Hashem avenge their blood.

Teach Me, Father

The following two stories were related by Rabbi Nissim Yagen zt"l. These stories, which Rabbi Yagen heard firsthand, give us a unique peek into the next world and provide us with powerful inspiration to keep the Torah and perform its mitzvos.

On a sunny Saturday afternoon, Ronen* and Chaggit drove with their three children along the winding country roads of the Catskills. It was a day off from work, and this Israeli couple was happy to be surrounded by nature, taking in the clear, sweet mountain air. Inside Chaggit, however, there was a gentle tug of guilt, for in the home in which she grew up, Shabbat was always something special. Her family was not religious, but still, the seventh day of the week was Shabbat—not Saturday.

These were the thoughts that were creeping into the edges of Chaggit's consciousness as Ronen set out to drive the family back home to New York. Suddenly, a sharp pain spread across Chaggit's chest. For some reason, she felt certain that the pain was related to her family's driving on Shabbos.

"Let's not drive home now, Ronen," she urged her husband. "This pain…it's Shabbat. Maybe it's not right for us to drive. Maybe Hashem is telling me…let's wait until Shabbat is over."

Ronen had no religious upbringing at all, and his wife's sudden revelation confused him. Nevertheless, she was frightened by the pain in her chest and adamant about curtailing the trip, and so he relented.

When the family finally set out that night, the weather had taken a turn for the worse. As they drove, a pounding rain turned the roads slick and cut down visibility to nearly zero. Ronen struggled to follow the winding roads, but in one horrifying moment, he lost control. The car skidded off the side of the road, tumbled down a steep embankment, and flipped several times before it smashed into a boulder and came to a halt.

For a moment, the car was filled with a dreadful silence. Chaggit knew she was badly hurt, and she realized that her husband had been killed. Then, to her relief, she heard the cries of her children—all three of them—calling out for her in pain and fear.

Chaggit knew she needed help immediately, but how would she attract attention on this dark, rainy night as she lay in the rubble of her car at the bottom of an embankment? She reached over to the car's horn and pressed with all her strength. It blurted out its raucous noise, but no one was close enough to hear. Chaggit turned her attention to her children, whom she extricated one by one through the shattered side window. She honked and honked some more, until finally, a car pulled over to the side of the road and the driver, seeing the tragic scene below, called for an ambulance.

The emergency responders used a strong rope to bring the four survivors back up to the road. Chaggit helped her children and then ascended herself, collapsing in pain as soon as she reached the top.

When she awoke, she was in the hospital. Her children had been spared any serious injury, but for Chaggit, the road to recovery was long. As she endured multiple operations and treatments, her father sat by her bedside, giving her strength and comfort.

One day, she asked her father, "*Abba*, could you bring me a *Sefer Tehillim*? I need to say *Mizmor L'Sodah* (a Song of Thanks) to thank Hashem for keeping my children and me alive."

The miracle of having survived the accident was not lost on Chaggit. She realized that this open display of Hashem's mercy and love demanded a response from her, and when she emerged from the hospital, her life took a new turn. She took her family and returned to Israel, where she enrolled her children in yeshivah. In her new life, there was no more Saturday. The seventh day was Shabbat.

Though their hearts were devoted to living a Torah life, the adjustment was not easy. One day, Chaggit's son Yonah came home from yeshivah with a downcast expression on his face. Chaggit noticed the gleam of tears on his cheeks.

"Yonah, what's the matter?" she asked her son.

"Tomorrow I am going to have a big Gemara test, and I don't know the Gemara at all, and have no one to learn it with," he said dejectedly. He seemed so forlorn, and in fact, he was right. Chaggit could not learn Gemara, nor could she afford a tutor.

"Listen, Yonah, try to study yourself and I am sure you'll do fine on the test," she said with as much assurance as she could muster.

"*Ima*, the Gemara is too hard. There is no way I can learn this on my own. Is it my fault that I don't have a father to teach me?" Yonah's quiet tears turned to soft weeping as he headed to his room to try to learn on his own.

An hour later he returned to his mother, his eyes bleary and his spirit more deflated than ever. "You see, *Ima*, I tried, I really tried, but it didn't work. I can't understand a word of the Gemara. I am going to fail the test again and the whole class will think I'm stupid."

Chaggit had no advice left to offer. "Yoni, just try your best tomorrow," she said softly. "Now it's late. Get a good night's rest and hopefully you will succeed. Good night, Yoni," she said. "Have sweet dreams."

The next morning, Chaggit arose early to prepare breakfast for her children before they went off to yeshivah. She shook her head in despair as she thought of the frustration and humiliation Yoni was facing. She hoped that his situation would seem a little more hopeful in the morning light.

Soon, Yoni wandered into the kitchen to eat his breakfast. Much to Chaggit's surprise, he wore a broad grin on his face.

"I'm so glad to see you smiling, Yoni," she said to her son. "What happened?"

"*Ima*, you are not going to believe it," said Yoni as he sat down at the kitchen table. With the relish of one who knows a mysterious secret, he announced, "I know the whole Gemara."

The incredulous response he was waiting for came quickly. "You do? How? I thought you said you couldn't figure it out. What happened?"

"*Abba* came to me last night and taught it to me," Yoni stated simply.

"*Abba* came to you? Oh, come on Yoni, please don't play such tricks on your poor mother."

"No, really, *Ima*, I am not lying!"

Chaggit didn't know what to believe, but she knew that Yoni was not the type of child to lie. He went on with his story.

"You see, *Ima*, last night after I went to sleep, *Abba* came to me in a dream. He asked me why I looked so sad. I told him that I have a big Gemara test tomorrow and I don't know it. So *Abba* said, 'Come, Yoni, we'll learn it together.'

"I asked him, 'How can you learn Gemara with me, *Abba*? You never learned Gemara.'

"So he told me that even though he had never learned Gemara in his life, the minute you sent me to yeshivah, *Ima*, they allowed *Abba* to enter the *Yeshivah Shel Maalah* (Heavenly Yeshivah). When I started to learn Gemara, *Abba* started learning the exact same Gemara!

"Then *Abba* began to teach me the entire Gemara that's on the big test. Now I feel that I really know it and that I am going to easily pass."

Chaggit stood speechless as Yoni confidently strode out of the house toward school. Could it be as he said?

Her answer came a few days later when she got a call from Yoni's rebbi.

"His mastery of the material is just incredible!" the rebbi enthused. "I don't know what happened, but whatever it is, he should keep it up!"

"Well, let me tell you what Yoni told me." Chaggit repeated Yoni's account of his dream.

Skeptical about this strange tale, the rebbi tested Yoni orally to see if he could come up with the right answers on his own. What he discovered was that Yoni not only knew what he had been taught in yeshivah, but was also able to offer many novel insights into the material.

Strange as it seemed, the truth of the matter was obvious. Yoni's Torah was indeed Heaven-sent.

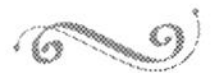

Seeing the Light

At Kibbutz Hashomer Hatzair, where Sharona grew up, there were many things about which the residents were "religious." They religiously cultivated their land, built up their community, took care of one another, and served in the army, all with the single-minded devotion of true zealots. Practices like eating kosher, keeping Shabbos, or even fasting on Yom Kippur, however, were simply not on the agenda. This was the new, modern way of Jewish life, freed from the bonds of ancient tradition, strong and independent, and firmly planted in the physical world.

The problem with the system, though, was that it left a gaping void. Some people didn't really feel it, but others did. They were the young people who left Israel to travel the world in search of something—anything—that would speak to their souls. From the

Buddhist monasteries of Thailand to the Hindu temples of India, Sharona, like many of her friends, traveled the world searching not only for adventure, but also for meaning.

After a long period of traveling the East, Sharona returned to Israel to find a path for herself as she embarked on adult life. She married and began a career; endless possibilities seemed to lie before this intelligent and talented young woman. Then in one flashing moment, the possibilities evaporated.

She was walking down a street in Tel Aviv, on her way to meet some friends, when a frantic shout erupted from somewhere high above her.

"Look out below!" someone screamed. "Run!"

Sharona looked up, and in one horrifying second, saw a massive wooden beam plunging to the sidewalk, right above her head. She froze in terror, uselessly covering her head as the beam crashed down upon her and left her sprawled upon the sidewalk, a pool of blood quickly spreading out around her skull.

She heard nothing of the commotion that instantly let loose around her. "Get an ambulance!" people were yelling. "Hold her head up!" "Don't touch her!" "I think she's dead!" Soon the siren's jarring sound screamed down the street and a team of emergency responders snapped into action. Finding no pulse, they desperately tried to resuscitate the young woman. But surveying the scene and examining the beam that had fallen, they realized that no one could have survived the blow.

Sharona's limp body was borne on a stretcher into the ambulance.

"She's gone," said one of the rescuers.

"No! Hey, listen to me. I am not dead!" Sharona heard herself crying out. "I can't be dead! I still have so much to do!"

No one heard her voice. It was as if the sound were trapped in a tightly enclosed space, and no matter how hard she yelled, nothing was heard. "Please don't give up on me," her silent scream called out. "Bring me back!"

When the body arrived at the hospital, the doctors could not find a pulse.

"There's nothing we can do for her," she heard a doctor say.

"No, please don't give up on me. I'm not dead!" she insisted to her unhearing audience.

"Put her body in the morgue until the *chevrah kadisha* comes," the doctor ordered.

The next perception Sharona experienced was somewhere far, far away from the hospital. A brilliant light surrounded her, as if the thousand brightest days in all of creation had been concentrated into one. From somewhere within the light, a voice boomed forth. "Sarah bas Leah, are you prepared for your final judgment by the Heavenly Court?"

Sharona felt her heart contract within her chest, sending a surge of fear throughout her being. Was it really too late? Could she somehow rescue her soul?

"Please, no! I'm not ready. Until this day, I was searching for the truth. Now everything has become clear. Please give me another chance!" Tears streamed down her cheeks as she begged to be returned to life. "Don't let them bury me, or it will all be over."

Despite her forlorn pleas, the proceedings went forward. Sharona saw her entire life unfold before her. Every good deed she had ever done was recounted, as were her many sins. In the final accounting, her sins far outweighed her mitzvos.

"Now you must sign your name to this accounting," Sharona was told. "Then you will receive your judgment." With no other choice before her, she signed the document. Yet something inside her would not give up the hope that perhaps she could have another chance.

"That was me," she admitted. "But I didn't know anything. I never had a chance to learn. Please, let me try again now that I do know. I promise, I'll do *teshuvah* and live a good life."

The judges in the Heavenly Court recognized the sincerity of Sharona's plea. Indeed, she had never been given the opportunity to learn about the mitzvos, and now that she did know, she seemed determined to live her life differently. On that basis, the judges agreed to give her one more chance at life.

The next thing Sharona perceived was the cold, hard slab upon which she had been laid. There were dead bodies all around her, but as she moved her hands and toes and stretched her limbs, she realized that she was no longer among them. She was alive! As soon as she could move, she managed to get up, leave the hospital, and head for home.

A short while later, the members of the *chevrah kadisha* arrived at the hospital to perform their duties. They checked the morgue for Sharona, but did not find her there. Perhaps she had not been taken there yet, or maybe someone had claimed her body. They located a doctor and asked for Sharona's whereabouts.

"She's in the morgue," the doctor informed them.

"No, she is not," a member of the *chevrah* replied.

"How could that be? Where could she be?" the doctor asked in alarm. No one could figure out what had happened. A few days later, when Sharona returned to the hospital for treatment of her injuries, the mystery of her disappearance was solved. The deeper mystery, however, remained. How could she have walked away from the hospital after she had been pronounced dead?

Sharona never related her experience to her doctors, but she did seek out Rabbi Yagen to find out how she should go about keeping her promise to the Heavenly Court. He advised her to cover her hair and to begin observing Shabbos and the mitzvos. He also provided Sharona with a pair of tefillin for her husband.

"Someone who has been given such a revelation as you have has to do something with it," he advised her. "It's not enough for you to change yourself. You've seen the truth, and you can be tremendously powerful in getting other people to change as well."

Sharona followed his advice, and today, her life's story unfolds in a completely different manner than it did on her last appearance at the Heavenly Court. Now, not only are her mitzvos plentiful, but they're multiplied day and night by the thousands of mitzvos of those who have been inspired by this special woman and her unique story, to recognize the truth and to live by its light.

Eyes to See

At the Avinu Malkeinu event, an evening of inspiration that took place last year before Rosh Hashanah, Rabbi Zecharia Wallerstein related this powerful mashal that teaches us how to develop an appreciation for our neshamah. This precious gift from Hashem can never be taken for granted, and must always be handled with great care.

Chana was born blind. However, she never let her disability define her. She went to a mainstream Bais Yaakov, worked hard at her studies, and gathered a large group of close friends along her journey.

When she came of marriageable age, she hoped to find a husband who would also not let blindness define her, but would see her character, talents, and warm personality instead. Fortunately, it did not take long for her to meet Moshe.

After just a few dates Moshe and Chana knew clearly that they had each found their *bashert*. They were engaged, and a few months later, they began their new life together as husband and wife.

Moshe was a loving and devoted husband who wanted to do anything he could to make Chana's life easier. One day, they were listening together to the radio, and they heard a news story about a doctor in New York who had discovered a way to perform eye transplants.

All of a sudden, a new hope burst forth in Chana. While she had always accepted her blindness, now it appeared that there might actually be a possibility for her to see. She could barely contain her excitement as she urged her husband to help her find this doctor and see if she would be a candidate for this surgery.

Moshe gladly complied. However, he soon discovered that the procedure was more theory than reality, for there were very few sources for donor eyes, while there were many people longing to see. Therefore, the waiting list for the surgery was long, and the estimated wait was about 20 years.

When Chana heard the news, she was utterly broken. Her first breath of hope had been quickly extinguished, and now her blindness felt more like a burden than it ever had before. She cried bitterly at this broken dream, and Moshe's heart ached for his wife's sorrow.

A month later, Moshe came home and burst through the front door calling, "Chana! Chana! I have some great news! You're not going to believe this, but a miracle occurred, and for some reason, you were moved to the top of the list! You are the next one in line to get an eye transplant!"

"Oh, I can't believe it!" Chana cried out in excitement. "Hashem! Thank you! What a miracle!"

Only a few weeks later, Moshe and Chana were on their way to a Manhattan hospital for the operation that would change Chana's life forever. Once the admission procedures were completed, Chana was brought to her hospital room, where she would be given the preparatory tests for the surgery that was scheduled for the next day. She lay on her bed, barely able to believe it was real, while Moshe sat silently by her side.

At last, Moshe broke the silence.

"Chana, I want to tell you something that I have never told you before," he said. "It's something very serious."

"Moshe, what is it?" she said with concern in her voice.

"I want you to know that…you are not the only one who is blind. I too am blind," he announced. "I didn't want you to know. I was afraid you wouldn't respect me, that you'd think of me as pitiful. I never knew how to break the news to you while we were dating and finally, I just asked everyone to keep it a secret. But now that you are going to have this operation and will able to see, I felt you had to know. I also felt that if one of us should be able to get this transplant, it should be you, not me. My day hopefully will come soon, and I too will get a transplant."

Chana was shocked by the revelation, but was glad Moshe had told her the truth. Now she was truly astounded by the care and love he had lavished on her all these years, since he was really in no better a situation than she was. Her heart overflowed with gratitude and love for her giving, compassionate husband.

Early the next morning, Chana underwent the operation. The complex procedure took several hours, but when it was over, it was pronounced a success. Chana's eyes were taped shut to promote healing; she was told that in five days, the tape would be removed and she would slowly gain the ability to see.

After five days of almost unbearable suspense and anxiety, the tape was removed and Chana looked at the world for the first time through seeing eyes. Little by little, light, shapes, and forms began to define themselves, and by the end of one week, Chana saw her husband's face for the first time.

Now that I can see, she thought, *I will do everything to make my dear husband's life as easy as possible. I will return everything he's done for me a thousand times over!*

Seeing, however, gave Chana a new zest for life. There was a wide world out there that she had never explored, and she wanted her opportunity to discover it. And yet, she couldn't. Moshe needed her to take him to shul. Wherever they went, she had to walk slowly by his side, guiding him. She could not just leave her beloved husband behind, and yet, she was beginning to feel trapped by his blindness. Feelings of resentment began to cloud her heart, and a rift began to form between them.

One fateful day, Chana decided that she had had enough of disability and its restrictions. As she now viewed the situation, she would have to divorce Moshe if she wanted to lead a normal, healthy life.

Although she made the decision with a heavy, guilty heart, she felt sure that it was the right one. Was she not entitled to live? Nevertheless, she could not bear to tell him in person. She could not bear to see his expression, his pain. Therefore, she chose to speak to him over the phone.

"Moshe, I have to tell you something," she told him abruptly when he picked up her call. She was afraid that if she did not dive right into the conversation, she would lose her courage. "I'm sorry, but I can't be married to you anymore."

"What? What do you mean? Why?" asked the astounded voice on the other end.

"I simply need to be married to someone who can see! Even though I can see, I can't live a free life, because I'm bound by your blindness. I want a different life, and as long as we are married, I can't have it. This is it, Moshe. We only get one life, and I want to live mine! I am so sorry, but I can't hold back these feelings any more."

"I can't say that I agree with your decision," Moshe responded quietly. "But I respect it. If that's what you want, then I am willing to go to *beis din* and give you a *get*."

"I am really, really sorry Moshe. You are such a *tzaddik,* such a wonderful man. It's just me...I can't live like this anymore."

"I'll pack my stuff and leave tonight," Moshe concluded.

Late that night Chana, returned to an empty house. All of Moshe's belongings were gone. She cried for the loss of her devoted husband, but she was relieved and happy that this difficult, seemingly inevitable decision had been made.

It's best for the both of us, she thought. *He doesn't deserve a wife who resents him.*

When she entered her bedroom, she noticed a letter resting on her pillow. She recognized Moshe's handwriting and quickly opened it up. As she read along and comprehended the letter's message, a sense of deep, sick remorse spread throughout her entire being.

> *Dear Chana,*
>
> *I want you to know that I respect your decision and understand that this is what you had to do. I want you to know that I still love you and will always love you no matter what. There is one big favor I have to ask of you, though. There is one thing that I feel you have to know. Perhaps if you would have known this before, things would be different.*
>
> *Make sure to always take good care of those eyes, Chana, because not too long ago those eyes. . .were mine.*
>
> *There was a 20-year wait for an eye transplant, but I loved you so much and so dearly wanted you to be happy, that I decided to give you my eyes. For what wouldn't I do for my beloved Chana?*
>
> *Love, Moshe*

Rabbi Wallerstein expounds:

There is a verse in *Bereishis* (2:7): *And Hashem G-d formed the man of dust from the ground, and He blew into his nostrils the soul of life.*

It was not just any soul, but His soul. Hashem gave us life. He gave us a transplant; He gave us His own soul. What do we do with that soul? Yes, we go to shul to daven and we learn, but why are we so busy trying to see the world? We tell Hashem that we appreciate the soul He has given us, but taking care of it is holding us back. We need to be busy with our gadgets and entertainment. We love to be busy with anything but Him!

But we must remember that Hashem writes us a letter and tells us:

Dear . . .

"Remember that I am the One Who gave you those eyes, I am the One Who gave you that soul. Make sure to take good care of it because that soul was once Mine."

We must ask ourselves this big question: "Did we take good care of those eyes? Did we take good care of that soul this year? Or were we perhaps like Chana, busying ourselves with the distractions of the world and forgetting where we came from? Did we remember who gave us the light to see and the abilities we use for our aimless running?"

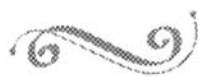

Rabbi Wallerstein concludes:

"I asked my rebbi, Rav Gamliel Rabinowitz, "What *kavanah* should we have when the shofar is being blown?"

Rav Gamliel answered that when the *baal tokei'a* blows "*tekiah*," the long blast, one should think, "I'M SORRY," a shout of sorry, a long sob. I'm so sorry for not treating the *neshamah* You gave me properly this year.

For *shevarim*, the broken sound, think, "I'M SORRY I'M SORRY I'M SORRY"—broken sobs of regret for what I have done.

For *teruah*, a continuous sob of regret, think, "I'M SORRY, I'M SORRY, I'M SORRY."

While the *baal tokei'a* blows the shofar, your soul is crying in pain for the things you did throughout the year.

Finally I asked my rebbi what we should think about during

tekiah gedolah. He replied, "One doesn't cry during *tekiah gedolah*, because that is when the Heavens cry out for all the souls that left the path of Hashem. But in the year when Mashiach comes, Heaven doesn't cry. Rather, it announces Mashiach!"

If we do our best to change what is going on in our soul, and try to come close to Hashem, then with the help of Hashem, this year we will hear that tekiah gedolah, the announcment of Mashiach Tzidkeinu, bimheirah viyameinu. Amen.

Chapter 4: Hear My Voice

Rav Shimshon Pincus teaches that there is a unique format of prayer referred to as "tze'akah," or "crying out," which is a vocal manifestation of the very depths of one's heart. It is the most potent and effective of prayers, as it emerges directly from the soul of a person who is so overburdened with sorrow and hurt that language falls away in the face of a primal, wordless cry. When a person channels this pain into a prayer to Hashem, there is no truer expression of a neshamah longing to reach Hashem. Surely, if such a person were to continue pounding at the doors of Heaven, his prayer would get through.

Says Rav Pincus: If a person reaches such an exalted state of prayer, he should not stop praying! To do so would be similar to a man who quits digging for a treasure right after his shovel hits something solid. Would he only have continued his efforts, he would have realized that he had reached the top of the treasure chest itself.

The reason we must simply never give up is that we can never know if we are, right at this very moment, banging against the top of that treasure chest. In this chapter, we will meet people who took this lesson to heart, and did not stop praying until Hashem ultimately heard their voices.

Daven for Me

From their earliest years, every Jewish child knows the dictum, "Ve'ahavta l'rei'acha kamocha, Love your friend as you love yourself." But what does that really mean? In the following story, Rivky Shainfeld helps us define the boundless concept of "love." It is a bond that endures through good times and bad, the fuel that spurs a person to true greatness, stirring him to action in his friend's time of need. And, it is the ticket to redemption, because each act of love between one Jew and another brings the geulah sheleimah ever closer.*

For as long as I remember, I harbored a glowing, detailed vision in my mind of the life I would live when I got married. I could picture the beautiful home, a true *bayis ne'eman b'Yisrael,* where I would lavish my love and attention, my efforts and energies, on my husband and children. Whenever I would see a young mother with her children, I would see myself in her place, pushing a carriage, drying a tear, sharing a laugh; I could not wait until I could become this wife and mother of my dreams.

When I met my *bashert* and settled down into married life, the dream seemed to be on the verge of fulfillment. Never could I have imagined that eight long years later, I would remain on the verge, still waiting to become a mother.

My first response, as the situation became clear to me, was one of disbelief. How could I, who had been mentally preparing myself for motherhood for so long, who was so very ready and able to care for a child, be the one denied this gift? What had I done to deserve such a fate? I countered these thoughts in the best way I could, trying to reinforce my faith in Hashem and my belief that whatever He does is for my ultimate good. My husband tried to calm me and provide the emotional support I so desperately needed. Nevertheless, the longing in my heart created a constant ache, which sometimes intensified into a sudden stab of grief that literally made me cry out in pain.

Throughout all these years, I prayed to Hashem for a child. The pages of my *siddur* and my *Tehillim* were stiff and crinkled from the tears that had dried upon them. Prayer after prayer, year after year, my life went on. My friends and siblings brought their children into the world, celebrated *brissim* and *kiddushim*, birthday parties and *upsherins*, while I salved my broken heart and waited.

Naturally, my husband and I sought the best medical assistance we could find. We willingly consulted with any doctor and treatment that provided a glimmer of hope. In tandem with our efforts on the medical front, we waged a mighty battle on the spiritual front as well. We spared no effort in seeking *berachos* from *tzaddikim* and trying the many *segulos* that were suggested to us. We hoped, we tried, we suffered yet another crushing disappointment, and yet, we remained willing to try again.

One day, I heard about the great *tzaddik* Rav Moshe Neuschloss, of blessed memory, who had exerted great efforts during his lifetime to build a *mikveh* in Monsey, N.Y. He had promised that anyone who would contribute money to support this *mikveh* would be blessed with children, and I was told that there were many recorded instances of this *segulah* working, turning childless couples into grateful parents. Was this worth a try, I wondered? Should I set myself up for another disappointment? On the other hand, if there was still something that offered hope, how could I not give it a shot?

Several days later, I traveled to the cemetery where the *tzaddik* was buried and found his grave. There I stood, alone in this quiet spot, pouring out the pain and longing that had been mounting in my heart for the previous eight years. After regaining some composure, I spoke:

"I am going through a very hard time now. I have been suffering in silence for years, hoping to raise a family of my own. I just can't bear this situation any longer. I will *bli neder* donate $5,000 to your *mikveh*—money that I do not have now, but I will do anything for the *zechus* of having a child. Daven for me! Please, please daven for me! In your *zechus* and in the *zechus* of your *mikveh*, may Hashem answer my *tefillos*!"

I said some more *Tehillim*, and then I picked up a rock and placed it on the gravestone. Lifting my eyes to heaven, I whispered "Please, Father in Heaven, answer my call. Please, I beg of you!"

Ten months later, my prayers were miraculously answered; I gave birth to a healthy baby boy. It seemed at that moment that the world was awash in joy. It overflowed from the hearts of myself and my husband, and from those of our family and friends as well. For days, I delighted in the exultant feelings we all shared, for it was clear that we had witnessed a miracle and the living, breathing answer to years of heartrending prayer.

There was one friend, however, who could not share my joy, nor could she hide the pain that my good news stirred within her. She was among my closest friends in the world, a woman named Shani, whom I had met in the course of our mutual struggles with childlessness. Our relationship was forged on sympathy, support, encouragement, and shared tears. Shani knew the interior of my heart the way a person knows the interior of his own home. And I knew her as well. Somehow, naively perhaps, I had expected her to unequivocally rejoice for my miracle and find in my story an extra dose of hope for herself.

Instead, Shani clearly felt abandoned in the dark world of childlessness. It was as if I had broken free of prison and left her behind. Of course, once I realized that my baby's birth was painful for her, I tried to deal with the situation sensitively. Over time, I was sure, she would realize that my baby had not taken anything away from her, not even my friendship and empathy.

Despite Shani's coldness, I kept calling her as any friend would, taking an interest in what was going on in her life and sharing as much of my own life as I could. On Shani's side, I knew the effort was appreciated, and yet if she heard my baby cry in the background, or if I spoke about him in any way, the conversation would abruptly end with, "Okay, I've got to go now"—click.

I couldn't let my friend do this to herself. It was like watching someone I loved drowning at sea, refusing all offers of help. I would not let her push me away. One night, I decided that I was finished tiptoeing around Shani's bitterness. I had help to offer, and even if she felt it was presumptuous of me to do so, I was going to offer it. I dialed her number and she picked up.

"Listen. Shani," I told her firmly. "Do you know how it happened that after all these years, I was finally able to have a baby? It was a *segulah*—yes, *another segulah!* But Shani, it worked! And it can work for you too!"

I told her about Rav Neuschloss and his *mikveh*, and the promise he made to those who contributed money to support it. I related the story of my journey to his gravesite, my prayers, and my pledge.

"It was 10 months from that day that my Moshe was born, Shani. Why don't you do the same?"

But Shani was not as inclined toward mysticism as I tended to be, with my Chassidish background. To her, it was all superstition. Still, I persisted, speaking several more times to her about the *segulah*.

One night, she finally lost patience. "Rivky, I've heard enough from you. Leave me alone. It's just not meant to be. Some people are *zocheh* to children and some people are not. The doctors told me that I should just give up already and stop causing myself such frustration. I don't have the strength to fight anymore. I've been married for 10 years already and nothing is going to change now. Hashem doesn't want me to have children. Period. You can't change fate!"

I realized that she was not going to follow my advice, and yet, I still could not give up the idea that there was a miracle awaiting her, too.

"Okay, Shani, I'm done nagging. But if you aren't going to go to Rav Neuschloss' grave to daven for yourself, then I am going to go there and daven for you!"

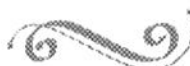

It felt strange to be traveling back to the cemetery, to walk the same quiet pathways and stand once again before Rav Moshe Neuschloss' grave. The memories of the pain and desperation that had accompanied me to this spot only a year before seemed so distant, now that I was at last a mother. Yet when I thought of Shani's emptiness, and the despair into which she was falling, tears once again sprung to my eyes. I wept for my friend as if I were weeping for myself.

"Rav Moshe, in your *zechus* I had a child, and for that I am forever grateful. However, my friend is still suffering. She also wants to have a baby more than anything in the world. I am willing to raise $3,600 as a *zechus* that my friend Shani should have a child. Be a *meilitz yosher* on her behalf."

I finished saying *Tehillim* and embarked on the long trek home. The trip was exhausting, both physically and emotionally, but by the time I arrived home, my heart felt lighter than it had in weeks. I had done something to help my friend.

When I called Shani to tell her what I had done, her hard wall of disbelief seemed to have crumbled. Hope was rising up in her once more, and she thanked me profusely for rekindling it for her.

"Be strong, Shani," I told her. "Just keep davening and keep going, because your *tefillos* will be answered soon."

"You know, I have an appointment with another specialist in Manhattan," Shani told me. "I was going to cancel it, I felt like, 'why bother?' But you know what? I'm going to keep it. Maybe this time will be different."

I wished her luck, certain in my heart that this was the opportunity to bring all our prayers to fruition.

On Tuesday of the next week, the day of the appointment, I picked up the phone to the sound of a frantic Shani.

"It's just not meant to be, Rivky, don't you understand?" She was sobbing and gasping, barely able to speak.

"What happened? What are you talking about?" I urged her.

"Didn't you hear? There was a terror attack on the World Trade Center. The whole city is shut down. No one is allowed into Manhattan. There's no way for me to get to this appointment. Hashem just does not want this to happen!"

It was September 11, 2001, and the city of New York was on fire. It was a tragic day in history, when so many innocent lives were lost and so many lives changed forever. Shani's appointment was among the lesser casualties, but to her, it loomed as an enormous sign from Heaven that motherhood would never be hers.

"Let's not get hysterical," I said, trying to remain calm in the face of both the horrifying news and my friend's despair. "Let's see what we can do."

After a volley of phone calls, we managed to obtain permission for Shani to enter Manhattan with a police escort. She was able to keep her appointment, which indeed turned out to be the channel through which her own personal miracle would flow. Ten months later, Shani gave birth to a beautiful baby girl. She was slightly premature and had to remain behind in the hospital until she was strong enough to go home, but even that could not dampen Shani's joy. She was at long last a mother.

Every day, Shani and her husband would go to the hospital to visit their little daughter When the baby was two weeks old, the couple received a call from the hospital in the middle of the night. It was a nurse in the preemie unit, calling to relate that the baby's health had taken a downward turn.

"The doctors are worried that it may get worse," the nurse related gently. "You should come as soon as possible."

I found out about the call moments later when my own phone rang and a brokenhearted Shani was on the other end.

"You see, Rivky, you see?" she wept. "I begged you to let it be. Now look what's happened. My baby is dying and there is nothing I can do about it. I went through all this just to watch my baby die. Why did I listen to you? First the World Trade Center and now this. Why didn't I see that it just wasn't meant to be?"

I could barely make out Shani's words through her choked sobs. She was hysterical, and she was certainly not doing herself or her baby any good this way.

"Enough, Shani!" I yelled into the phone. "Go to the hospital and say *Tehillim.* I will also daven for you. Hashem is going to get you through this, I promise. Don't give up yet."

In despair, Shani hung up the phone on me. I felt that there had to be something that I could do to help, but what?

Then I remembered the *tzaddik's* promise. Although it was the middle of the night, I resolved that as soon as morning dawned, I would travel to the cemetery where Rav Neuschloss was buried. Standing once again by his grave, I tearfully begged for a complete, true fulfillment of his promise.

"This was not the deal!" I argued. "You promised you would give a child to those who support your cause. I did my part, yet my friend's baby is dying. If her child dies, it will be all over for her. I don't think she will ever recover. Please don't let her baby die! Don't let her die! Please be a *meilitz yosher* for my friend's baby," I begged.

The words I cried out at the grave that night came from the deepest place I had ever touched within my soul. I felt a profound connection to Hashem, a true sense that my words were reaching Him and drawing down from Heaven the healing and *berachah* that Shani and her baby so desperately needed.

It wasn't long before the baby was fully recovered. My friendship with Shani became closer than ever. Now, 10 years later, Shani has several more healthy children and a beautiful, growing family to raise and love. And just as we spent so many years soothing each other's sorrows, we can now rejoice wholeheartedly with each other's happiness. We are best friends, and we always will be.

When I think back to that time of struggle, the ups and the downs of near victory and defeat, I realize that it taught me what it means to really daven for something. I felt a great closeness to Hashem throughout it all, and became sharply aware that everything is in His hands

I also believe that because I davened from the depths of my heart for Shani, because I really felt her pain, Hashem answered me and blessed her with children. Perhaps that is the segulah you should learn from my story: daven for your friend in need, show Hashem you really care and maybe your prayers will also be answered; if not this time, then perhaps the next time, or the time after that. Just keep pounding on heaven's gate until your tefillah breaks through and is answered.

May Hashem always hear our prayers.

Freedom!

When difficulties arise, we may feel locked up and unable to free ourselves from our situation. How does one overcome the challenge and break through the virtual chains surrounding him? Rabbi Chaim Klein, a mechanech for over 30 years, shares a story and a powerful lesson in gaining freedom for our soul.*

Standing in the midst of the *beis midrash*, eyes open wide in amazement, stood Avi Schoenberg and his father. Avi was the same age as the teenage boys who filled the *beis midrash*, and yet, as I observed his expression of wonderment, he appeared more like a young boy. The din produced by dozens of pairs of *chavrusas* hotly debating the points of the Gemara must have sounded to him like chaos.

At one point, Avi witnessed a debate so heated that he feared the boys would come to blows. He approached a rebbi and tried to get him to intercede before violence erupted.

"Don't worry," the rebbi explained. "They're not angry at each other. They're just defending their side of the argument. That's how Gemara is learned."

The animation in the boys' faces and voices made Avi's heart tingle with excitement. He imagined himself sitting there, filled with energy and confidence, holding his own in a debate over some fine point of Gemara. Some day, maybe.

It was a year later when Avi returned to the yeshivah, this time to take his seat among the students. He came with absolutely no learning skills, but a burning desire to succeed. I believed that, with such a strong desire, success would surely follow.

But things don't always progress as one would expect. Avi literally could not learn. Every word was a struggle. Every concept was an impossible knot for him to untangle, and somehow, even if someone untangled it for him, he managed to knot it up again. I surmised that he must have been afflicted with a severe learning disability.

The unbelievable part was that he never gave up. Late into the night, I would find him in the *beis midrash* trying to work his slow way through the Gemara. He would pass the entire night there, plugging away until 4:30 in the morning, and still the learning would not penetrate.

Seeing his devotion, the rebbeim and other *talmidim* all tried to learn with him. Everyone imagined that he would be the one to help Avi break through his learning block and soar to the heights he clearly longed to reach. But I must admit that in my own efforts to learn with him, I found the situation impossibly frustrating. It seemed like there was a stone wall blocking Torah from going in. But what was the wall made of? It certainly didn't come from a lack of desire: Avi had more desire than I had ever witnessed in any student. Neither did it come from a lack of intelligence. You could speak to him on any topic and have a perfectly intelligent conversation. He seemed perceptive and mature as well.

There was another mysterious aspect to Avi's personality that further confused me. It was his *tefillah.* In all my years in *chinuch,* I have certainly seen boys who possess an unusual amount of *kavanah.* But I had never seen anyone like Avi; the moment he stepped forward to start the *Shemoneh Esrei,* he would begin weeping profusely. It didn't begin at a certain point in the davening, but started right at the outset and continued until the end. I wondered what weighed so heavily on his heart that it burst through so forcefully each and every time he davened.

One day, Avi came to me and asked me to set aside a time to learn with him. "Any time at all would be fine," he said. "Whenever you can fit me in."

On one hand, of course I wanted to respond to this sincere boy's request. On the other hand, I was extremely busy, and reasonably sure that the time we would spend together would be fruitless. I decided to offer him a time slot he would be unlikely to take, thereby giving him the chance to be the one to refuse.

"Really, the only time I have available is Thursday night at about midnight, Avi. Is that too late for you?" I asked.

He told me that it wasn't too late, but it was a bit too early, because he had a learning session planned for that time. He would be finished at about 2 a.m. "Can I come then?" he asked.

I couldn't say no to such devotion. Thursday night arrived and I worked a long time on preparations for my *shiur*. I was sure that Avi would have forgotten about our appointment and gone to bed, but at 2 a.m., there was a knock on the door. Avi was there, ready to learn.

I chose a small *mesechta* to learn with him, hoping that eventually we could finish it and make a *siyum*. For the next few weeks, we learned together once a week in the wee hours of the morning, but Avi's dedication to our *seder* did not make it any easier to learn with him. He exhibited the same thickheadedness that had frustrated me on my many previous attempts to learn with him, but I tried mightily not to betray my impatience.

Finally, one week, I decided to at least try to unlock some part of the mystery that was Avi. I asked him point-blank, "Avi, why is it that every time you daven *Shemoneh Esrei*, the moment you begin, you burst into tears? What is it all about?"

"Well rebbi, you are a bit of a psychologist. What do you think it is?"

"I will tell you what I think. I think that in your life, you have had many challenges, unbelievable challenges that gave you no respite. You were never able to get away from your problems and the only time you have some freedom is during *Shemoneh Esrei*. That is when you have some time to yourself. That is when the thoughts of the challenge weigh on your mind and you are overcome with your problems."

"Rabbi Klein, you're absolutely right, only....only..." and he began to weep as he finished his thought, "you have no idea how bad it really is!"

At this point, Avi began a tale of unbelievable suffering at the hands of the one to whom most children turn for comfort: his mother. This woman, obviously bearing deep emotional scars of her own, had raised her son with an iron fist, with a loveless, merciless approach that left him feeling like a hated stranger in his own home.

"When I would go to school, my mother made me promise that I would never talk to another child. I would have to lie to her and tell her that I didn't speak to anyone. I was never allowed to have any friends—period, and certainly not in my home. Whenever I came home from school, my mother would take my homework and rip it up in front of my face. I was not allowed to have a mind of my own. If I wanted to eat something, I had to ask my mother for permission. If I didn't ask, then it would be taken away from me. I had to knock on the door and wait for permission from my mother to enter a room if she was there.

"I can't count how many times I was locked in a dark closet for the smallest sin. I suffered the worst treatment possible and was humiliated each and every day, but somehow I was expected to put on a smile and pretend that I was a happy and healthy boy. Can you imagine growing up all your life with a mother who treats you with such hatred? I had no childhood. My father didn't help me either. He would just tell me that he understood what I was going through, but claimed there was nothing he could do to help. I just had to suffer in silence.

"This past year, I went to Israel with my parents, and while I was there I went to the Kosel. That was the first time in my life that I burst into tears and let it all out. I davened so hard that I nearly lost control of myself. I poured out my soul to Hashem and begged Him to end my mother's abuse.

"And miraculously, my prayers were answered. The next day, my mother told me that she was thinking of sending me away to an out-of-town yeshivah. When I heard that, I pushed to her let me go here, because of the impression the boys made on me when I visited earlier in the year.

"So now, when I stand here in yeshivah and say *Shemoneh Esrei,* the moment I begin to daven, my heart overflows with the pain of my childhood."

At this point in Avi's story, I too was crying. It all began to make sense. This poor boy was tormented by his mother. He was not allowed to think on his own and was barely permitted to breathe on his own. He couldn't absorb Gemara because his mind had been twisted and torn to pieces by his mother.

The mystery was no longer why Avi couldn't learn, but rather, what kept him going? "How could you still be sane?" I asked him. "How could you have remained *frum*? Most people would have gone crazy or given up long ago!"

Avi had an answer, and it contained all the wisdom in the world.

"I would have given up long ago," he admitted. "But a rebbi once explained my situation to me in a way that really hit home. He said that everyone has his challenges in life. There is a reason Hashem gave you this challenge, and your job now is to overcome it. If you do it, and keep on trying and pushing and never give up, then the dam will burst, and all the *berachah* in the world will come your way. There is only so much trouble a person can go through before the *yeshuah* comes, but you have to give it your all and try your best to make it happen.

"I came to this yeshivah and realized that Torah couldn't make a dent in my mind, but I was committed to keep going at it until I finally would have that breakthrough. Rabbi Klein, I feel that you are my ticket to this breakthrough. I know that with your help, I can overcome this challenge, and that is why I wanted this learning session at all costs."

The tears were flowing freely from my eyes by this point. I was now willing to do whatever it took to help Avi climb up and over his mountain of trouble.

Avi stayed in yeshivah for a while and then moved on, and *baruch Hashem,* he began to see amazing improvement in his learning. Eventually he began *shidduchim.* One day, he called to tell me that he was seriously dating someone, and did not know how much he should reveal of his family life. I told Avi that he would have to sit down with his future father-in-law and tell him the whole story about his parents and the way he was treated.

He followed my advice, and after telling his story, he saw that his future father-in-law was regarding him with a very serious expression. He instantly began to panic. The whole thing was obviously about to be called off.

But instead of issuing the expected rejection, the girl's father said, "Avi, I want you to know that I understand exactly how you feel, because I went through the same thing in my life. And look at me, I made it. I am successful despite the fact I had such a difficult upbringing, and you will also be very successful with the help of Hashem."

Rabbi Klein concludes with this lesson: We all go through incredible challenges in our lives. There is not one person in this world who doesn't have a challenge that he feels is beyond his ability to overcome. It is at those times that we have to put in a 150-percent effort, as Avi did, so that the dam can burst and the berachah can come gushing forth. We become great people because of our challenges, which are tailor made by Hashem for us alone.

Going Vertigo

Reb Yosef loved to explore the deep sea off the coast of Israel. He made the greatest discovery of his life when, diving in deep water, he went vertigo, a condition in which the diver cannot tell whether he is traveling upward or downward. The analogy applies to everyone's life at one time or another, and through his story, Reb Yosef teaches us how to free ourselves from confusion and find our bearings once again.

As far back as I can remember, I have always loved nature. Nothing energized me more than being outdoors, under the sky, hiking in the wilderness, viewing the world from the mountaintops, and most of all, delving into the mysterious world beneath the sea. Yet my sense of wonder, so keen within my heart and mind, had never penetrated my soul. Never did I wonder, "*Mi bara eileh—who created these?*"

Such a question simply did not exist in the secular Israeli lifestyle in which I grew up. In my family home, the basics of Judaism were completely absent. There was no sense of any Divine power, any Creator or Ruler of the world. "Be a good person, do what is right, and find happiness" were our Three Commandments, and that was all.

As it turned out, however, my love of nature was instrumental in opening my eyes to Hashem, and changing my life forever. The episode that brought about this change started with a scuba-diving expedition that I and three friends undertook on one calm summer day. The undersea world, so splendid with color and novelty, beckoned to us, and yet we all felt the need for some new diving experience. Aiming to explore a new area of deeper water, we set out for a day of adventure.

To avoid wasting time and oxygen, my friend Doran and I offered to go on a reconnaissance mission to see if the new area held any novel features to explore. Dropping down into 35 meters of water, we began our descent, steadily moving closer to the seafloor. To our delight, we encountered what appeared to be the opening of a cave, a small world of possibilities just waiting for us to explore.

We did not need to see any more. We swam to the surface to share the good news with our friends. Everyone agreed that the cave would be a worthwhile destination, and so we quickly made our preparations. The first step for a diver is to make sure that he has enough oxygen for the length of time he intends to remain submerged. Our tanks were 75 percent full, which gave each of us a total of 40 minutes worth of oxygen. That meant we would have 35 minutes to reach the cave and to explore it, still leaving us 5 minutes to get back up to the surface.

The squeezing I felt in my stomach as we submerged was a feeling I recognized instantly as the sensation of thrill. We were on a seemingly endless downward glass elevator, and each level we passed revealed new vistas of exotic beauty. Fish drifted by in stunningly vivid schools, their purple, orange, and yellow hues rivaling the most glorious sunset.

As we went deeper, I began to feel a different kind of squeezing sensation. This was the result of the water pressure building all around me. Although I wasn't in any imminent danger at this level, the sensation reminded me that I had to be careful of resurfacing too quickly. A diver who does that can be seriously injured or killed by the sudden release of pressure on his organs and blood vessels. It's one of the risks a person faces when deep-sea diving, but adequate preparation and precautions are usually enough to avoid harm.

Another danger is vertigo. When you're surrounded by water, it is easy to become disoriented and lose track of which way is up. In that case, you might end up swimming deeper and deeper toward the seafloor when you think you are heading to the surface. To prevent vertigo, divers wear a special watch that indicates the right direction.

Despite the dangers, our descent to the seafloor was a safe and smooth journey through a world of visual delights. We quickly found the cave, and in our eagerness to enter its hidden world, we made an elementary mistake. Any diver knows that when you explore a cave, you must tether yourself with a rope to something outside the cave, so that you can always find your way back to the exit. Somehow, despite our considerable experience, not one of us remembered to follow this procedure. The only explanation is *hashgachah pratis.*

Unaware of our mistake, we drifted into a watery realm of otherworldly beauty. The sea all around us appeared so intensely blue that I felt as if I were floating within the interior of a liquid sapphire. Each arched entryway of the maze of caverns was framed with lacey formations of coral and rock, painted by nature with golden hues of orange and red. Unusual sea creatures swam with the gentle currents or hid in the crevices of their home. A visitor in an enchanted land, I could barely absorb the exquisite scene unfolding before my eyes.

Our intense curiosity kept us moving forward into the cave, unheeding of its mazelike structure that was leading us ever further from the entrance. We were in a dream, but we were roughly awakened by the sudden realization that one of our party was missing. We scampered around the silent depths, hoping to find him behind the next rock or inside the next cavern, but our efforts yielded no result. His name rose up in my throat; if only I could scream for him! But of course, that was impossible.

As our feelings of panic rose, we realized that our oxygen tanks were beginning to run low as well. There was only nine minutes worth of air remaining, just enough time to get out of the cave and back to the surface, if we could determine which way to go. I probed each hole we passed to see if it led out of the cave, but they were all dead ends. A sense of doom closed in on me. I felt like I was going vertigo. We would all die. There would be headlines tomorrow morning about the three divers lost at sea. So unceremoniously, we had reached the end of the line.

Four minutes worth of oxygen remained. Four minutes of life. I did not know what to do, until suddenly, from somewhere in the deepest depths of my soul, these astounding words burst forth. "G-d, save me from death!"

I looked up—that's what you do when you call out to G-d from the floor of the sea. And when I looked, I saw a beam of light shining into the darkness. It was the elusive opening that would take us to the surface. My friends and I swam as quickly as we could to the light, out of the cave and up toward the surface. I was aware that the speed of our ascent could spell trouble, but I could not believe that G-d would show me the way and then abandon me. I prayed again, "G-d, please save my life! For my wife and children, please get me home safely."

I reached the surface moments after my oxygen had run out. My friends were all there; we had all made it out alive. However, danger still lurked just below the surface of the placid sea, for this was shark-infested water. Our movements as we swam toward our boat would be all that was necessary to invite an attack. Again, my voice rose up in prayer, "Please, G-d, keep the sharks away from us."

And again, G-d answered. We swam to our boat unimpeded, a third miracle for me in my 10-minute-long career as a believer.

The entire experience shook me to the core of my being. Not only had I faced death, which was enough of an awakening, but I had encountered a part of my deepest self that I had never known existed. What was this voice that had emerged from me and had directed itself with such laser precision to its exact target in Heaven?

I was overcome with a desire to know this part of myself better, and that desire lead me to a seminar given by the outreach organization Arachim. There, I learned about G-d the Creator, G-d the Supervisor of everything, G-d the Author of the Torah. The things I learned at that seminar were like a bright light shed inside the dark room in which I had been stumbling during the course of my entire life. I was finally able to see the abundant love and unfathomable intelligence behind the "nature" I so adored. I was able to see purpose in my existence and in my struggles. Within a short time, I enrolled in yeshivah and rebuilt my life upon a whole new foundation.

As my life moved forward, the G-d Who had answered my prayers under the sea continued to answer me. At one point, my wife had given birth to a son, and he was soon thereafter diagnosed with cancer. I had not been religious for very long, and all my old acquaintances used this tragedy to point out the futility of my beliefs. "This is what you get for being religious?" they chided. "I'll stay the way I am."

Their words hurt, but they did not shake my faith. I was certain that G-d continued to guide me, and I held onto that belief through two difficult, frightening years of treatments. My child was barely holding on to life when we brought him to the hospital for a dangerous procedure.

Before my son was taken to surgery, I lifted him from his crib, pressed him to my heart and let my prayers and tears flow. Once again, I was lost at sea, faced with devastation. I wanted only to reach that deep place I had reached then, and pull from there a prayer that would bring just one more miracle into my life. "*Ribono Shel Olam,* please, You can take everything from me, but there is one thing you cannot take: my *emunah*. Please have mercy on my child."

Baruch Hashem, today my child is healthy and well. My *emunah* is strong and with the help of Hashem I will never experience vertigo again. Like the watch that prevents diver's vertigo, the Torah is our true guide. It keeps us oriented in the right direction, so that even when the deep waters surround us, we know which way Hashem wants us to go.

Mazal Tovs

In the following story, Ari Streicherman teaches us a lesson in being persistent yet patient in our prayers. We must always remember that Hashem sees the end result of everything, and when He does not seem to respond to our tefillos, there just might be a very good reason. Sometimes, like Ari Streicherman, we are privileged enough to see this reason with the utmost clarity.*

I had already been married for several years, and our state of childlessness was beginning to weigh heavily on my heart. On Shabbos or Yom Tov especially, when families got together and fathers brought their children to shul with them, I would plaster a smile on my face and then find a moment to squeeze my eyes shut and wonder when it would be my turn. When would I, too, have the pleasure of arriving for a *simchah* or a visit to a family friend with a car full of my children?

Then, when the holiday of Simchas Torah would arrive, I would feel a very keen sort of sadness. It seemed as though the entire shul was one buzzing mass of excited people and exuberant faces—everyone with his child on his shoulders—except for me. As a child, I had always looked forward to the special blessing of *Kol Hane'arim*, when all of us children would excitedly crowd under the tallis-canopy, but now, as an adult, my heart ached for the day when my own child could be similarly excited.

Perhaps it was for that reason that I decided, one year, to purchase the honor of *Kol Hane'arim*. Many childless couples had purchased it in previous years, and all of them seemed to have benefited from the renowned *segulah* and been blessed with children at last, so why not me? Why not now?

The bidding that year rose quite high, but with a silent prayer and determination, I won the honor of the *aliyah*. Elated, I poured all my *kavanah* into the *aliyah*; I felt certain that this year would mark the answer to my prayers.

Well, the year came and went, and no miracle occurred. My wife and I still did not have a child. Though I was shaken and anguished at the failure of what I thought would be a surefire *segulah*, I resolved that I would simply purchase *Kol Hane'arim* again the following year. Perhaps I only had to show Hashem that I had *bitachon,* and that I was placing my life in His hands.

The following Simchas Torah, however, I simply did not have the means to bid as I had the previous year. Luckily, I was able to make an arrangement with the Rav of a very small shul nearby who kindly agreed to grant *Kol Hane'arim* to me for a set fee. The *minyan* had just barely 15 men in it, and there would not have been much competition, anyway.

Simchas Torah morning arrived, and I began my walk to the small shul with a smile in my heart, as I knew that I was sure to receive the coveted *aliyah*. Perhaps this year would finally mark the end to my troubles. Lost in thought, I almost bumped right into my friend Ezzy, approaching the same shul from the other direction.

"Hey, Ezzy," I greeted him with curiosity, "what brings you to this side of town? Don't you live almost a mile away?"

"Hi, Ari," he smiled. "To be honest, I'm here because I think I might be able to get *Kol Hane'arim* this year for an affordable price. At my usual shul, there's no way I can afford the kind of money that the bidding demands, but this is a small place where no one else needs the *aliyah*, so I'll probably get it for almost nothing."

"Oh," I responded quickly, trying to hide the way his words had flustered me, "that's nice." My mind raced.

It's my *aliyah, and I'm not going to give it up! I'm through being the nice guy at my own expense...I already made this up with the Rav, and I'm sticking to it!*

Encouraged by my seeming sympathy, Ezzy began explaining his circumstances to me. He described how seven years of marriage had yielded no children, how he and his wife were at their wits' end, and how someone had suggested *Kol Hane'arim* to him as a *segulah* to end his pain.

"I would give *anything* for a child," Ezzy muttered gloomily. "You have no idea what it's like for us..."

I bit my tongue, hard, and continued listening as Ezzy poured his heart out before me. It was as though a dam had burst, and his eyes welled up as he tried to describe the inexplicable pain of childlessness—a pain I was far too familiar with, unbeknownst to my friend. And my heart went out to him. I realized that Ezzy needed this more than I did, and so I quickly excused myself, and then ran home to ask my wife if she would allow me to give my honor to Ezzy. She readily agreed.

When I arrived at shul, I wasted no time in my hurrying to inform the Rav that I wanted my *aliyah* given to Ezzy in my stead. Though he was surprised at my decision, he respected it and agreed to the change. I felt a thrill of pleasure rush through me as I assumed my seat, for I had remembered an even more well-known *segulah*: one who prays that another person be blessed with something that he himself needs will merit to see his own needs fulfilled. Certainly, I assured myself, if I were willing to surrender my coveted honor to another Jew in need, I too would have my prayers answered. It simply *had* to be; I was fully confident.

Well, I shudder to remember my devastation when another, further year came and went without a child to grace our home! Even more jarring was the speed with which Ezzy and his own wife had welcomed a baby boy into the world that same year. Of course, I rejoiced for them, but never had I felt as neglected by my Father in Heaven. I vividly remember Rosh Hashanah afternoon of that year, when some of my pain boiled over and I complained bitterly to my wife.

"It doesn't make sense! Why weren't we answered? I even gave up my *aliyah*, and any kid who reads storybooks can tell you that that means I should have been answered *first!* I just don't get it!"

My wife watched me silently, her own expression mirroring my pain and hurt. I realized then that it was unfair of me to put this bitterness upon her. She was suffering just as much, if not more, than I was, and there was no sense in bringing us both down about it. Resignedly, I prepared to attend the same shul on Simchas Torah as I had the previous year, once again settling on a price beforehand with the Rav.

This time, to my satisfaction, my purchase and recital of the *Kol Hane'arim aliyah* went off without a hitch. Now, once again, there was nothing to do but wait...

Well, wouldn't you know it...our dreams came true! A mazal tov came our way at last. But then, the shock: not one, but *three* mazal tovs arrived in the form of adorable triplet girls: three precious daughters! In the midst of my indescribable elation, understanding suddenly bloomed to life in my mind:

Hashem hasn't been silent at all these past three years—He said "yes," and He said it three times! He only wanted to wait for me to get Kol Hane'arim three times before it was time for His answer to my prayers! Thank You, Hashem for all three of my mazal tovs!

Sometimes, we may find ourselves wondering what Hashem has in mind for us, and sometimes, when the *berachah* suddenly comes through loud and clear, we are honored to see the Master Plan in all its glory, and we are awed by it.

Hashem is always there to answer us. Sometimes His answer is yes, and sometimes it is no, but then there are those special times when our loving Father smiles upon us and says, "Wait, and you will see."

Never Give Up Hope

When our tefillos aren't answered, we often feel disappointment and we might even lose our hope. Sometimes it feels like we are knocking our heads against the wall, to no avail. In this amazing story, Mrs. Sarah Bayler from Israel tells us of her own unique experience.*

For me, it had been 20 years. Twenty years of hopes, dreams, and fantasies of building a family of my own. For someone who struggles with childlessness, even five years is a very long time; 20 years is an eternity. Throughout that time, year after heartbreaking year, I bounced between specialists and false promises until the day came that I could stand it no longer. I simply gave up. I returned to my apartment in defeat; I could just stay there forever, for all I cared.

It just wasn't fair! What had I ever done to deserve such merciless punishment? Why could I not share the contentment of all those around me whose children could be heard playing, laughing, and running up and down the steps of my apartment building on their way to and from school? I had watched some of these children grow up and get married already, but there were always more children arriving, laughing in the halls on Shabbos afternoons, and stampeding through the building in the evenings, when their mothers called them from their games and their bicycles to return for supper.

I was alone in the dark. After 20 years of dashed hopes and broken smiles, I allowed sorrow to overcome me at last. I cried hysterically that day, the day I gave up. My anguish and pent-up hurt were too much to bear anymore; even my tear-drenched *Tehillim* offered only a modicum of solace in my haze of misery.

But then, in the midst of it all, a single thought blazed in my mind: *This is not what Hashem wants of me. He surely does not wish for me to give up hope. A Jew never surrenders all hope.*

I began to breathe a bit easier, wiping some of the tears from my eyes and face. *After all, can't Hashem do whatever He wants? If He wanted me to have a child, I simply would, as though there had never been anything wrong. Maybe this is worth one more shot.*

I washed my face, and then quickly snatched up my purse and my *Tehillim*. It was time to pay a visit to the Kosel and talk some *tachlis*. There was a river of tears inside me threatening to burst through its dam, but I was going to save those tears for the prayer of my life. I was going to confront my Creator as I never had before.

When I approached the ancient stones of the Kosel HaMaaravi, I was already shaking. As I pressed my lips to those cold stones that had nevertheless warmed so many hearts, I started to cry.

Yes, I had cried before, but this was much different. I felt *connected*. I understood, finally, what our matriarch Rachel must have felt when she turned to G-d about her barrenness. There she had been, hoping to build a great nation, and yet it seemed that Hashem was denying her the purpose of her life. I understood the crushing pain that Chana must have felt when she poured her heart out to Hashem so thoroughly that her fervent prayers were mistaken for inebriation. For once in my life, I truly felt my own pain in such a deep sense that I knew my soul itself was *talking* as I prayed, adding its own voice to mine as I petitioned the One Above to finally let my prayers through the Heavenly Gates.

I was almost unaware of how violently I trembled as I cried. It was truly the sobbing of a baby, in which the entire body shudders with the vibration of it and the tears flow completely uninhibited by shame or self-consciousness. It was right then, at the heights of my *neshamah's* plea, that I felt a soft tap on my shoulder.

I was bewildered for a moment, so lost in my prayer that I almost couldn't get my head around to see who had decided to interfere with someone so clearly focused on speaking to her Creator.

An old Sefardi woman wrapped in a shawl met my blurry gaze, smiling kindly at me, her gnarled hands clutching a faded book. Her face was so thoroughly wrinkled that there could be no way of determining her age. Something about her gave me the distinct sense that she wasn't a local, even though she addressed me in soft, tender Hebrew.

"*Biti, lamah at bochah?*" ("My daughter, why are you crying?")

For reasons that I didn't fully understand, I was suddenly awash with the certainty that I could trust this woman. I found myself opening up as I never had before, telling her how I had been married for 20 years and had not been blessed with children. I described the years and years of hoping, praying, and consulting with highly recommended doctors, and I added that I had finally given up today, since I could bear it no longer.

The old woman gazed into my eyes with a warm, knowing smile and said, "My daughter, you no longer have anything to worry about. Hashem has heard your cries, and He has connected with your prayers. Your prayers for a child have been answered."

I stared at this unknown woman, wondering who she was and why I felt completely compelled to believe every word she said. It was then that I happened to glance down at the faded *sefer* she was holding, and I was startled to read the Hebrew name engraved upon it:

Serach bas Asher.

My eyesight blurred, stinging with tears, and I quickly spun to grab some tissues from my purse to blot at them. When I swiveled my head back around to find out more about this old woman with the peculiar *sefer*, I found myself facing empty air. I did a complete

360-degree turnaround, but the old woman was gone as though she had never been there at all…

That year, I gave birth to a healthy baby girl.

Today, I have a beautiful family of four children, for whom I pray daily that Hashem shower them with blessing. After all, I've learned my lesson. Never give up hope in Hashem, just as He never gives up hope in us.

Keep davening, keep smiling, keep the faith, and your prayers, too, will surely be answered.

Chapter 5:
Forever Inspired

Everyone experiences inspiration at some time or another. It arrives as the proverbial bolt from the blue, illuminating our consciousness for only a short, valuable time before disappearing. Our job in this world is to seize these precious moments and make them last a lifetime.

Rav Chaim Shmulevitz expands upon this, explaining that this is how we may understand the reaction of Rebbi to the death of Elazar ben Durdeya (Avodah Zarah 17a), who had traveled the world for the sole purpose of engaging in sin, but was inspired to do teshuvah. At first, Elazar ben Durdeya, who had no doubt spent many years assuming that spiritual work was something other people did, simply approached the mountains, the sun, and other natural entities and begged them to beseech mercy for him from Above. When he finally arrived at the shocking realization that the matter depended solely on him, that teshuvah must be done by the person himself, he became so distraught over his sinful past that he cried until his neshamah departed from his body. A Heavenly voice cried out, "Elazar ben Durdeya has a place in the World to Come," at which point Rebbi declared, "Yeish koneh olamo b'shaah achas." ("There are those who earn their portion in the World to Come in a single moment.")

This, explains Rav Shmulevitz, is exactly the lesson. Some experience moments of inspiration that dissipate as quickly as they appear, but others can make that moment last by constantly reminding themselves of the clarity they experienced at that moment. In this chapter, we will meet people who stretched their moments into a lifetime of inspired avodas Hashem, and who have most certainly acquired a beautiful portion in the World to Come.

A Priceless Picture

At a gathering for mechanchim, Rabbi Leibish Langer related a fascinating story that he heard from a menahel of a large yeshivah. This is a story that highlights the profound effect a rebbi can have on his talmidim. As Rabbi Langer was my rebbi when I was a fifth-grader in the Mirrer Yeshivah, I can certainly attest to the impact of a rebbi's love and warmth.

It was the first day of yeshivah, and Rabbi Feingold* was determined to hit the ground running. The sixth-graders of the Chassidishe *cheder* Lev Torah* seemed poised to do the same, with their Gemaras opened, their fingers firmly on the place, and their faces shining with eagerness to learn Torah.

Rabbi Feingold began the day with a short speech about what he expected of the boys and how much they would accomplish and grow now that they were learning Gemara. Then, without further ado, the class began to learn. The rebbi circulated through the rows of his *talmidim*, chanting the opening words of the *perek* and listening with pleasure as the boys repeated them. It was always an inspiration to introduce young boys to Gemara, to see their excitement as they followed along.

As the rebbi surveyed his class, his gaze was drawn to the corner of the room, where Dovid* sat hunched over, his Gemara partially obscuring him from view. Something about the telltale way the boy's hands stayed hidden behind the Gemara alerted the seasoned rebbi that something was not right. Rabbi Feingold casually made his way over to a closer vantage point, and his mouth dropped open as Dovid's hands moved into view. The boy was engrossed in sorting through a pile of baseball cards. Instead of peering intently into his Gemara as the other boys were doing, Dovid was using it as a barrier to hide his misdeed.

"Dovid!" thundered Rabbi Feingold, his shock overwhelming his usual self-control. "What is going on here?"

Dovid jumped guiltily and then recoiled as Rabbi Feingold snatched the stack of cards from his hands.

"It's the first day of yeshivah, Dovid!" the rebbi shouted. "Everyone here is learning Gemara, and this is what you decide to do?"

It was one of the most important days of the year, Rabbi Feingold well knew, and first impressions were always the strongest. It was the time to set the tone: the boys had to learn what would and would not be tolerated in his classroom! Before tens of pairs of wide eyes, Rabbi Feingold tore the cards into pieces.

Frightened by his rebbi's harsh reaction, and deeply ashamed of himself, Dovid buried his face in his arms and began to cry.

Though his anger had receded, Rabbi Feingold did not surrender to his impulse to comfort his crying *talmid*. He wanted the class to understand that this sort of disrespect for *limud Torah* would never be acceptable. Class continued on for another 10 minutes, and then the sixth-graders—with the exception of Dovid—filed out for recess. Soon, the only ones left in the classroom were Rabbi Feingold and his chastened *talmid*, whose face was still firmly buried in his arms.

The rebbi went to stand beside him. "Dovid," he said quietly, "I'd like to talk to you."

The boy lifted his head reluctantly, revealing a reddened face that was still quite damp with tears.

"Dovid," Rabbi Feingold began, "I wanted to say that I'm sorry for tearing up your cards, but I do hope you understand that you should not have been playing with them behind your Gemara."

Dovid avoided his rebbi's eyes uncomfortably. "Rebbi, I know I did the wrong thing, but why did you have to tear them up? Couldn't you have just taken them away and then given them back to me later?"

Rabbi Feingold sighed. "I shouldn't have torn them up, Dovid, but I was simply shocked that you could be playing with baseball cards on the first day of class! I didn't expect any of my *talmidim* to behave that way. Still, I am sorry for going that far, and I'd like to make it up to you somehow."

The boy hung his head morosely. "You can't, rebbi. Those cards were my special collection. They were worth money, and you can't even get them anymore. They were my prized possession!"

The rebbi was quiet for a moment, and then he heaved another sigh. "Well, now that I understand the whole picture, I can only repeat what I told you. Somehow, I promise to make this up to you. I'm sorry about what happened, but I do hope you've learned a lesson today."

"I did," replied Dovid, his voice soft with his shame and dejection. "I'm very sorry, too."

The following day, Rabbi Feingold returned to his Lev Torah classroom with a mysterious black bag in his hands. Once the boys were seated and quiet, he placed the bag in front of him on his desk. The class waited expectantly.

"What I have here," announced Rabbi Feingold, "is something far more precious than baseball cards."

The sixth-graders followed their rebbi's every motion as he withdrew a framed picture of a *gadol* from the bag and held it up for easier viewing.

"This is my most prized possession," Rabbi Feingold told them, with feeling. "It's a picture of the Vizhnitzer Rebbe, the Imrei Chaim, alongside his two sons, Reb Moshe and Reb Mottel. I took this picture myself, which means it is extremely rare. There is none other like it in the world! Dovid, I'd like you to come up to the desk, please."

Dovid approached the desk timidly, but Rabbi Feingold smiled warmly at him and ceremoniously handed him the picture. "Dovid, I want you to have my most prized picture because I took yours away. One day, I promise you that this picture of the Vizhnitzer Rebbe will mean much more to you than those baseball cards ever did."

Dovid smiled shyly as he accepted the gift, and Rabbi Feingold offered a silent prayer of thanks that he had found some way to mollify his *talmid* after having acted out of anger the day before.

In the year after this incident, Dovid's family relocated to England, and Rabbi Feingold lost touch with the young boy. Twenty years came and went as Rabbi Feingold continued his labor of love with as much vigor as always, introducing young boys to Gemara and rejoicing in their journey toward true *hasmadah*. Though countless *talmidim* passed through his classroom doors, Rabbi Feingold still occasionally thought of young Dovid and wondered what might have happened to him.

Then, one morning in shul, Rabbi Feingold got his answer.

It was the end of davening, and Rabbi Feingold was preparing for another day in Lev Torah. He had said his "*Shalom aleichem*" to the Rav, and now he chatted with some acquaintances as he closed his tallis bag and began making his way to the door.

A young Chassidishe gentleman was waiting for him there, a delighted smile lighting up his face as Rabbi Feingold approached him.

"*Shalom aleichem*, Rebbi," the young man pronounced, reaching out to shake Rabbi Feingold's hand warmly.

Rabbi Feingold returned the smile and the handshake, but his eyebrows knitted in puzzlement. The younger man caught the expression and laughed.

"I see that the rebbi doesn't recognize me. I am Dovid Churnowitz,* and you once gave me a beautiful picture of the Vizhnitzer Rebbe."

Recognition flooded over Rabbi Feingold as he mentally added 20 years, a beard and *peyos* to the face of the young boy from so long ago. It was hard to believe, but this stately looking man had indeed been in his sixth-grade classroom!

"*Shalom aleichem,* Dovid," laughed the older man with obvious pleasure. "It is you, of course! What a wonderful surprise to see you again after all these years! Tell me, what brings you back to the neighborhood?"

"Well, I learned in Bnei Brak for a few years and just now got married," began Dovid, "and we decided to return to the old neighborhood. I'm going to join a *kollel* here, but I'm also looking for a part-time job to bring in some *parnassah*."

"What are you looking for, specifically?" inquired Rabbi Feingold after a moment.

Dovid smiled. "You know what? I'd actually love to be a rebbi. It's a dream of mine, but I'm well aware of how hard it is to find an opening anywhere nowadays..."

"Actually," cut in Rabbi Feingold with enthusiasm, "your old *cheder* is looking to hire! They need a rebbi who can get through to today's kids, who understands how to be strict and warm at the same time. I think you'd be perfect for the position. It's not a standard full-time job, but it's in the neighborhood and the pay is good."

The smile had slipped from Dovid's face, and his gaze was serious. "Are you offering me a job, Rebbi?"

"I believe I am," answered the other man warmly. "I think you'd be a great role model for the *talmidim*."

Dovid's mouth twisted a little, and he looked troubled. "Well then...I'm flattered by the offer, but I'm afraid I can't accept it."

It was Rabbi Feingold's turn to frown. "But, why not?"

"I'm not the person you want if you're looking for a role model, Rebbi. I have somewhat of a past."

"It's no matter." Rabbi Feingold waved a dismissive hand. "The man I see before me now looks like he'd be a great rebbi."

Dovid cast his eyes down. "Look, Rebbi, I'm completely serious: you don't want me. Let me tell you my story, what happened to me over the last 20 years. You can let me know afterward if you still think I'm 'perfect' for the job. I feel I owe you an explanation, since I wouldn't be standing here in shul if it weren't for you."

"Me?" echoed Rabbi Feingold. "What could I have done?"

"Well, for one thing, there was that beautiful picture of the Vizhnitzer Rebbe." Dovid met his former rebbi's eyes this time, and there was a small smile on his face. "But there's more to the story...":

The move to England was not an easy one for me. The troubles with school began almost immediately. The idea of fitting in with a completely new school and a strange group of kids seemed like a mountain I could never climb, and it wasn't long before I simply gave up. On my way down, I picked up a large number of fellow misfits who were also turned off to the school and yeshivah system and tried to rebel in every way possible.

Once I began to rebel, I did it all the way. I wouldn't listen. In fact, anyone who tried to scare me or humiliate me into doing the right thing only pushed me out onto the streets even faster. My parents were ashamed of me and furious, but there was little they could do. My *peyos* and yarmulke disappeared, I stopped keeping mitzvos, and I found a new home in an apartment I shared with a few of my new friends. We would spend our days looking for thrills and committing petty crimes, and at night we just went from party to party, losing ourselves in alcohol and drugs.

But the street lifestyle eventually loses a lot of its appeal, and it wasn't long before my friends and I drifted apart and headed to various other parts of the world to find something more exciting.

One guy went to India, one to Tibet, another one went to Thailand, and I decided to check out Israel. I found my way over to Kibbutz Shomer Hatzair, one of the best-known antireligious kibbutzim in the country. Because of my feelings toward religion and my appetite for a new life, my move to the kibbutz was the easiest transition of my whole life. I blended in immediately and felt right at home.

Of course, by this time my parents were in despair. They sent friends and relatives to visit and talk to me, but I sent them away, telling them to leave me alone and let me live my life. Meaningless as this life was, I believed that it was just the thing I had always wanted. My days were spent working the land, and my weekends and evenings were spent on the beaches of Tel Aviv or Eilat, always surrounded by my big, loose circle of friends.

But then, the unbelievable happened: I started to feel empty. Nothing I did seemed to have any flavor anymore and nothing could hold any excitement. One fateful weekend, I finally declined to follow my friends to Eilat. I simply wasn't interested anymore.

Instead, I spent the day sitting alone in my apartment, confronted with my own inner thoughts for the first time in years; there were no friends to distract me and no activities to occupy me. I was amazed to find my thoughts traveling back in time to my parents' Shabbos table in England. I was so sure I never wanted to see it again, that I never wanted to have any responsibilities thrust in my face by parents or rebbeim...and yet, there was...*something* there that I sorely missed. There was a certain happiness to it all, a certain sense of peacefulness and love. I found myself picturing that table, and then the *sefarim* shelf nearby, filled with my Bar Mitzvah gifts. I startled myself by suddenly remembering that picture of the Vizhnitzer Rebbe that my own rebbi had given me so long ago, in a different lifetime. I remembered the circumstances of my receiving it, and I could suddenly hear my rebbi's voice as clearly as if sixth grade had happened yesterday:

One day, I promise you that this picture of the Vizhnitzer Rebbe will mean much more to you than those baseball cards ever did.

What was so meaningful about a picture of the Vizhnitzer Rebbe anyway? I wondered. I suddenly knew that I had to find out. Although the Vizhnitzer Rebbe in the photo had departed the world long before, I knew that his son—only a child in the picture—was now leading the Chassidus in Bnei Brak. I had distinct recollections of people from my past discussing what an incredible experience it was to attend the Vizhnitzer's Shabbos *tisch*. Right then, in the middle of a dreary Friday afternoon in Shomer Hatzair, I knew where I was going for Shabbos.

I dug a white shirt and black pants out from somewhere in the depths of my closet and tied my wild hair into as neat a ponytail as I could manage. Slinging a backpack over one shoulder, I set out on my way to this weekend's big adventure: Vizhnitz in Bnei Brak.

Let's see what it's all about, then.

I arrived at the Vizhnitz Beis Midrash as Shabbos was drawing close. With my ponytail and my backpack standing out loudly in the sea of Chassidim, it wasn't long before a *bachur* approached me and asked what I needed.

"I'm here to see the Vizhnitzer Rebbe," I announced.

"It's only hours to Shabbos," the young man apologized, "and the Rebbe is too busy to see anyone. I'm sure if you come back later tonight, he'll be able to see you."

"I'll need somewhere to stay for Shabbos, then," I told him.

"Let me get the *mashgiach*," replied the *bachur*, disappearing immediately back into the crowd of Chassidim.

The *mashgiach* appeared minutes later, smiling kindly as he shook my hand. His smile deepened when I answered his questions in fluent Yiddish, and he assured me that a room and meals would be found for me. I was soon set up in someone's *dirah*, right on time to greet the first Shabbos I had kept in a very long time.

I ate a nice Friday-night meal with a local family, but then I immediately said goodbye and thanks, and left to do what I had come for: attend the Vizhnitzer Rebbe's Shabbos *tisch*.

The scene, when I arrived, was like nothing I had ever seen before. There was a feeling of electricity buzzing around the crowded room as the throngs of Chassidim swayed together and sang Shabbos *zemiros* in a wave of sound. I found myself singing right along with them, tears in my eyes as I sang with total strangers the words I had nearly forgotten. I'm sure I stood out sharply with my appearance, but for once, I felt completely at ease: welcomed and accepted, not judged.

Soon it was time for the Rebbe's *l'chaim*, and the Chassidim pushed inward to get hold of some portion of the food or drink that their Rebbe had blessed. Someone must have whispered to the Rebbe about my presence, because he suddenly looked up and stared me right in the eyes, smiled, and motioned for me to come closer to him.

I was embarrassed at the attention already, but I didn't feel that I had a choice. My doubts dissolved when the Rebbe clasped my hand warmly and wished me a "gut Shabbos" in a way that left no question that he meant it. For the first time I could remember, I was overcome with emotion and a feeling of longing. It was as if I had been living inside a shell for all these years, and now that shell was gone. I could feel something stirring inside me, something demanding my attention.

At *shalosh seudos*, I felt a magnetic pull to return to the Rebbe's *tisch*. Again I felt my soul soaring with the beautiful melodies and harmonies of the *zemiros*. They somehow seemed to be expressing exactly what I was feeling. I was truly sad to see the *Havdalah* candle extinguished at the end of the night. I found myself thinking almost desperately that it couldn't be over *already*.

With all this emotion going on inside me, I clasped the Rebbe's hand to wish him a "gut voch" and asked when I might be able to see him again. The Rebbe smiled and answered that he hoped I could be their guest again very soon. At these words, that were so very sincere, I couldn't hold back anymore. The voice inside me that had been growing louder and louder all Shabbos long burst out of me with the bitter, unashamed tears of a child, and I cried for my soul to the Rebbe.

The Rebbe clasped my hand even more firmly and met my eyes. "Don't go back there," he said softly. "We need you over here."

At this point, my body and soul made a unanimous decision.

"All right," I agreed, my voice shaking, "I will stay."

Well, I never did return to Kibbutz Shomer Hatzair; I was too busy turning my life around until I became a Vizhnitzer Chassid myself. I stayed in Bnei Brak for several years, learning as much as I could and recapturing what I had lost. In time, a fine girl from a good family was suggested for me, and I soon merited to add the joy of building a *bayis ne'eman* to the joy of *limud Torah*. Finally, I was done wandering.

"So tell me," Dovid asked Rabbi Feingold, hoarse with emotion, "do you really think someone with a story like that is fit to be a rebbi in his old *cheder*?"

Rabbi Feingold smiled incredulously. "Reb Dovid...no rebbi could understand as well as you could how valuable a Torah education is. No rebbi besides you could possibly provide just the kind of love, warmth, and understanding that today's children need. You ask if you're 'fit'? We would be lucky to have you! Consider yourself hired."

A mechanech and a parent both must remember never to underestimate the incredible power that love and effort have upon a child. With children, there is no such thing as a lost cause. You may not see it now, but a precious seed has been planted, and with nurturing and caring, your precious student or child can grow to become a mighty tree of life.

Keep on planting, hoping, believing. . .Vezakeinu legadel banim uv'nei vanim oskim b'Torah u'v'mitzvos. May we merit to raise children and grandchildren who involve themselves with Torah and mitzvos.

Earning Your Wings

Every year, Rabbi Benzion Klatzko travels to Israel with Jewish American college students in order to give them a taste of their heritage and perhaps ignite a spark in their souls that might bring them closer to Torah and mitzvos. Discovering one's roots is always emotionally moving, and Rabbi Klatzko usually returns from these trips with stories of students who have experienced personal revelations that often turn out to be life-changing. The following are the stories he shared with me after his most recent trip.

It had been a really amazing couple of weeks in Israel. We had quite literally traveled the country, from the Kosel to the mountains of Ein Gedi, and we felt as though we had seen all there was to see. This was to be our last Shabbos meal together before returning to America, and so the students and I were sharing a somewhat melancholy *seudah shelishis* in Ramat Beit Shemesh.

This final Shabbos meal is always a highlight for me, as it is the best way to assess the impact made on the young men and women I had brought to the Holy Land. We started off the meal with some heartfelt melodies, followed by a Torah thought from me and then a truly delicious spread. Finally, as Shabbos was winding down to a close, it was time.

"Friends," I began, "I'm sure it has been a beautiful trip full of rich experiences for us all. I would like to go around the table now and ask anyone who feels like it to share his or her most meaningful and inspiring memory from our time here."

A young woman was the first to speak.

"My name is Amanda," she introduced herself shyly, "and I just want to say that this is most amazing experience of my life. I felt a connection to Judaism that I've never felt at any time before this trip. But what I *really* want to tell you about is one little incident that made a very deep impression on me, and I don't think I'll ever forget it.

"It was when we were in Jerusalem. I was walking down the street in a neighborhood that's mainly *charedi*. The truth is, I've always considered these *charedim* to be very selfish people. I've always believed that they cared only about themselves or other very religious people. I was sure that people like me were nothing in their eyes, maybe not even Jews.

"Well, as I was walking, I noticed a *charedi* man, complete with the long black jacket and beard, hefting two arms full of shopping bags to his home. As he shifted his bundles to pull his keys out of his pocket, I noticed his wallet tumbling to the ground. I guess because he was so preoccupied with the bags, he himself didn't realize. I felt immediately obligated to tell the guy what had happened, so I yelled, '*Slichah, slichah*,' and, when he turned around, I pointed excitedly at the ground.

"He looked at me for a second, bent down to retrieve his wallet, and then simply disappeared inside without so much as a nod. Well, you can imagine how I was fuming! Okay, *maybe* I could make peace with the fact that *charedim* hate all non-*charedim*, but there's such a thing as common decency! And not even to say 'thank you' to someone who saved your wallet, well…! That was just unbelievable!

"Just as my mind was working itself into a fit of anger, the door reopened and the same man was standing there with his hands still full, but this time with the largest pomegranate I have ever seen. He approached me with a beaming smile and handed me the fruit ceremoniously. '*Todah rabbah, todah rabbah*,' he said. No further words were necessary.

"The man disappeared back into his apartment, but I stood in place holding the pomegranate, tears blurring my vision. I was wrong, you see. These people really *do* care about us. It was a really awesome moment for me, because I finally felt proud to be a Jew."

The next young woman to raise her hand was a girl named Debby.

"My most inspiring moment was when we went to the burial place of Rabbi Akiva's wife, Rachel."

Rachel's *kever* was always a particularly inspirational trip for my group. I would share the story of how she had given up a life of luxury in order to marry a man who hadn't even learned to read Hebrew until he was 40. Rachel believed in him, though, and supported his journey to Torah and mitzvos even at the cost of her family's approval. She willingly waited 24 years as Rabbi Akiva left her to grow in greatness and acquire thousands of students. When Rabbi Akiva finally returned with his legions of disciples in tow, he told his *talmidim* about Rachel, "*Sheli v'shelachem shelah hi*, What you and I have acquired is hers." This was a story that never failed to inspire.

Debby continued: "To me, though, the most inspiring part of Rachel's story was what happened after we heard it. See, the group of rabbis leading this tour went into a kind of huddle after the story, and then told us they had an announcement to make. They said that they, too, were grateful to their wives for allowing them to pursue *chinuch* and *kiruv* programs, and that they never would have gotten where they were without them. They all resolved to bring their wives the same present when they returned to the U.S.: a necklace with the Hebrew inscription, *Sheli v'shelachem shelah hi.*

"To me, that was the most touching moment, because I finally understood why it is said that G-d's presence rests in the home of a Jewish couple with a happy marriage. I have never seen anything so beautiful."

The final speaker was a man named Jack who had recently finished a stint in the U.S. Army and had decided to join our trip to Israel. His story left the crowd rapt with emotion.

"I had joined the army a couple of years back, and just a few months ago I found myself in Iraq. I wasn't the only Jew there; we actually had a pretty nice group of guys, and I felt very proud of myself for serving my country.

"One day, this Israeli commander visited our base with the goal of training soldiers to be paratroopers. In fact, he offered us an unheard-of incentive: anyone who agreed to train for the next three weeks to learn how to be an Israeli-style paratrooper would receive his very own Israeli wings! For those of you who don't know, 'wings' are a medal that a soldier receives for being an outstanding paratrooper, and it is a tremendous honor. I was very excited at the prospect of getting this medal; in fact, as a Jew, I felt especially drawn to the idea of earning my 'Jewish wings.'

"I accepted the offer and immediately began my training. It was grueling, frightening, and exhausting, and I still don't know how I pulled through those three weeks, but I was finally ready to take the test. I approached my commanding officer to ask about the nearest opportunity to take it.

" 'I'm really sorry,' he told me, 'but the Israeli official returned to Israel just last night. It's too late to do any kind of test.'

"Well, you can imagine how crushed I was. I had just spent three weeks training harder than I had ever trained before, and for what? Just like that, my opportunity had gone. Shortly after this goal slipped away from me, so did my desire to serve in the army altogether. My tour was over in a few weeks, and I returned to America, no longer sure what I wanted to do with my life until I heard of this trip to Israel. I always did want to know a little more about my heritage, so I signed up.

"Not long after I got here, I struck up a friendship with our *madrich,* Yosef. I found myself telling him what had happened to me in Iraq and how disappointed and disillusioned I had become. Yosef heard me out, and then suddenly told me he would be back soon.

"A little while later, Yosef came back and told me that he had a present for me. 'I used to be an Israeli paratrooper myself,' he said, 'and when I heard what you've been through, I realized how much you deserve these.'

"He opened his hand to reveal a pair of Israeli wings, which he then proudly pinned on my shirt. 'This is a gift from one soldier to another,' he said. Then he reached into a bag and pulled out a pair of olive-green army-issue *tzitzis*. He placed this last gift over my shirt and told me how to make a *berachah*. I did, and then I gave the *tzitzis* a kiss. It was the first time I had ever worn *tzitzis*, and Yosef told me they would protect me from danger."

The room had grown quiet and somewhat teary eyed as Jack told his story, but the soldier still had one more point to make.

"You know," Jack said quietly, gesturing at his lapel, "at the beginning of this trip I was so proud of myself for getting these wings. I believed they were the most important wings I could achieve. But now..."

Jack's voice caught with emotion as he grasped the strings of his *tzitzis*, holding them up for all to see. "...now I realize that *these* are my wings, because nothing else I own lets me soar up to the skies!"

Everyone in the room burst into spontaneous claps and cheers. At that moment, I believe every single soul in the room knew exactly what kind of wings were more important, and how crucial it is that we all take pride in our various ranks and medals in the great army of Hashem.

A Little Warmth, a Lifetime of Inspiration

At this year's Agudah Convention, speakers explored the theme of "Lev Avos Al Bonim—For the Sake of Our Vulnerable Youth." It was an uplifting weekend dedicated to understanding and upholding our great role in influencing our children's lives. The consistent message of the speeches is that our most powerful tool in reaching our children's neshamos is the warmth we display toward them. Here are three stories that touched me, and I'd like to share them with you. The first is from Rav Yaakov Bender, rosh yeshivah of Yeshivah Darchei Torah.

Many years ago, there was a 15-year-old boy who used to daven at the old yeshivah building of Torah Vodaath when it was still located in Williamsburg. The boy had lost his father, and on the day this story took place, he had come to the yeshivah to daven Minchah.

As he waited for Minchah to begin, the boy noticed a distinguished-looking, elderly man walking into the *beis midrash*. Instantly, the boy recognized that this regal-looking *talmid chacham* was the great Ponevezher Rav, Rav Yosef Shlomo Kahaneman.

The Rav noticed the boy as well, and much to the boy's pleasure, the Rav asked him for a favor. "I have *yahrtzeit* today and need the *amud,*" he told the boy. "Can you please try to arrange it for me?"

Immediately, the boy approached the *gabbai* and related that the Ponevezher Rav was there and wanted to daven for the *amud*.

The *gabbai* was happy to accommodate the revered Rav, and Minchah soon began.

When davening was finished, the Rav made another request of the boy. "I have to go to the Satmar Rav's house, but I don't know my way around here," he explained. "Could you help me find the address?"

What a privilege this mission was for the boy! He arranged a ride for the Rav and even accompanied him to the meeting, hoping to be of further assistance. And indeed, his presence was needed again after the meeting, this time to arrange for transportation to Boro Park. The boy hailed a taxi. As the two were settling into their seats, the boy explained to the Rav that he would not be able to accompany him all the way to his destination. He would have to disembark before the taxi reached the highway.

When the time came for the boy to get out of the taxi, he turned to the Rav and said, "Before I leave, can the Rav give me and my mother a *berachah*. I am a *yasom* (orphan) and my mother has to raise our family on her own."

The Rav exclaimed, "You are a *yasom*!" He threw his arms around the boy, gave him a big hug, and then showered the boy and his mother with *berachos*. There was no mistaking the spirit flowing from the Rav to the boy; it was sincere love, for a child he barely knew. For those few moments, the boy felt as though he were as treasured as the Rav's own son.

Concluding this story, Rabbi Bender thundered to the crowd assembled at the Agudah Convention, "*Rabbosai*! It has been many years since the Ponevezher Rav gave me those hugs and *berachos*, but I can still feel the love and warmth. Smother your children with warmth and they, too, will never ever forget it!"

The next story is based on the speech of Rav Yitzchok Scheiner, rosh yeshivah of the Kamenitzer Yeshivah in Yerushalayim.

I was born in Pittsburgh in 1922. The state of my Yiddishkeit in those days was a reflection of the state of Yiddishkeit throughout America. There were 60,000 Jews in Pittsburgh at that time, many of them *frum,* but only a handful would remain that way. If they did, it was a miracle. My miracle came about because of a few words of concern from one person.

Things would have turned out very differently if I had simply followed the track I was on. I attended Rogers Elementary School for eight years and went on to Peaberry High School, struggling to stay *shomer Shabbos* as I shared my day-to-day life with non-Jews.

However, in one Shabbos, my life switched tracks. Here is how it happened: Ours was the only kosher home in the east end of Pittsburgh, so we often played host to *frum* Jews in need of a place to stay. It was for that reason that one Shabbos, my parents and I found ourselves sitting around the table with a guest from out of town. I had mentioned during the meal that I had just graduated high school and would be attending the University of Pittsburgh in the coming year.

The guest was in the midst of a conversation with my parents when he turned to me and asked, "Why university? Why not yeshivah?"

Those few words, uttered by Rav Avrohom Bender, the grandfather of Rav Yaakov Bender, changed my life. I decided to go to New York to find a yeshivah. I spent the summer in a camp mesivta, where I met Rabbi Yitzchok Karp and Rabbi Moshe Yechezkel Samuels. With their guidance, I decided to attend Yeshivah Torah Vodaath, under the leadership of Rav Shraga Feivel Mendelovitz.

Five words spoken by a man at my Shabbos table—five words spoken with sincere concern for the fate of a Jewish boy's *neshamah*—opened my heart to a whole new realm of possibilities. Of course, I'm sure that my mother's prayers that I should not follow the path of my many friends, who had dropped Yiddishkeit and intermarried, were also a powerful part of the equation. But the message we should take from this story is that a few warm words can change the course of history.

There is a similar lesson in a story told about the great *tzaddik,* Rav Shlomo Zalman Auerbach. A friend once commented to the Rav, "I don't understand. We sat on the same bench in Yeshivah Eitz Chaim, and I was superior to you. Yet 30 years later, you are a *gadol hador* and I am nothing. Please tell me your secret, so I can teach it to my children and grandchildren. How did you do it?"

Rav Shlomo Zalman smiled and said, "The secret is a glass of hot milk and a hug and a kiss."

"No, really!" the friend insisted. "I'm serious!"

"I am being very serious," said Rav Shlomo Zalman. "Every day when I came home from *cheder*, my mother was waiting for me at the door. She would give me a hug and a kiss and she would ask me about my day. I would tell her that I had a good day and had learned well. Then she would tell me to take the glass of hot milk and snack that awaited me on the table. This routine repeated itself every day. I would go to sleep each night as if I were floating on a cloud, warmed by her hug and kiss and glass of hot milk. I felt this warmth from my mother throughout my yeshivah years, and it was due to her love that I became who I am today."

So remember to stay alert to a child's need for love, because you too will encounter the opportunity to change the world with a few warm words.

After hearing Rav Scheiner's inspiring words, I walked outside of the convention hall for a break, and was pleasantly surprised to meet my good friend Rabbi Benzion Klatzko. He had come to promote his organization "See You on Shabbos," a website that sets up nonreligious Jews with religious Jews for a Shabbos experience. After greeting each other, he said, "Binyomin, you have to hear what happened this Shabbos at my home."

It was just a few hours before Shabbos, and I was expecting a group of 30 *frum* girls from out of town for a Shabbaton we were hosting. While we were getting everything ready, I got a phone call from a local girl who was part of another group. These were girls who had left Yiddishkeit and were just hanging on or starting to come back in various degrees. And they wanted to come to my house for a Shabbaton also.

Well, I knew it would be a little tight, but at least they were all girls. I thought it might work out nicely for both groups, but I was in for a surprise.

During the meal, some sort of argument broke out between one of the religious girls and a girl from the other group. Pretty soon everyone was taking sides, and I could see that it could lead to big trouble. Just to keep things from exploding, I found the nonreligious girls a place to sleep at one of my neighbors' homes. They left for the night, but not without first threatening revenge on the other group.

True to their word, they came back on Shabbos morning and declared they were taking their belongings and leaving right then and there. Even though I pleaded with them to wait until after Shabbos, they took their things and began to leave. As they were heading to the door, I heard the out-of-town girls shouting, "Hey! They took our stuff!"

Unbelievably enough, they had stolen money and other items from the out-of-town girls, and we could not do anything about it until after Shabbos. Not only weren't these girls ashamed of taking the property, but they even threatened to come back later with some boys who would even the score for their insulting treatment.

Needless to say, the beautiful, warm Shabbos we had expected was turning into a nightmare. The girls were frantic and the mood was anything but peaceful. I tried to assure them that they would get back their belongings before they left, but it was hard for them to put the episode out of their minds.

The group of nonreligious girls returned as promised, later on Shabbos afternoon, accompanied by three large young men dressed like street thugs. I don't know what they thought they were going to accomplish, but I was fairly sure that their presence was mostly for dramatic effect. I went out to speak to them.

"Look," I told them, "the stuff the girls took from my guests has to be returned. If it isn't, then I will reimburse them from my own pocket. You'll literally be taking food from my children's mouths. Is that what you really want to do?"

By the end of the whole episode, we did indeed get back most everything the girls had taken, but that's not the real ending of the story. When the whole gang showed up at my house, it was just about time for Minchah, and I was short a few men for a *minyan*. There was no time for me to hunt down the extra men, so I decided to appeal to the three men who were already there, standing outside my door.

At first, they acted like they didn't know what I was talking about. They even claimed that they weren't Jewish. But I knew one of them, and I knew he was Jewish. It was pretty safe to assume that the other two were Jewish as well. Anyway, after a few minutes of coaxing, amazingly enough, they agreed to join our *minyan*.

They donned yarmulkes for the occasion, and I gave two of them an *aliyah*. The third young man, named Jason, got *hagbahah*. When he stepped up to perform his part, I could see that he was moved. His eyes were tearing and his face lit up as he lifted the Torah into the air.

Davening concluded without incident, and the boys left my house, clearly in high spirits. They were no longer looking for blood, and I hoped that the experience might even have had some sort of long-term effect on them.

Later that night, right before *Havdalah*, there was a knock on the door. I opened it to find big Jason standing there with a yarmulke on his head.

"Can I come inside to hear *Havdalah*?" he asked.

"Sure, come on in," I answered.

When it was all over, Jason gave me a bear hug. "Rabbi," he said with emotion in his voice, "thank you so much. That was exactly what I needed."

If I were to compare my hopes for this Shabbos to what it actually turned out to be, I would have to say that it was a disaster. The out-of-town girls had expected an inspiring Shabbaton, and instead, they were put into a state of panic by the other group of girls.

But if I just think about it from the goal of bringing people closer to Hashem, the episode with Jason puts a whole new spin on it. He seemed so far away from his heritage, and yet it was so clear that there was still a small flame burning inside him. If it's true for him, it's true for every Jew, and Jason proved that with enough love, those small flames can become a fire that will light up their souls.

May we all be *zocheh* to spread the warmth of *ahavas Yisrael* to those who need it most, and bring them back to *Hakadosh Baruch Hu*.

I walked away from the Agudah Convention with those three stories on my mind, and a new understanding of chinuch and human nature. Every bit of energy we invest into our children, our students, and our friends can have an everlasting impact on their lives and future generations. A little warmth is a seed that is planted deep within a person. Little by little the seed can grow and make an impact. The impressions we make today can determine someone else's, and our own, tomorrow.

Quality of Life

Every morning when we arise, we thank Hashem for returning our neshamah to us. Chazal teach us that we are obligated to thank Hashem for each and every breath we take. In this penetrating story that I heard from Rabbi Yonason Schwartz, we learn just how far that sense of gratitude goes.

Tethered by dozens of tubes and wires to a frightening collection of medical equipment, 19-year-old Moshe was fighting for his life. That he lay there alive at all was a miracle, after the high-speed car accident on an Atlanta highway that had turned his car into a crushed accordion, with Moshe enclosed in its folds. Emergency technicians had managed to extricate him and keep him alive, but now, he lay there in the Intensive Care Unit, looking no more viable than his totaled car.

With a fractured skull, a punctured lung, and broken hands and feet, he had been rushed into emergency surgery upon his arrival. The doctors managed to stabilize him, but bringing him back to productive life would be a long, hard climb. He would need more surgery and a long course of difficult, painful physical therapy. Even then, it was doubtful that he would ever walk normally or speak normally again.

To keep him alive and work toward his remediation, the hospital would have to commit tremendous resources. Before the doctors took that aggressive course of action, they held a meeting to decide if, in fact, the expenditure of time, effort, and care made sense, in light of the dim prognosis for Moshe's future.

One morning, 20 of the hospital's top doctors gathered at an "ethics committee" meeting to discuss Moshe's case.

"Let's look at this realistically," said one doctor. "In his weakened state, with all the wounds and all the surgery he'll need, he is very prone to infection. That alone is likely to cause tremendous problems. He'll need 24/7 care and months of therapy—hundreds of thousands of dollars worth—and for what? His survival, even with all of that, is iffy. And this is a boy who, sorry to say, will never have a quality of life again. Is it right to put him through all this and to run up these kinds of costs just on the off-chance that he might survive to be an invalid?"

The other doctors picked up their cue from the first one, and soon, all had agreed that the most ethical, humane course of action was to give Moshe "palliative care," that is, to provide him with as much pain-killer medication as he needed to rest comfortably until the end came.

When the experts were done offering their opinions, one lone doctor raised his voice.

"Just one more minute!" said Doctor Fried. He was the only religious Jew on the entire hospital staff, and his "ethics" were not subject to committee vote.

"I don't understand what right we have to throw this young man's life away! You say it is because he will lack quality of life! How can you judge that, gentlemen? Who says he won't have a quality of life? What kind of quality do *you* have?

"Why don't we take a survey right now? How about you, Dr. Morgan, on a scale of 1 to 10, 10 being the best quality of life, how would you rate your life?"

"That's a tough question for me at the moment," Dr. Morgan replied in a muted tone. "You know, I was recently divorced, and right now my children don't want anything to do with me. I'm kind of all alone out there. I guess I'd say my life is about a 6."

"How about you, Dr. Bernard?" Dr. Fried inquired.

"Well, I would also have to say that my quality of life doesn't rate more than a 7," he replied. "After all, I have a child who has Down syndrome, and taking care of him has really taken over my life."

As Dr. Fried went around the room, he discovered that no one was able to claim a quality of life higher than 7.

"Okay, gentlemen, so everyone has their troubles in life. Why don't we go to Moshe now and ask him to rate his quality of life?"

Despite Moshe's dire condition, his mind was sharp and he was able to speak audibly enough to be heard. The doctors gathered at his bedside, each of them looking hopelessly at the sight before their eyes. In this 19-year-old, previously vibrant young man, they could not see life, only imminent death.

Moshe saw the doctors enter en masse, and recognized Dr. Fried, among them.

"Moshe, can you answer an important question for us?" Dr. Fried asked him,

Moshe nodded.

"On a scale of 1 to 10, 10 being the highest and 1 being the lowest, how would you rate your quality of life?"

Moshe's eyes lit up. "Ten!" he said "Ten-plus!"

"But how can you feel that way?" Dr. Fried persisted.

"Dr. Fried, look what I've been through and still, I'm alive," Moshe strained himself to continue. "When I say *Modeh Ani,* I thank Hashem for each and every day He grants me, for each and every breath I take. That is the greatest quality of life I could ever imagine, especially in my situation."

Moshe's words left Dr. Fried with no more need to convince the others. They were ready and motivated to do everything in their power to keep this young man alive, and return to him as many of his abilities as possible. Even according to their own ethics, that was now their obligation, for Moshe had a greater quality of life than any of them could imagine.

Mi k'amcha Yisrael. Even in the darkest of times, a Jew can be the happiest man alive, if he puts it all in the right perspective.

Bas Mitzvah Wish

Michal's imagination was working overtime. Tomorrow was her Bas Mitzvah, and she could already envision the scene. She imagined herself in her beautiful new outfit, opening the door to her family's Jerusalem home to greet each friend and relative as they arrived. They would be bearing gifts, of course, and her mind wandered over the hundreds of delightful possibilities arising from that fact. Some pretty jewelry? Nice new clothes? Money to spend and money to save?

Her mind was conjuring up the scene so vividly that it was as if she were in the midst of a dream. In just one fraction of a second, however, she was thrust from her dream into a nightmare, by the palpable, sickening thud of an explosion somewhere nearby. A familiar, dead silence filled the next few seconds, and then the air erupted into a cacophony of sirens. The sequence had become perversely normal for residents of Jerusalem in that summer of 2001, when the Palestinian uprising known as the *intifada* was exacting its bloody toll on a daily basis.

Even against that backdrop, however, the commotion following this particular explosion was unusual. The waves of ambulances just kept coming, and Michal surmised that the attack must have been a particularly destructive one. Her heart trembled at the thought of the inevitable casualties, the misery and sorrow inflicted on ordinary people trying to go about their lives.

Her assumptions were tragically correct, for the explosion she had heard was that of the deadly suicide bomber who had placed himself inconspicuously in line for pizza at a downtown Sbarro restaurant during lunchtime. Fifteen souls were lost in the attack, and 130 Jewish men, women, and children were wounded. Hundreds of lives would never be the same.

At the scene of the explosion, rescuers worked under battlefield conditions of controlled confusion. Stunned onlookers, saved from harm by such seemingly random decisions as eating elsewhere or eating later or earlier, watched as casualties borne on stretchers emerged from the rubble. Those left standing were shellshocked into silence. Others wept quietly, while others sobbed out loud.

The explosion's powerful impact had created a gruesome collage of blood, food, personal possessions, glass, and rubble, spattered across a wide swath of the downtown district. As the news and the images spread throughout the country, a sense of deep mourning and bewilderment set in.

The tragic event weighed heavily on Michal's heart. Her dreams of a party and presents seemed so frivolous when she knew that so many families had been plunged into unspeakable sadness and suffering. Her heart was not tuned in to a celebration; rather, it was with those who were hurting. She pondered the situation, wondering how to balance the arrival of her personal milestone—a true *simchah*—with the pain that pervaded her own heart and the collective heart of the Jewish people.

In a sudden moment of inspiration, she understood how to reconcile these two forces. With a self-awareness and maturity that testified to her arrival into Jewish adulthood, she decided to cancel her celebration and ask her parents to devote the money they would save to helping the victims of the attack. Then she contacted all those who were to attend her party and asked that, instead of spending money on a gift for her, they should donate the money to help the victims.

The seed of *chesed* that Michal planted took root. She and her family launched an all-out mission to continue raising money for the victims, and within just a few weeks, a new organization called "Onefamily" was born. Today, "Onefamily" is a large, volunteer-based organization that provides all types of assistance to thousands of terror victims throughout Israel.

Michal thinks back to the crucial moment in 2001 when she decided to give up her Bas Mitzvah party and gifts in favor of helping the victims of the Sbarro bombing. She doesn't recall feeling any regret about her sacrifice. In fact, the 12-year-old Michal did not see it as a sacrifice at all. It was an exercise in *chesed*, and that, she always knew, could only lead to a happier, more fulfilling life.

Even at that age, she knew that acts of hatred and violence have only one productive response: to create a greater, more powerful counterforce fueled by loving-kindness. "Onefamily" is a testimony to the compassion of the Jewish heart, a trait that will outlast every tragedy, outlive every enemy, and protect us until the time when there will truly be but one family on earth.

The Hug

Sometimes when a parent can't seem to get through to his struggling child, love can succeed where logic fails. In this story, Rabbi Avi Fishoff shares an incident that occurred on Erev Rosh Hashanah a few years ago, which proved how far a little love can go.

It was Erev Rosh Hashanah and the streets of Flatbush were clogged with cars as everyone hurried to complete their last minute pre-Yom Tov errands. Stuck behind a red light at an intersection, I was scanning the passing pedestrians when my eye caught sight of Jake.*

The truth is, you couldn't miss Jake. He was a giant of a guy: six-foot four at least. I had gotten to know him over the course of the past few years, as a result of my efforts to reverse his precipitous spiritual decline. His rebellion was somewhat of a mystery; he came from a fine family and had been given everything a boy needs to succeed. In fact, he was a sweet kid.

Despite that, somewhere in Jake's heart, there was a hole. Little by little, he started looking outside the yeshivah world for something to fill the hole. At this point, he had stopped keeping Shabbos, stopped putting on tefillin, and basically, had stopped living as a Jew altogether.

Still, he seemed willing to let me be his friend. So I gave my horn a light tap to get his attention and shouted out my window, "Jake! Can I give you a lift?"

He ran to the car and climbed in before the light changed. We got into some small talk.

"So what are your plans for Rosh Hashanah?" I asked him.

He shrugged and raised his eyebrows as if to say, "You think I care?" I knew he hadn't heard the shofar or even fasted on Yom Kippur for several years.

"Listen, I'm heading into Boro Park. Do you want to come along?" I offered.

"Sure, I've got nothing else to do," he replied.

We continued plowing through the Brooklyn traffic. As we crawled into the even thicker traffic of Boro Park, I asked Jake, "Doesn't your grandfather live near here?"

Jake's grandfather—his mother's father—was a *tzaddik* of some renown. No doubt, there were plenty of Jews seeking his blessings for a good new year as the Day of Judgment approached.

"Yeah, he's somewhere around here," Jake confirmed. "But I haven't seen him in years. We're not exactly close."

"Well, that may be," I replied. "But you know, it is Erev Rosh Hashanah and I just had a good idea. Everyone knows that your grandfather is a big *tzaddik*. Wouldn't it be great if you got a *berachah* from him for a sweet new year?"

"No I don't think so, Rabbi," said Jake. "And I don't think he would want to see me. He thinks I'm a *sheigetz*."

"I don't believe that, Jake. Every grandfather loves his grandchild."

Then I heard Jake mumble to himself, "Yeah, right, love. Never in my life did anyone ever show me love. Never did I get a hug or a kiss from my family."

"What did you say, Jake?"

"Oh, nothing, Rabbi. Just that my family doesn't really love me."

"Listen, Jake, let's go to your grandfather for a few minutes. I'll wait for you outside while you get your *berachah* and then we will leave."

Jake finally agreed.

As we drove to his grandfather's house, Jake kept talking to himself about how no one loved him and how he never got any hugs. It would have been comical to hear this hulk of a man revealing his craving for a hug, except that it was so very sad.

A few minutes later, we arrived at his grandfather's home and Jake went inside. As soon as he disappeared behind the door, I called his mother and told her how I had picked up Jake and took him to her father's home for a *berachah*.

Then I asked her if she could enlighten me about Jake's mumbled conversation with himself.

"Is there any reason why your son feels like he never got any hugs or show of love from his family?" I asked her.

"Of course we show him love," Jake's mother replied. "But you know, Rabbi Fishoff, we're not the touchy, mushy type. We're not a family that hugs. Neither my husband nor I are that type."

"I see. But I have to tell you that even so, it seems to be the thing Jake really needs. I'm sure you love him, but he's not reading that message."

I got off the phone quickly, realizing all at once what I had to do. I ran up the stairs, hoping to catch Jake before he left his grandfather's presence. I got to Jake just in time, just as he was getting up to leave. Jake was heading to the door, with his back already turned to his grandfather. I caught the grandfather's eye and began motioning, wrapping my arms around myself and mouthing, "Give him a hug! Give him a hug!"

The grandfather saw and seemed to understand what I wanted him to do. As Jake reached the door, he turned back toward his grandfather to say goodbye. His grandfather looked at him and started to raise his hand up toward Jake's shoulder. Jake gazed, perplexed, at his grandfather's outstretched hands, and finally understood that the elderly *tzaddik* wanted to give him a hug.

He leaned his giant form forward and gently embraced his grandfather, his face flushing red with emotion. He said goodbye and went down the stairs; when he sat down in the car, he looked as if he were in shock. For a few long moments, he couldn't say a word.

Then, shaking his head as if he had seen a mirage, he said, "He gave me a hug. I can't believe he really gave me a hug."

"Wow, Jake, that's really great," I replied blandly. I didn't want to interfere with his thoughts. I just wanted that feeling to sink in and take hold. As we drove through the crowded streets, Jake kept repeating how he couldn't believe that his grandfather had hugged him. Then the car fell silent, and Jake seemed deep in thought.

Finally, at a red light, Jake said words that, in my wildest dreams, I would not have expected to hear—at least for many months or years into the future.

"Rabbi, I've been thinking maybe I should start putting on tefillin again. You know, to start the year off right. Maybe it's time for me to keep Shabbos again too."

Well, Jake kept that Rosh Hashanah and then he fasted on Yom Kippur. And he has put on tefillin and kept Shabbos ever since that day.

There is no way to assess the value of that one hug; it was priceless, in the truest sense of the word. But what this incident really taught me was how very much our children need to know that we love them. It is indeed the one ingredient essential to their success in life.

So don't hold back: give your kid a big hug, even if you think he is too big for hugs. Don't wait for him to ask, because by then, so much opportunity can be lost.

Glossary

abba — father
ahavas Yisrael — love of Jews
aliyah — being called to the Torah
amud — lectern; podium
aron kodesh — holy ark
ayin tov — a good eye
baal teshuvah — a penitent returnee to Jewish life
baal tokei'a — one who blows the shofar
bachur (pl. *bachurim*) — young man
baruch Hashem — thank G-d
bashert — destined mate
beis din — rabbinical court
beis medrash — study hall
berachah — blessing
biur chametz — destruction of leaven
bris — circumcision
chag same'ach — happy holiday
chametz — leaven
charedim — religious Jews
chassan — groom
chasunah — wedding
chavrusa — learning partner
cheder (pl. *chadarim*) — elementary school
chesed — kindness; acts of beneficence
chevrah kadisha — burial society
chizuk — encouragement
Chumash — Five Books of Moses
chuppah — loosely, the marriage ceremony
churban — destruction
daven(ing) — pray(ing)
derech — path
emunah — faith
frum — observant of Jewish law
gabbai — synagogue sexton; attendant of a Rebbe
gadol (pl. *gedolei*) *hador* — Torah giant of the generation
Gemara — loosely, a synonym for the Talmud as a whole
get — bill of divorce
Hakafos — the dancing in the synagogue on Simchas Torah
halachah — Jewish law
hashgachah pratis — Divine providence
Havdalah — ceremony marking the end of Shabbos or Yom Tov
ima — mother
Kaddish — prayer sanctifying G-d's Name, often recited by mourners
kallah — bride
kavanah — intent concentration
kedushah — holiness
Kiddush — blessing recited over wine expressing the sanctity of Sabbath and festivals

kiddush Hashem — sanctification of G-d's Name
kiruv — outreach
Klal Yisrael — Jewish people in general
Kosel — the Western Wall in Jerusalem, the only standing remnant of the Holy Temple complex
l'chaim — "to life"; traditional toast
limud Torah — learning of Torah
machlokes — discord
madrich — leader, guide
malach — angel
mashgiach — spiritual mentor in a yeshivah
mechanech — educator
mentch — "a person"; i.e. one with good traits
mesechta — tractate
mesirus nefesh — *self-sacrifice*
middos — traits
mikveh — ritual bath
minyan — quorum of ten men for prayer service
mishtarah — police
nachas — satisfaction, enjoyment
navi — prophet
neshamah — soul
p'sak — ruling of Torah law
parnassah — a livelihood
peyos — sidelocks
rasha — evil person
refuah sheleimah — a full recovery
Ribono Shel Olam — Master of the World, i.e., G-d
seder — period of learning in a yeshivah
sefer (pl. *sefarim*) — book
Sefer Torah — Torah scroll
segulah — spiritual remedy
semichah — rabbinical ordination
seudah shelishis — the third meal of Shabbos
seudas hoda'ah — meal tendered in thanks for a special event
shadchan — matchmaker
shailah — halachic query
shlaom aleichem — lit. "Peace unto you"; a traditional greeting; liturgical song sung on Friday night
shalosh seudos — the third meal on Shabbos
Shemoneh Esrei — the prayer containing 18 blessings, recited three times a day
shidduch — marriage match
shiur (pl. *shiurim*) — lecture; lesson
shivah — seven-day period of mourning
shliach — messenger
shomer Shabbos — one who observes the Sabbath
shul — synagogue
siddur — prayer book
simchah — joy; celebration
siyata d'Shmaya — Heavenly assistance
slichah — excuse me
sofer stam — scribe who writes Torah scrolls and mezuzos
tallis — prayer shawl
talmid (pl. *talmidim*) — student
talmid chacham — Torah scholar
tefillah (pl. *tefillos*) — prayer
tefillin — phylacteries
Tehillim — Psalms
tekias shofar — the blowing of the shofar

teshuvah — repentance
tzaddik — righteous person
tzitzis — fringes required by the Torah to be placed on a four-cornered garment
upsherin — cutting of a 3-year-old boy's hair
Vidui — confession of sins
yahrzeit — the anniversary of a person's passing
Yamim Noraim — High Holy Days
yarmulke — skullcap
yason — orphan
yeshuah — salvation
yetzer hara — evil inclination
Yid — Jew
Yiddishkeit — Jewishness
yimach shemo — may his name be obliterated
yiras Shamayim — fear of Heaven
z'man — semester of learning
zechus — merit
zeida — grandfather
zemiros — songs sung in honor of Shabbos
zocheh — to merit

This volume is part of
THE ARTSCROLL SERIES®
an ongoing project of
translations, commentaries and expositions on
Scripture, Mishnah, Talmud, Midrash, Halachah,
liturgy, history, the classic Rabbinic writings,
biographies and thought.

For a brochure of current publications
visit your local Hebrew bookseller
or contact the publisher:

Mesorah Publications, ltd
4401 Second Avenue
Brooklyn, New York 11232
(718) 921-9000
www.artscroll.com